DOCTOR WHO

THE ELEVENTH DOCTOR

VOL 6: THE MALIGNANT TRUTH

"Amazing! It hit all the right notes, and got the Doctor perfect! 9/10"
COMIC BOOK CAST

"A truly fantastic *Doctor Who* adventure that rewards loyal readers and long-time fans of the show."
POP CULTURE BANDIT

"Fun, energetic events liven things up with some thrilling twists!"
SNAPPOW

"A riveting story with magnificent set pieces and dazzling imagery!"
BLOGTOR WHO

"Excellent script with great artwork. I've become a fan of Alice Obiefune – what a character she has become!"
TM STASH

"The tone of the Eleventh Doctor is strong in this one."
WARPED FACTOR

"Very true to *Doctor Who*, but with a willingness to be weirder and achieve greater scale than the TV series is capable of. Fun, weird, and exciting!"
CAPELESS CRUSADER

"A great job creating a companion who can keep up with the Doctor. 10 out of 10!"
PROJECT FANDOM

"Nails the tone and spirit right out of the gate!"
COMIC BOOK RESOURCES

"I have never seen a *Doctor Who* story quite like this, and I cannot wait for more."
4 GEEKS LIKE YOU

"Full of dramatic reveals."
SCI FI ONLINE

"9.5 out of 10!"
NERDS UNCHAINED

"Very unsettling visuals, brilliantly done."
NERDLY

TITAN COMICS

SENIOR COMICS EDITOR
Andrew James

ASSISTANT EDITORS
Jessica Burton, Amoona Saohin

COLLECTION DESIGNER
Andrew Leung

TITAN COMICS EDITORIAL
Tom Williams

PRODUCTION ASSISTANT
Peter James

PRODUCTION SUPERVISORS
Maria Pearson, Jackie Flook

PRODUCTION MANAGER
Obi Onuora

ART DIRECTOR
Oz Browne

SENIOR SALES MANAGER
Steve Tothill

PRESS OFFICER
Will O'Mullane

COMICS BRAND MANAGER
Lucy Ripper

**For rights information
contact Jenny Boyce**
jenny.boyce@titanemail.com

**DIRECT SALES &
MARKETING MANAGER**
Ricky Claydon

COMMERCIAL MANAGER
Michelle Fairlamb

HEAD OF RIGHTS
Jenny Boyce

PUBLISHING MANAGER
Darryl Tothill

PUBLISHING DIRECTOR
Chris Teather

OPERATIONS DIRECTOR
Leigh Baulch

EXECUTIVE DIRECTOR
Vivian Cheung

PUBLISHER
Nick Landau

Special thanks to Steven Moffat, Brian Minchin, Mandy Thwaites, Matt Nicholls, James Dudley, Edward Russell, Derek Ritchie, Scott Handcock, Kirsty Mullan, Kate Bush, Julia Nocciolino and Ed Casey for their invaluable assistance.

BBC WORLDWIDE

**DIRECTOR OF
EDITORIAL GOVERNANCE**
Nicholas Brett

**DIRECTOR OF CONSUMER
PRODUCTS AND PUBLISHING**
Andrew Moultrie

HEAD OF UK PUBLISHING
Chris Kerwin

PUBLISHER
Mandy Thwaites

PUBLISHING CO-ORDINATOR
Eva Abramik

DOCTOR WHO: THE ELEVENTH DOCTOR
VOL 6: THE MALIGNANT TRUTH
HB ISBN: 9781785857300
SB ISBN: 9781785860935
Published by Titan Comics, a division of
Titan Publishing Group, Ltd. 144 Southwark Street,
London, SE1 0UP.

A CIP catalogue record for this title is available from the
British Library.
First edition: March 2017.

10 9 8 7 6 5 4 3 2 1

Printed in China.

Titan Comics does not read or accept unsolicited
DOCTOR WHO submissions of ideas, stories or artwork.

www.titan-comics.com

BBC

DOCTOR WHO
THE ELEVENTH DOCTOR

VOL 6: THE MALIGNANT TRUTH

**WRITERS: SI SPURRIER
& ROB WILLIAMS**

**ARTISTS: I.N.J. CULBARD
& SIMON FRASER**

**COLORISTS: MARCIO MENYS
& GARY CALDWEL**

**LETTERS: RICHARD STARKINGS AND
COMICRAFT'S JIMMY BETANCOURT**

TITAN
COMICS

BBC

DOCTOR WHO
THE ELEVENTH DOCTOR

ALICE OBIEFUNE

Alice Obiefune is a former Library Assistant. She has saved the Doctor from himself and others on multiple occasions, but of late, she feels useless and unwanted. She has just hurled herself back into the Time War, at great personal cost...

THE DOCTOR

When is a Doctor not a Doctor? When he's the battle-weary Time War incarnation, a man who has rejected the promise implicit in a name that served him well in previous lives. But has he truly turned his back on his former selves?

THE SQUIRE

An eccentric armor-clad warrior who claims to have fought alongside the Doctor. Truly does not know who she is, or how she remembers the Doctor. The Squire in the present timeline is dead... but perhaps there's still a past self who could provide the answers?

PREVIOUSLY...

The Overcaste blamed the Doctor for the death of their people, and hired The Then and The Now, a temporal bounty hunter, to punish him. The Squire is dead. Alice is now lost in the Time War, having piloted the Master's wounded TARDIS back through the Time Lock. River's life hangs in the balance. And Daak is almost certainly going to kill the Doctor for letting Alice go. Now it's time for the Time War to give up its answers.

How was the Malignant created? Who killed the Overcaste? What great crime was the Doctor responsible for? But, most importantly, will they be the answers that Alice – and the Doctor – want to hear?

When you've finished reading the collection, please email your thoughts to doctorwhocomic@titanemail.com

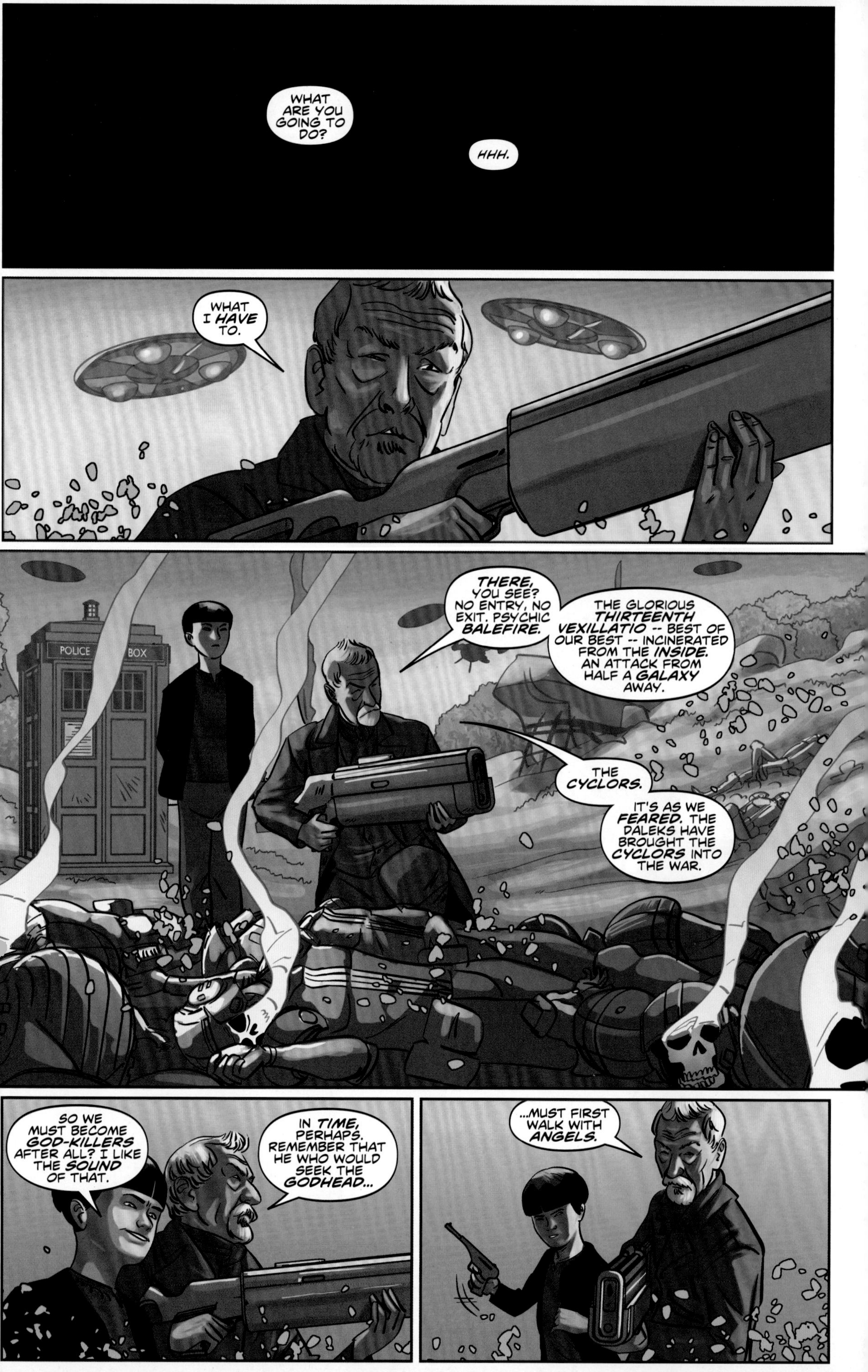
WHAT ARE YOU GOING TO DO?
HHH.
WHAT I HAVE TO.
THERE, YOU SEE? NO ENTRY, NO EXIT. PSYCHIC BALEFIRE.
THE GLORIOUS THIRTEENTH VEXILLATIO -- BEST OF OUR BEST -- INCINERATED FROM THE INSIDE. AN ATTACK FROM HALF A GALAXY AWAY.
POLICE BOX
THE CYCLORS.
IT'S AS WE FEARED. THE DALEKS HAVE BROUGHT THE CYCLORS INTO THE WAR.
SO WE MUST BECOME GOD-KILLERS AFTER ALL? I LIKE THE SOUND OF THAT.
IN TIME, PERHAPS. REMEMBER THAT HE WHO WOULD SEEK THE GODHEAD...
...MUST FIRST WALK WITH ANGELS.

THE ORGAN GRINDER

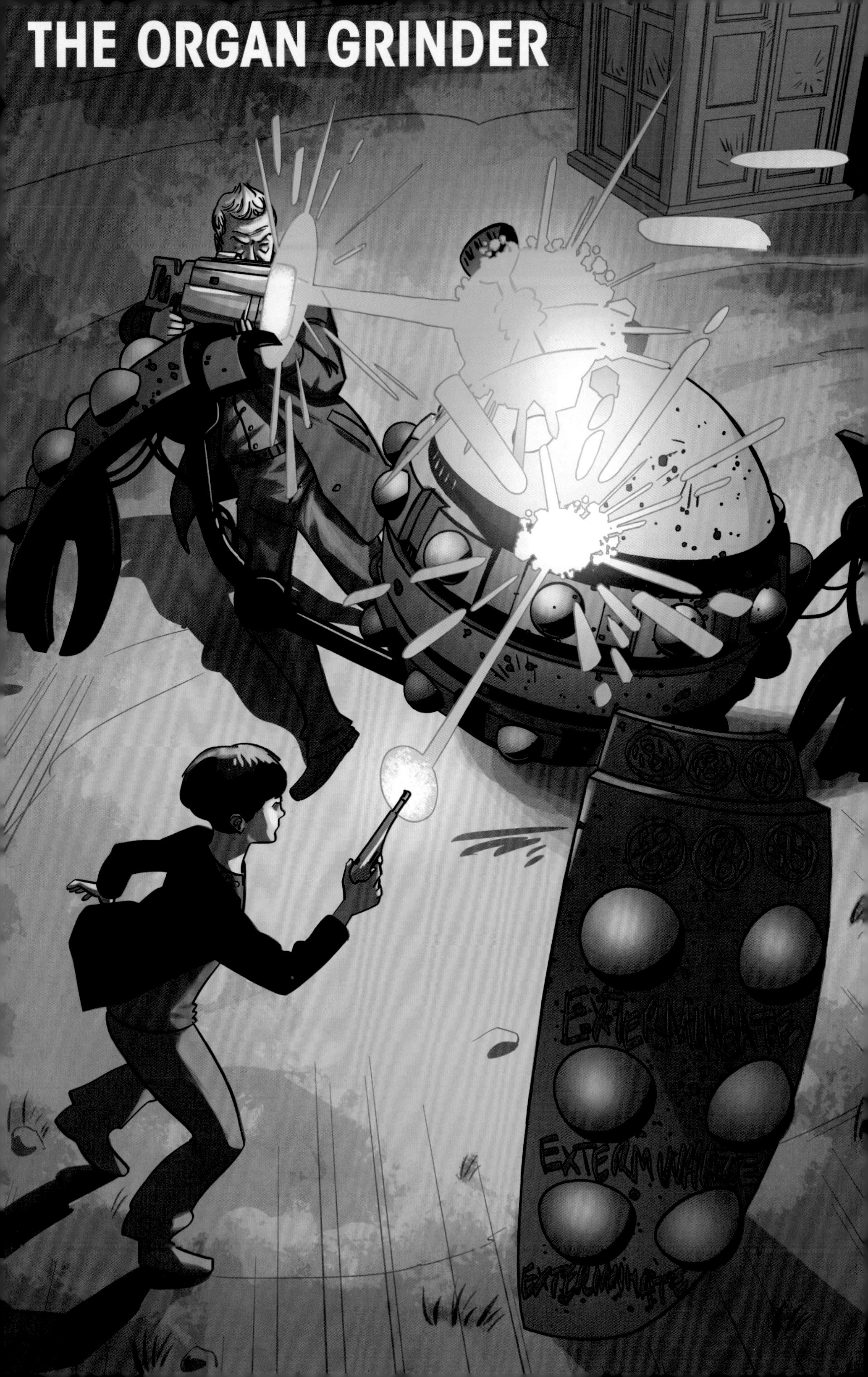

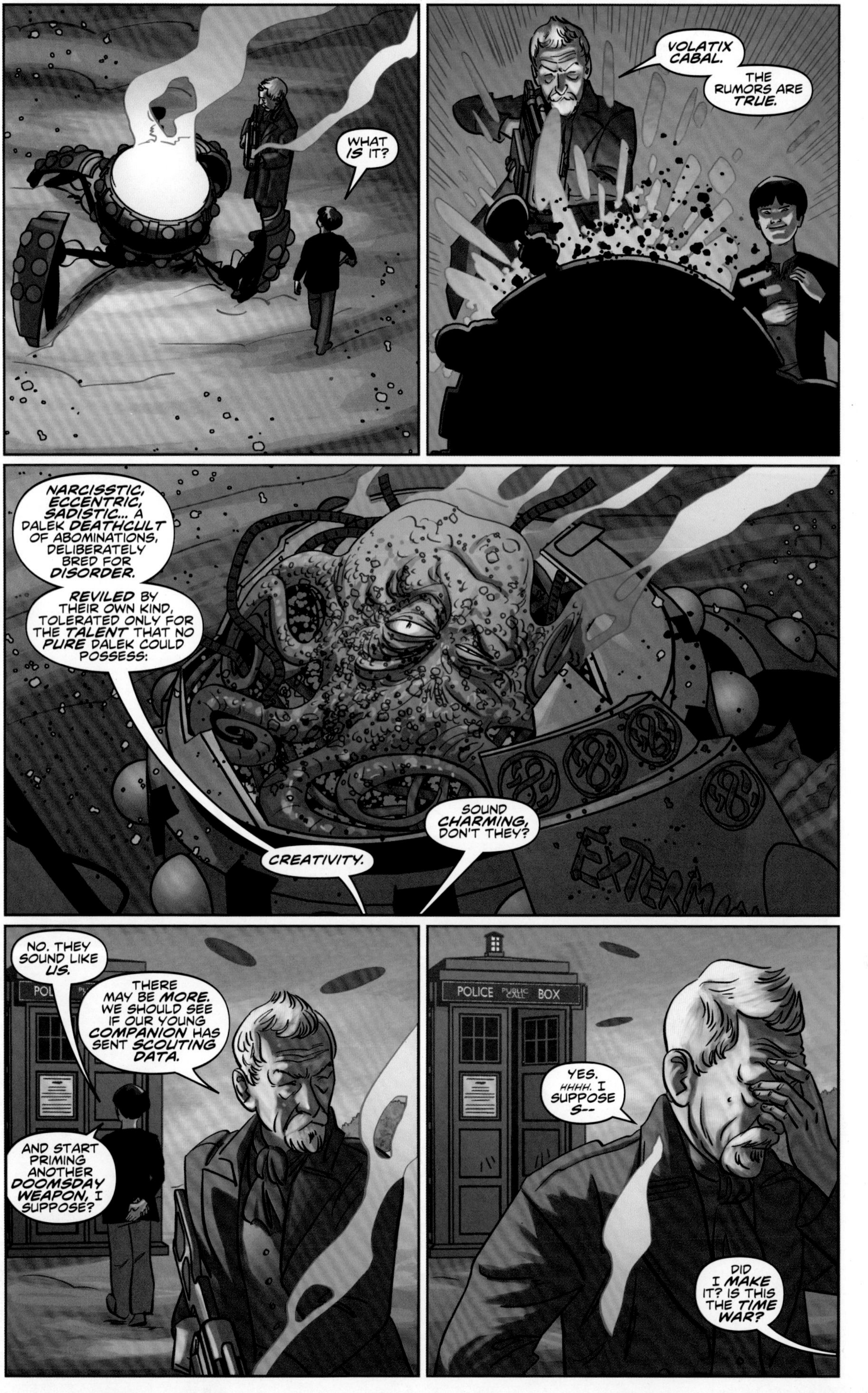
WHAT IS IT?
VOLATIX CABAL.
THE RUMORS ARE TRUE.
NARCISSTIC, ECCENTRIC, SADISTIC... A DALEK DEATHCULT OF ABOMINATIONS, DELIBERATELY BRED FOR DISORDER.
REVILED BY THEIR OWN KIND, TOLERATED ONLY FOR THE TALENT THAT NO PURE DALEK COULD POSSESS:
CREATIVITY.
SOUND CHARMING, DON'T THEY?
NO. THEY SOUND LIKE US.
THERE MAY BE MORE. WE SHOULD SEE IF OUR YOUNG COMPANION HAS SENT SCOUTING DATA.
AND START PRIMING ANOTHER DOOMSDAY WEAPON, I SUPPOSE?
POLICE PUBLIC CALL BOX
YES. HHHH. I SUPPOSE S--
DID I MAKE IT? IS THIS THE TIME WAR?

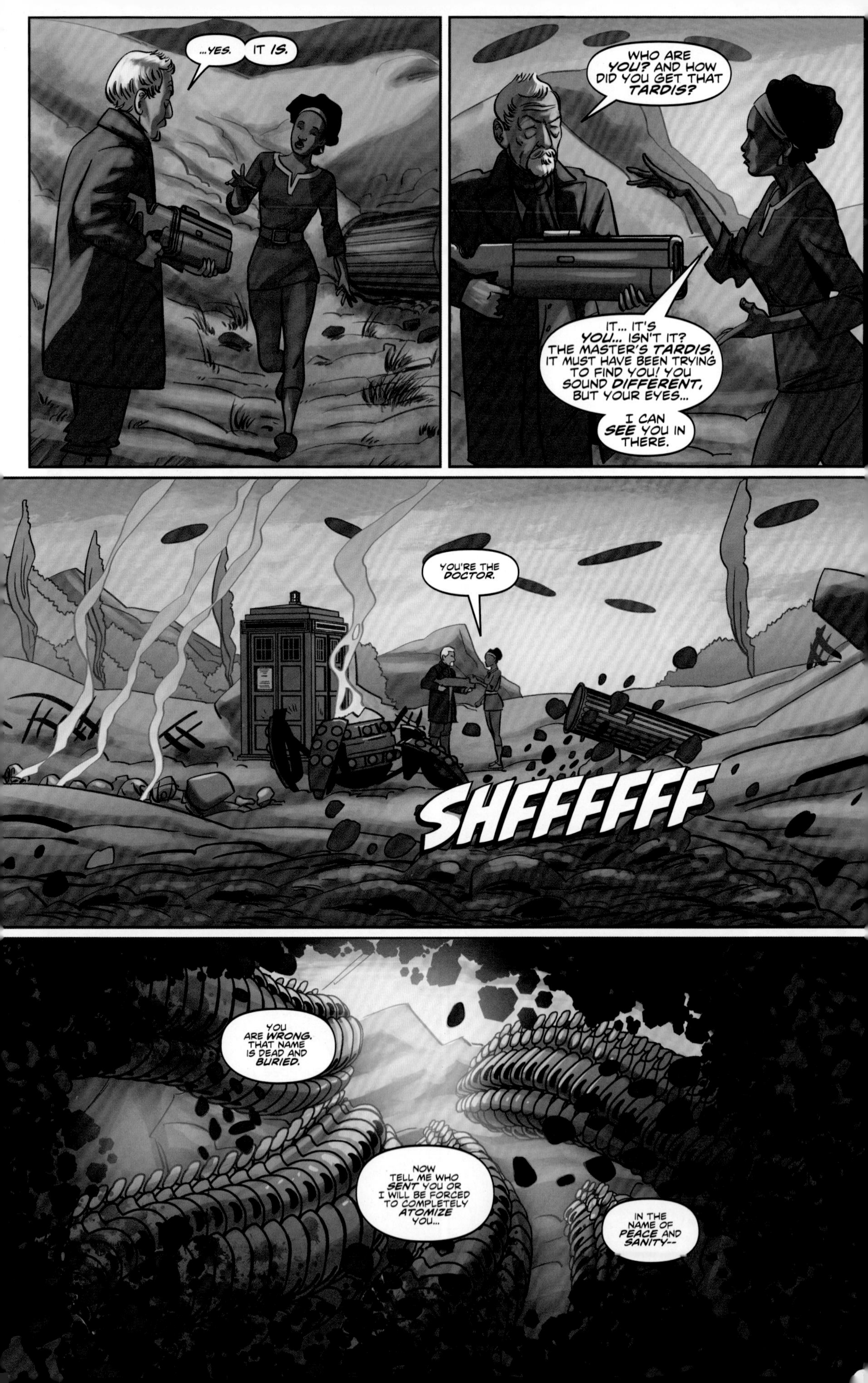
...YES. IT IS.
WHO ARE YOU? AND HOW DID YOU GET THAT TARDIS?
IT... IT'S YOU... ISN'T IT? THE MASTER'S TARDIS, IT MUST HAVE BEEN TRYING TO FIND YOU! YOU SOUND DIFFERENT, BUT YOUR EYES...
I CAN SEE YOU IN THERE.
YOU'RE THE DOCTOR.
SHFFFFFF
YOU ARE WRONG. THAT NAME IS DEAD AND BURIED.
NOW TELL ME WHO SENT YOU OR I WILL BE FORCED TO COMPLETELY ATOMIZE YOU...
IN THE NAME OF PEACE AND SANITY--

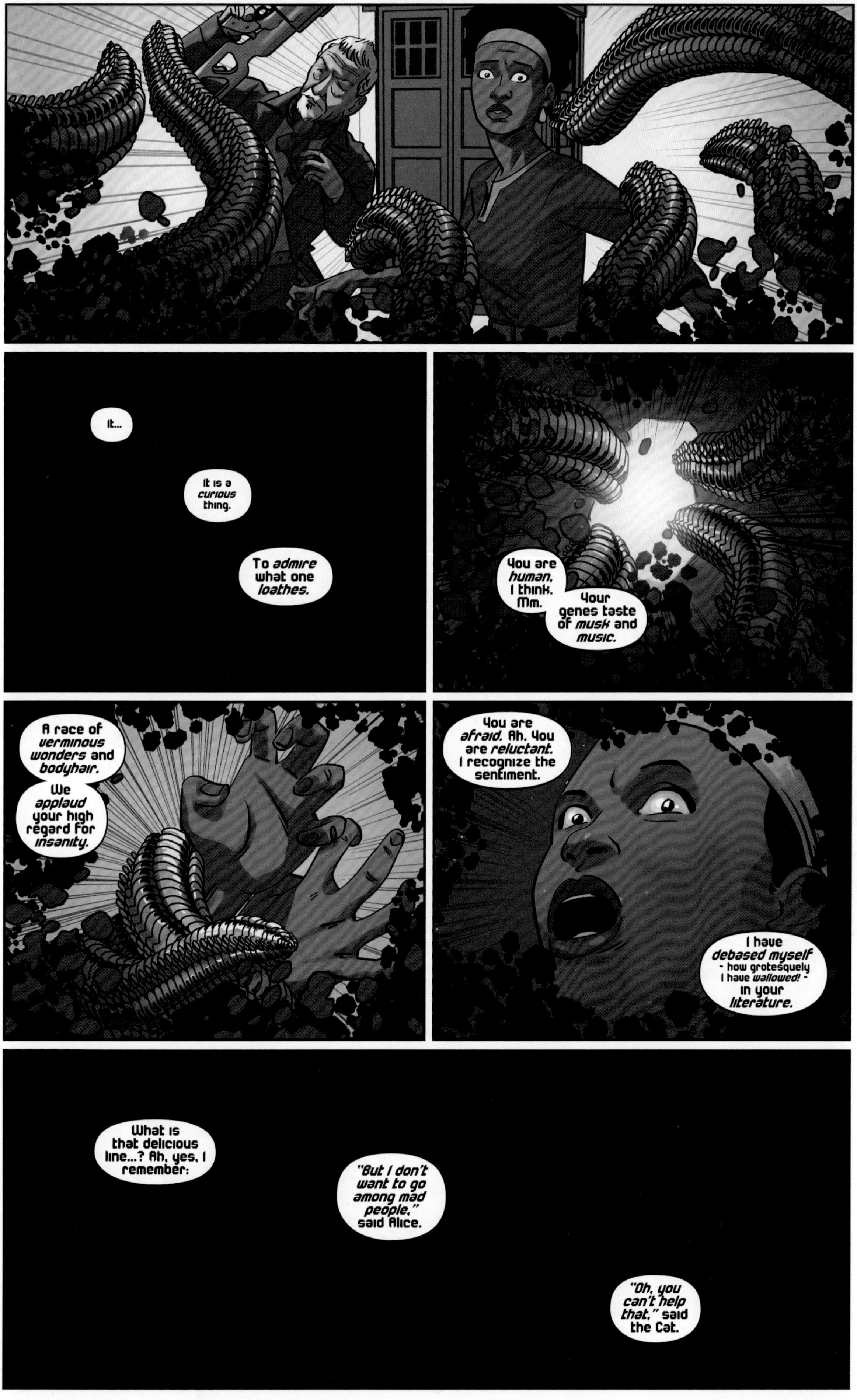

It...
It is a *curious* thing.
To *admire* what one *loathes.*
You are *human,* I think. Mm.
Your genes taste of *musk* and *music.*
A race of *verminous wonders* and *bodyhair.*
We *applaud* your high regard for *insanity.*
You are *afraid.* Ah. You are *reluctant.* I recognize the sentiment.
I have *debased myself* - how grotesquely I have *wallowed!* - in your *literature.*
What is that delicious line...? Ah, yes, I remember:
"But I don't want to go among mad people," said Alice.
"Oh, you can't help that," said the Cat.

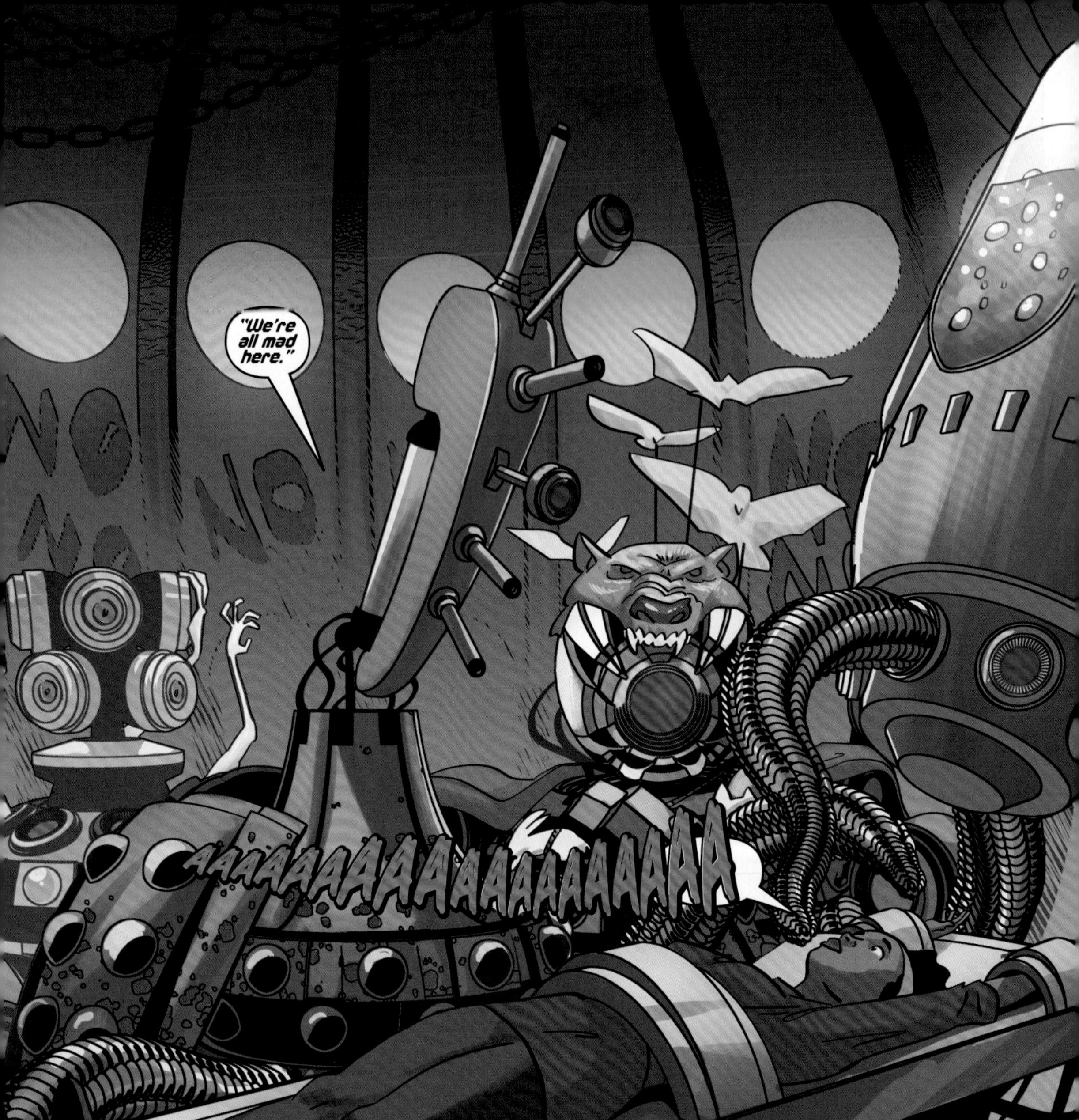
"We're all mad here."
NO NO NO NO NO NO
AAAAAAAAAAAAAAAAAAAA

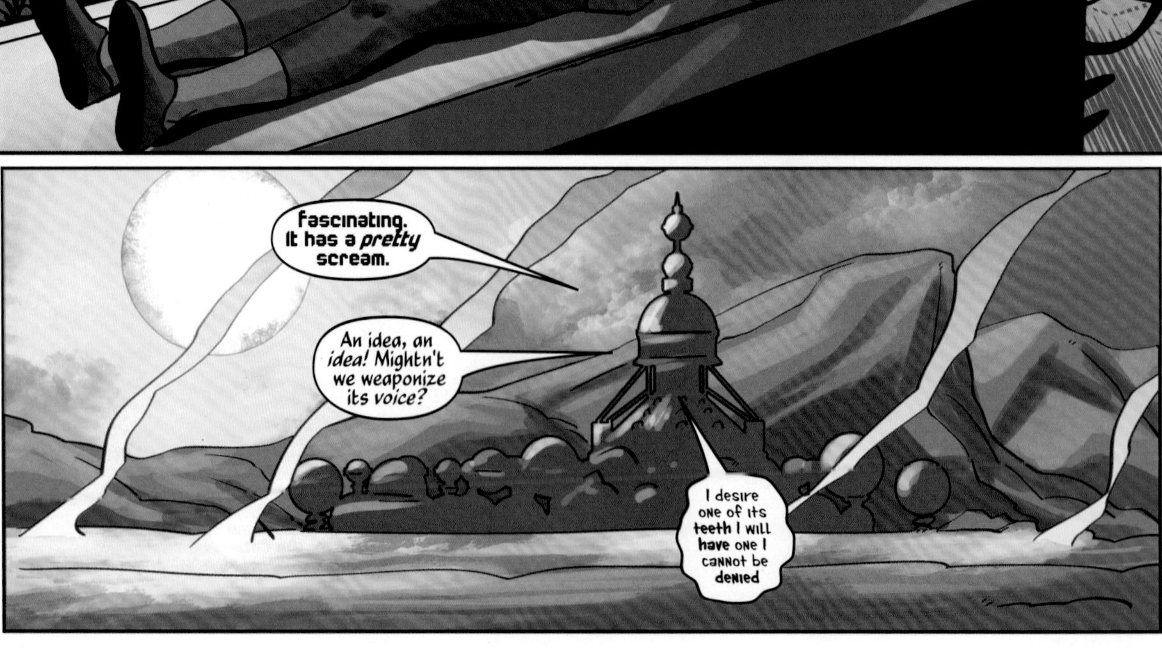
Fascinating. It has a *pretty* scream.
An idea, an *idea!* Mightn't we weaponize its voice?
I desire one of its **teeth** I will **have** one I cannot be **denied**

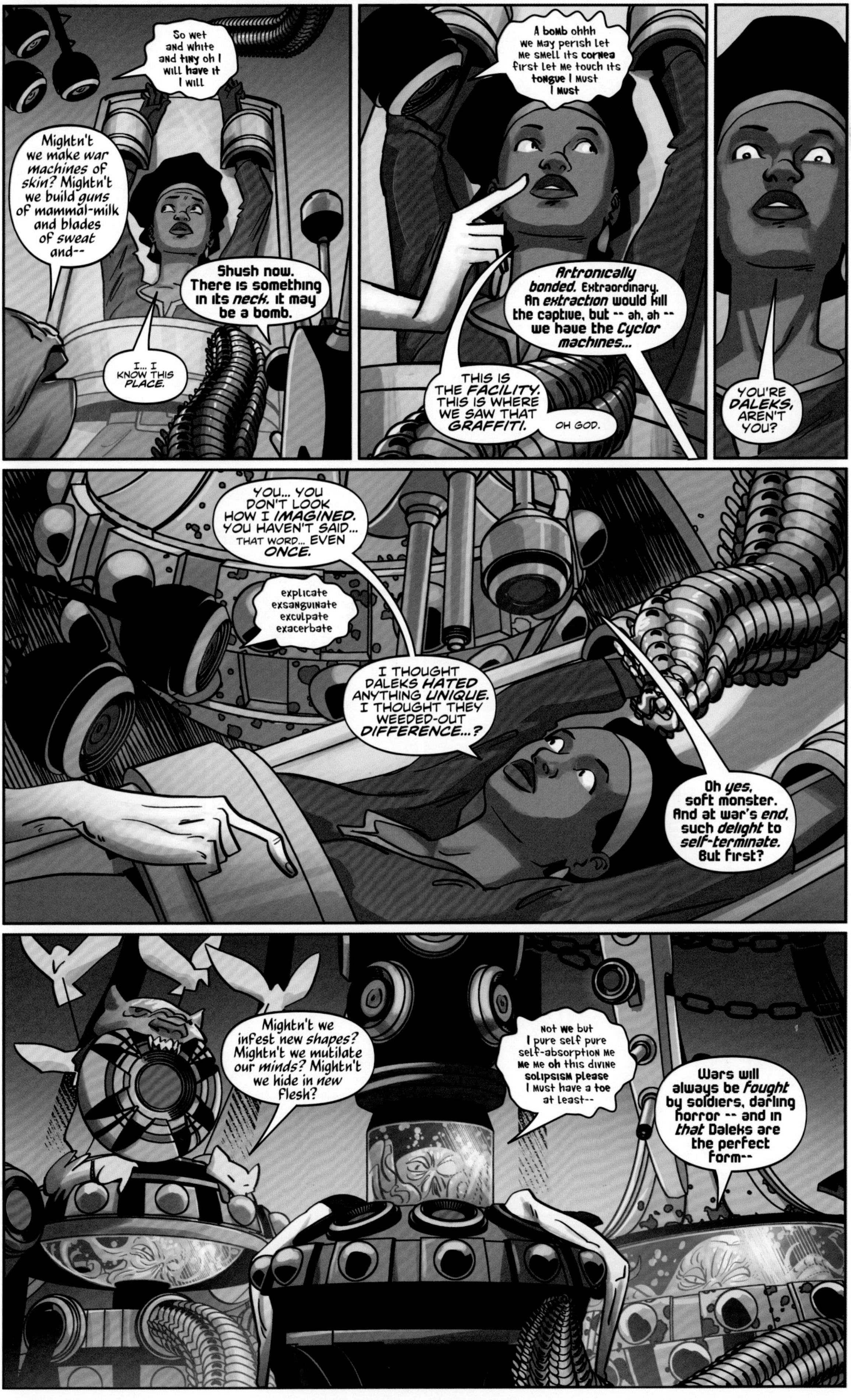

So wet and white and tiny oh I will have it I will
Mightn't we make war machines of skin? Mightn't we build guns of mammal-milk and blades of sweat and--
Shush now. There is something in its neck. it may be a bomb.
I... I KNOW THIS PLACE.
A bomb ohhh we may perish let me smell its cornea first let me touch its tongue I must I must
Artronically bonded. Extraordinary. An extraction would kill the captive, but -- ah, ah -- we have the Cyclor machines...
THIS IS THE FACILITY. THIS IS WHERE WE SAW THAT GRAFFITI.
OH GOD.
YOU'RE DALEKS, AREN'T YOU?
YOU... YOU DON'T LOOK HOW I IMAGINED. YOU HAVEN'T SAID... THAT WORD... EVEN ONCE.
explicate exsanguinate exculpate exacerbate
I THOUGHT DALEKS HATED ANYTHING UNIQUE. I THOUGHT THEY WEEDED-OUT DIFFERENCE...?
Oh yes, soft monster. And at war's end, such delight to self-terminate. But first?
Mightn't we infest new shapes? Mightn't we mutilate our minds? Mightn't we hide in new flesh?
Not we but I pure self pure self-absorption me me me oh this divine solipsism please I must have a toe at least--
Wars will always be fought by soldiers, darling horror -- and in that Daleks are the perfect form--

--but wars are won by madmen.

AAAAAAAAA

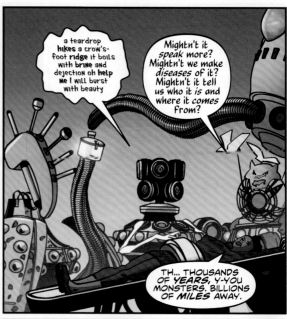
a teardrop hikes a crow's-foot ridge it boils with brine and dejection oh help me I will burst with beauty

Mightn't it speak more? Mightn't we make diseases of it? Mightn't it tell us who it is and where it comes from?

TH... THOUSANDS OF YEARS, Y-YOU MONSTERS. BILLIONS OF MILES AWAY.

≥Tk≥ Thousands. Billions. It still thinks in base-10.

born with ten fingers poor worm let me grow it Dalek tentacles let it count in twelves let it be as holy as I let me cut it

Mightn't its brain shatter? Mightn't duodecimals crush its reason? Mightn't we peer into its head first?

nf. This is nothing. A tracker beyond its range. A disappointment. Dull.

≥sigh≥ Very well. Let us pry-open its mind...

...let us see what it has seen.

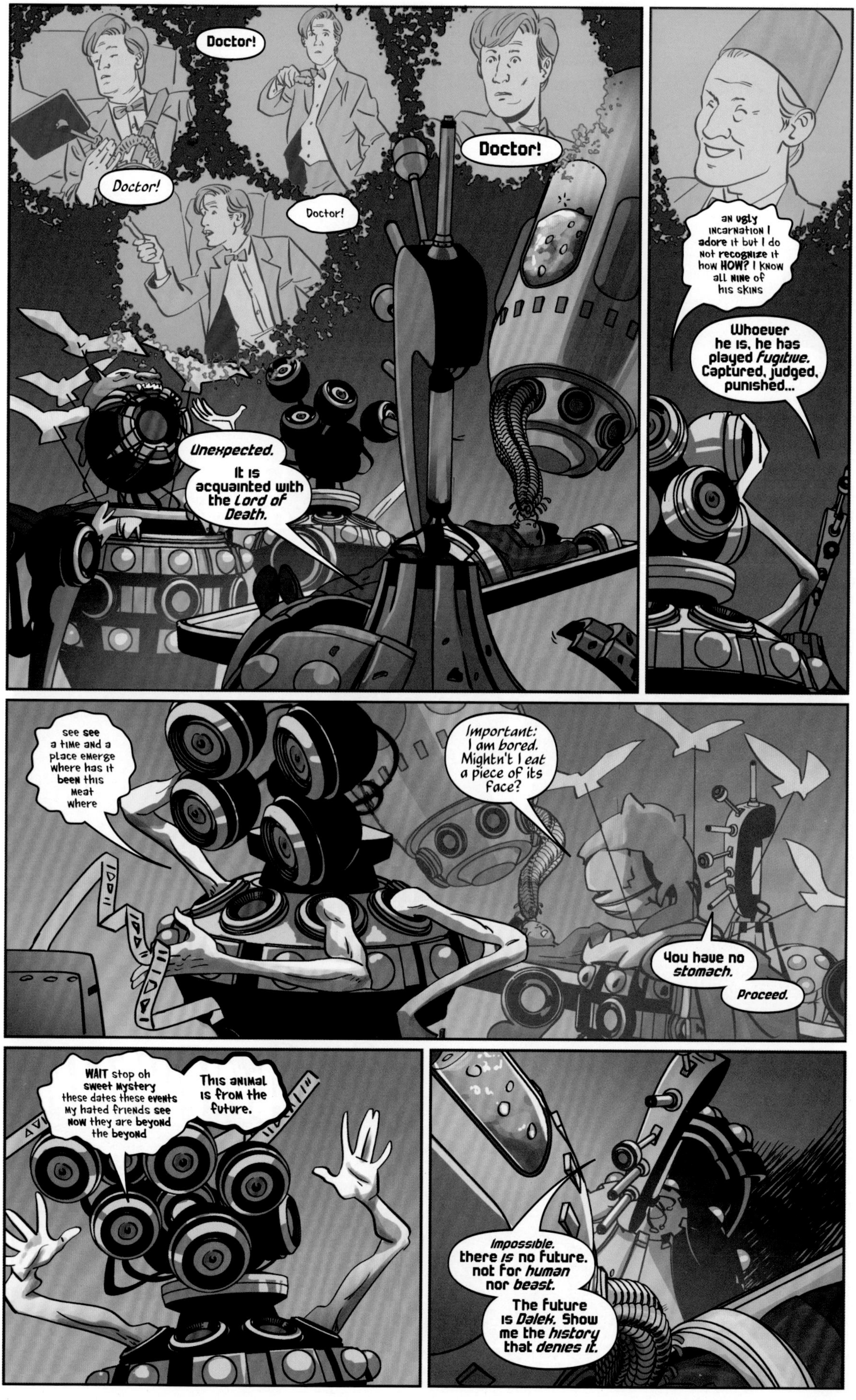
Doctor!
Doctor!
Doctor!
Doctor!
Unexpected.
It is acquainted with the Lord of Death.
an ugly incarnation I adore it but I do not recognize it how HOW? I know all NINE of his skins
Whoever he is, he has played fugitive. Captured, judged, punished...
see see a time and a place emerge where has it been this Meat where
Important: I am bored. Mightn't I eat a piece of its face?
You have no stomach.
Proceed.
WAIT stop oh sweet Mystery these dates these events My hated friends see NOW they are beyond the beyond
This animal is from the future.
Impossible. there is no future. not for human nor beast.
The future is Dalek. Show me the history that denies it.

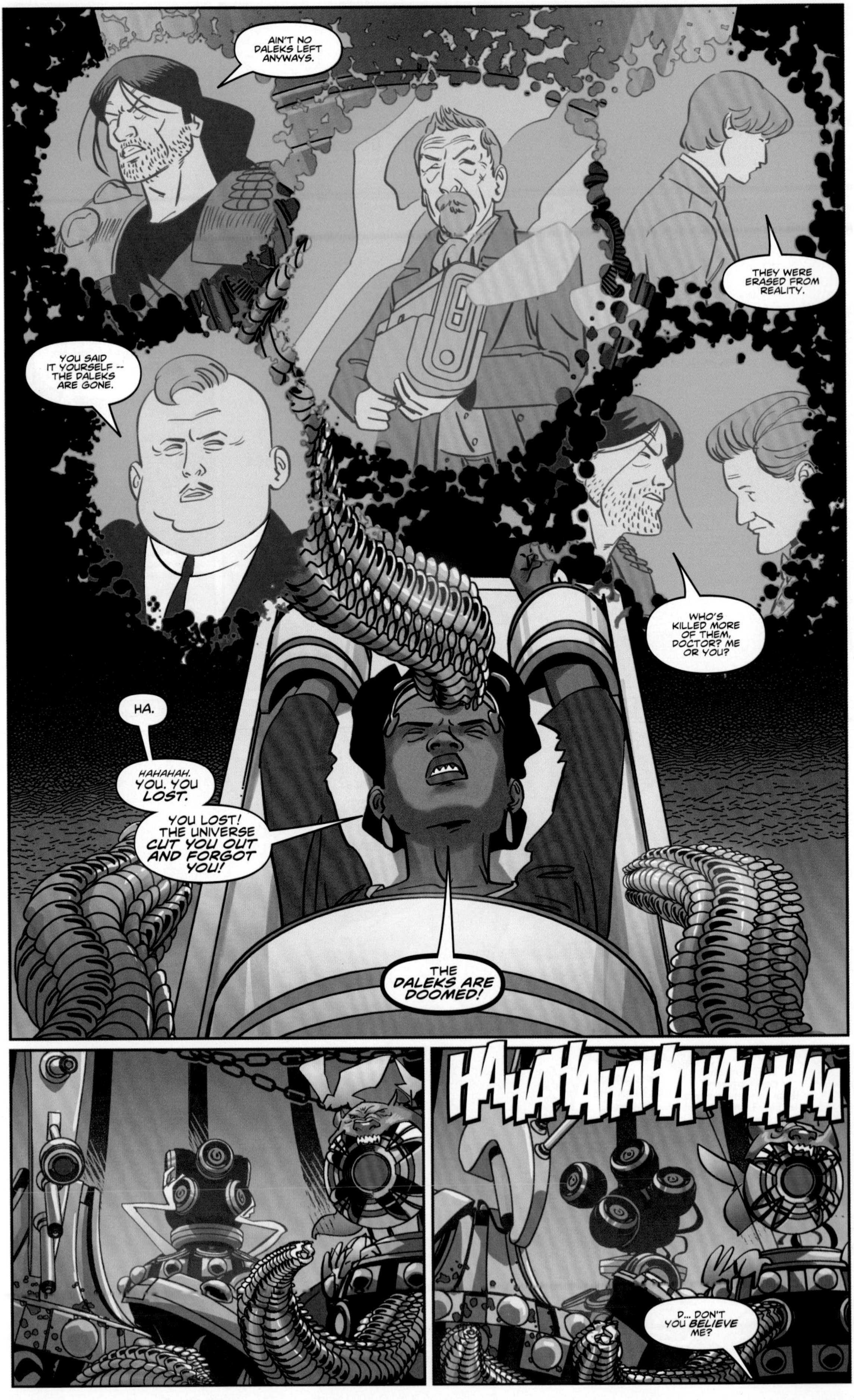

AIN'T NO DALEKS LEFT ANYWAYS.
THEY WERE ERASED FROM REALITY.
YOU SAID IT YOURSELF -- THE DALEKS ARE GONE.
WHO'S KILLED MORE OF THEM, DOCTOR? ME OR YOU?
HA.
HAHAHAH. YOU. YOU LOST.
YOU LOST! THE UNIVERSE CUT YOU OUT AND FORGOT YOU!
THE DALEKS ARE DOOMED!
HAHAHAHAHAHAHAHAHAA
D... DON'T YOU BELIEVE ME?

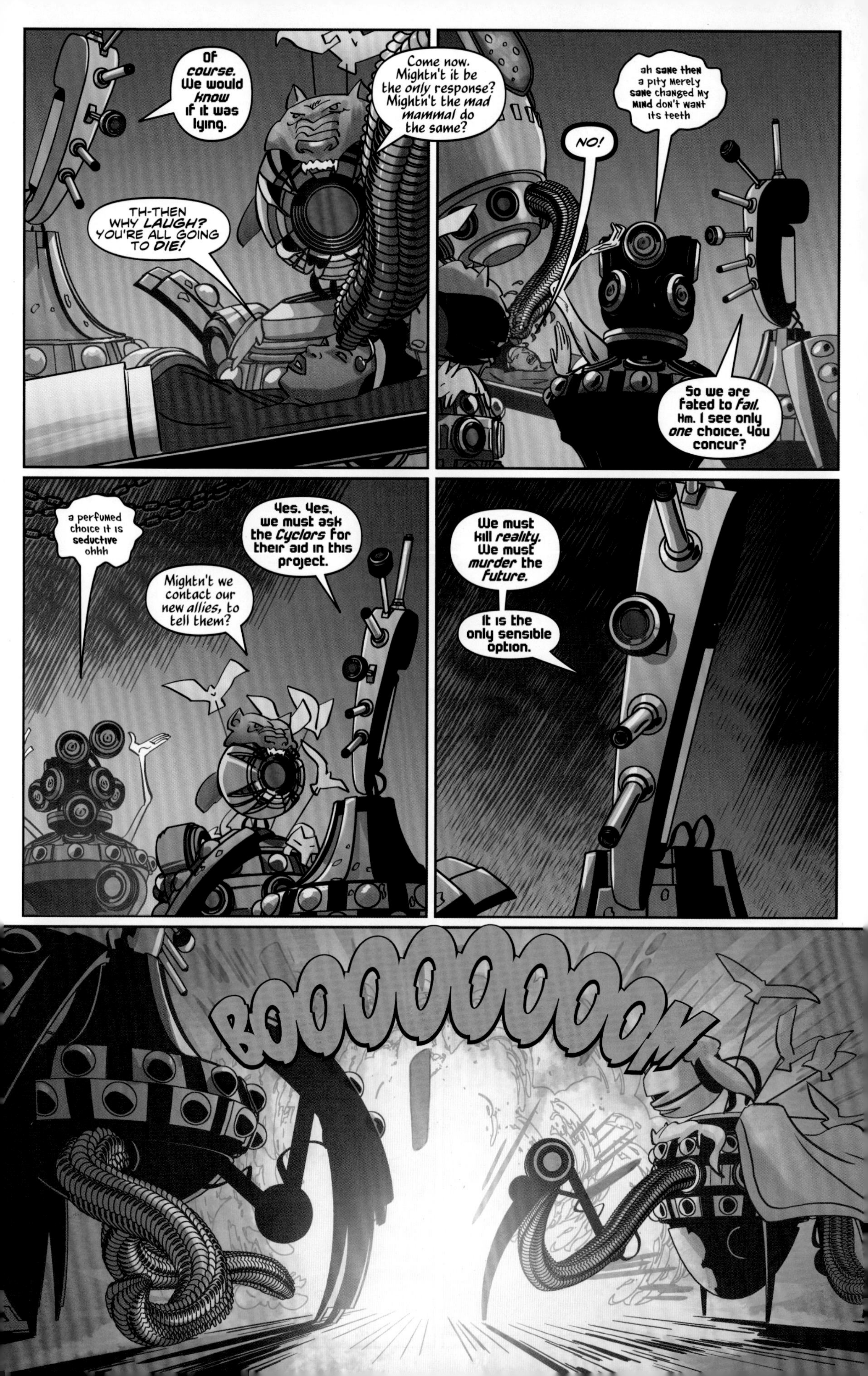

Of course. We would know if it was lying.
TH-THEN WHY LAUGH? YOU'RE ALL GOING TO DIE!
Come now. Mightn't it be the only response? Mightn't the mad mammal do the same?
NO!
ah sane then a pity merely sane changed my MIND don't want its teeth
So we are fated to fail. Hm. I see only one choice. You concur?
a perfumed choice it is seductive ohhh
Mightn't we contact our new allies, to tell them?
Yes. Yes, we must ask the Cyclors for their aid in this project.
We must kill reality. We must murder the future.
It is the only sensible option.
BOOOOOOOOM

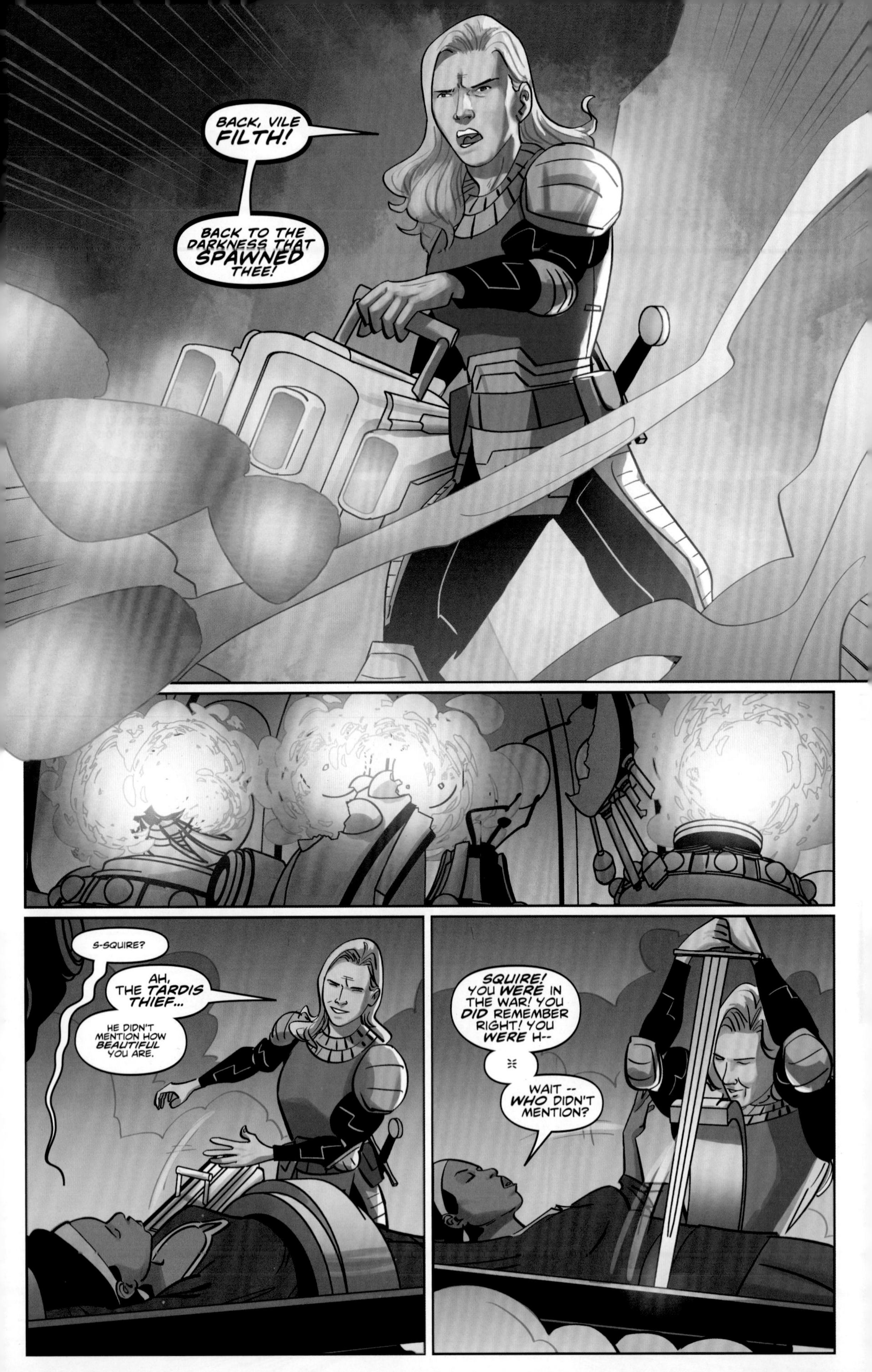
BACK, VILE FILTH!
BACK TO THE DARKNESS THAT SPAWNED THEE!
S-SQUIRE?
AH, THE TARDIS THIEF...
HE DIDN'T MENTION HOW BEAUTIFUL YOU ARE.
SQUIRE! YOU WERE IN THE WAR! YOU DID REMEMBER RIGHT! YOU WERE H--
WAIT -- WHO DIDN'T MENTION?

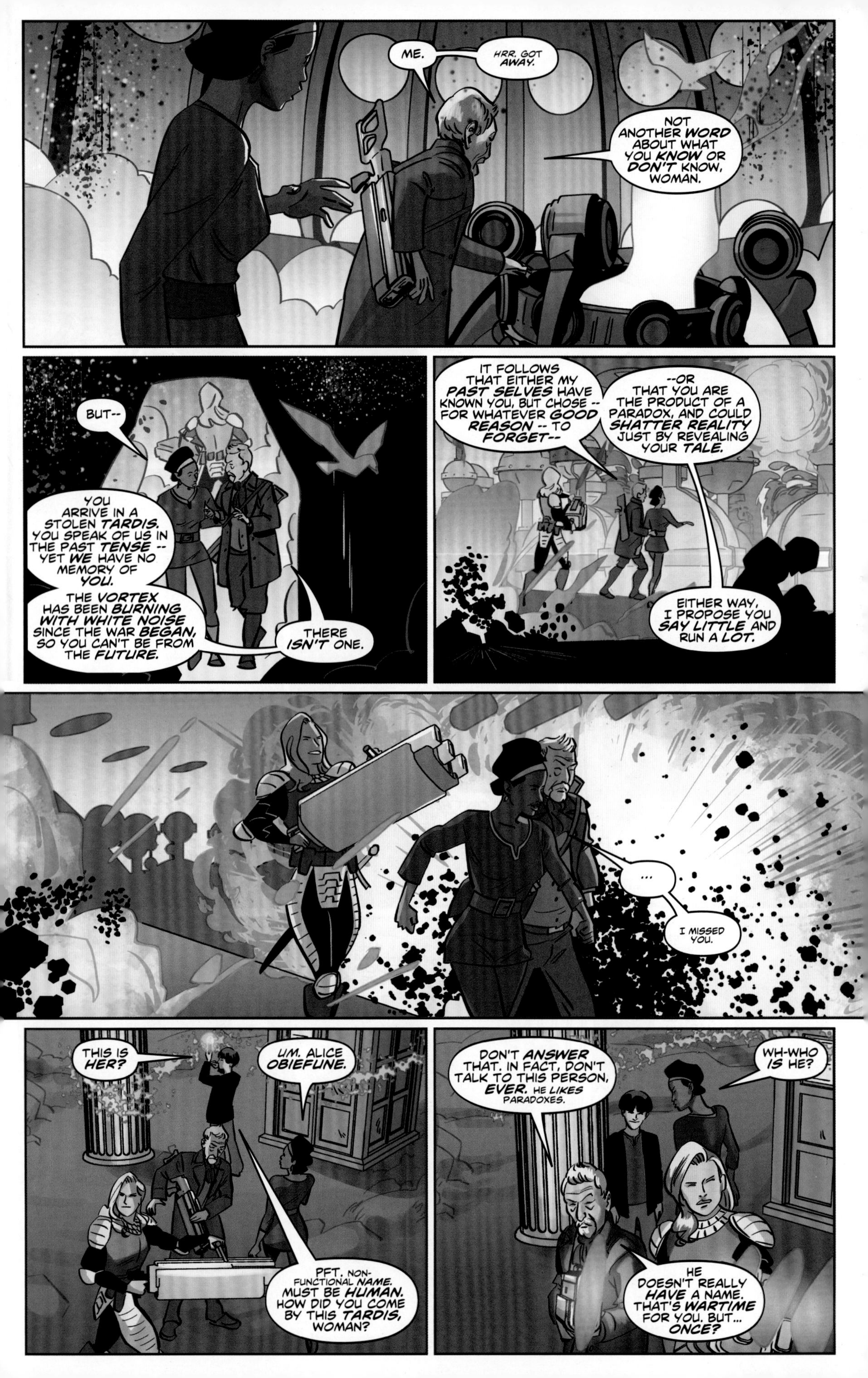
ME.
HRR. GOT AWAY.
NOT ANOTHER WORD ABOUT WHAT YOU KNOW OR DON'T KNOW, WOMAN.
BUT--
YOU ARRIVE IN A STOLEN TARDIS. YOU SPEAK OF US IN THE PAST TENSE -- YET WE HAVE NO MEMORY OF YOU.
THE VORTEX HAS BEEN BURNING WITH WHITE NOISE SINCE THE WAR BEGAN, SO YOU CAN'T BE FROM THE FUTURE.
THERE ISN'T ONE.
IT FOLLOWS THAT EITHER MY PAST SELVES HAVE KNOWN YOU, BUT CHOSE -- FOR WHATEVER GOOD REASON -- TO FORGET--
--OR THAT YOU ARE THE PRODUCT OF A PARADOX, AND COULD SHATTER REALITY JUST BY REVEALING YOUR TALE.
EITHER WAY, I PROPOSE YOU SAY LITTLE AND RUN A LOT.
...
I MISSED YOU.
THIS IS HER?
UM. ALICE OBIEFUNE.
PFT. NON-FUNCTIONAL NAME. MUST BE HUMAN. HOW DID YOU COME BY THIS TARDIS, WOMAN?
DON'T ANSWER THAT. IN FACT, DON'T TALK TO THIS PERSON, EVER. HE LIKES PARADOXES.
WH-WHO IS HE?
HE DOESN'T REALLY HAVE A NAME. THAT'S WARTIME FOR YOU. BUT... ONCE?

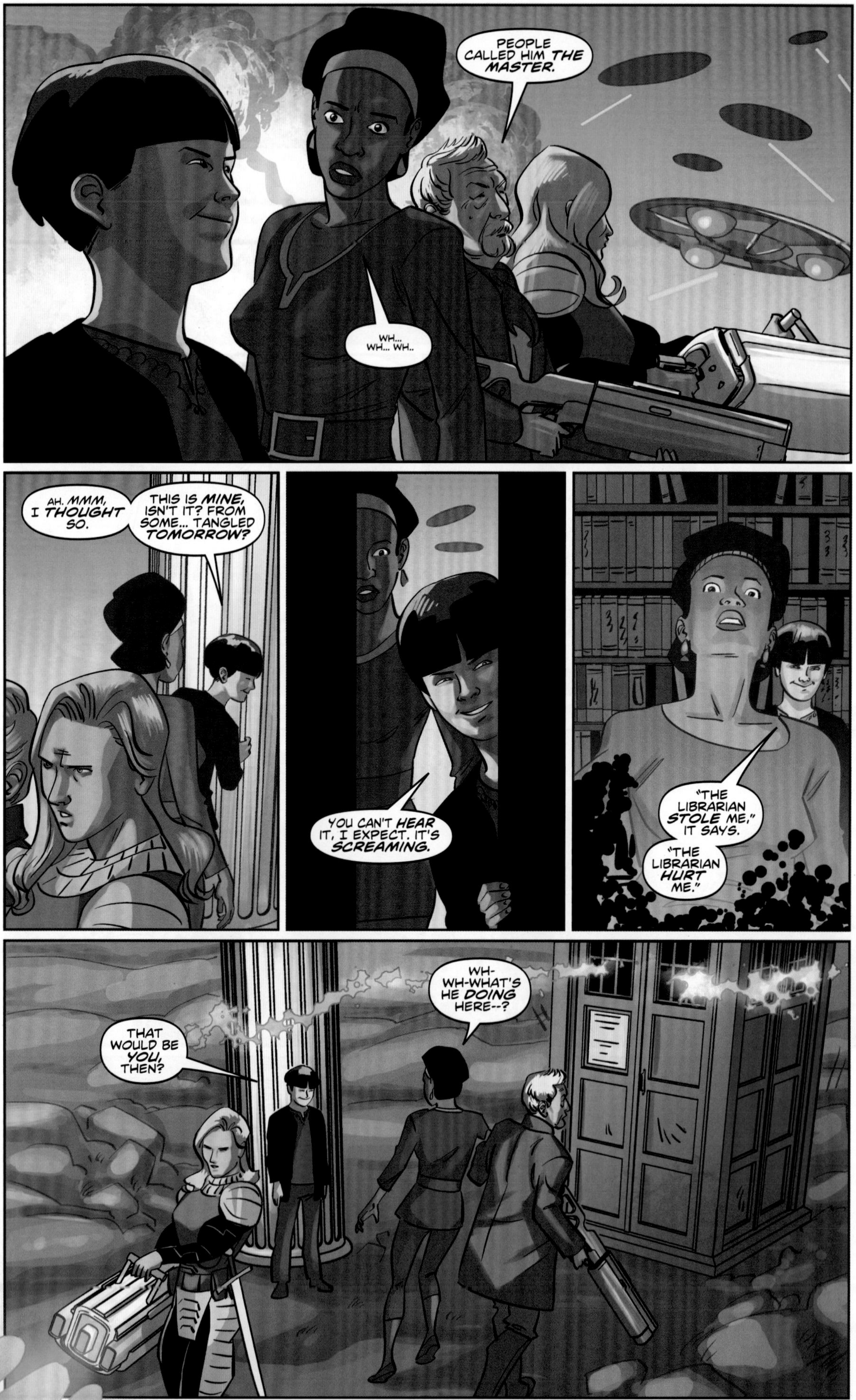
PEOPLE CALLED HIM THE MASTER.
WH... WH... WH..
AH. MMM, I THOUGHT SO.
THIS IS MINE, ISN'T IT? FROM SOME... TANGLED TOMORROW?
YOU CAN'T HEAR IT, I EXPECT. IT'S SCREAMING.
"THE LIBRARIAN STOLE ME," IT SAYS.
"THE LIBRARIAN HURT ME."
THAT WOULD BE YOU, THEN?
WH- WH-WHAT'S HE DOING HERE--?

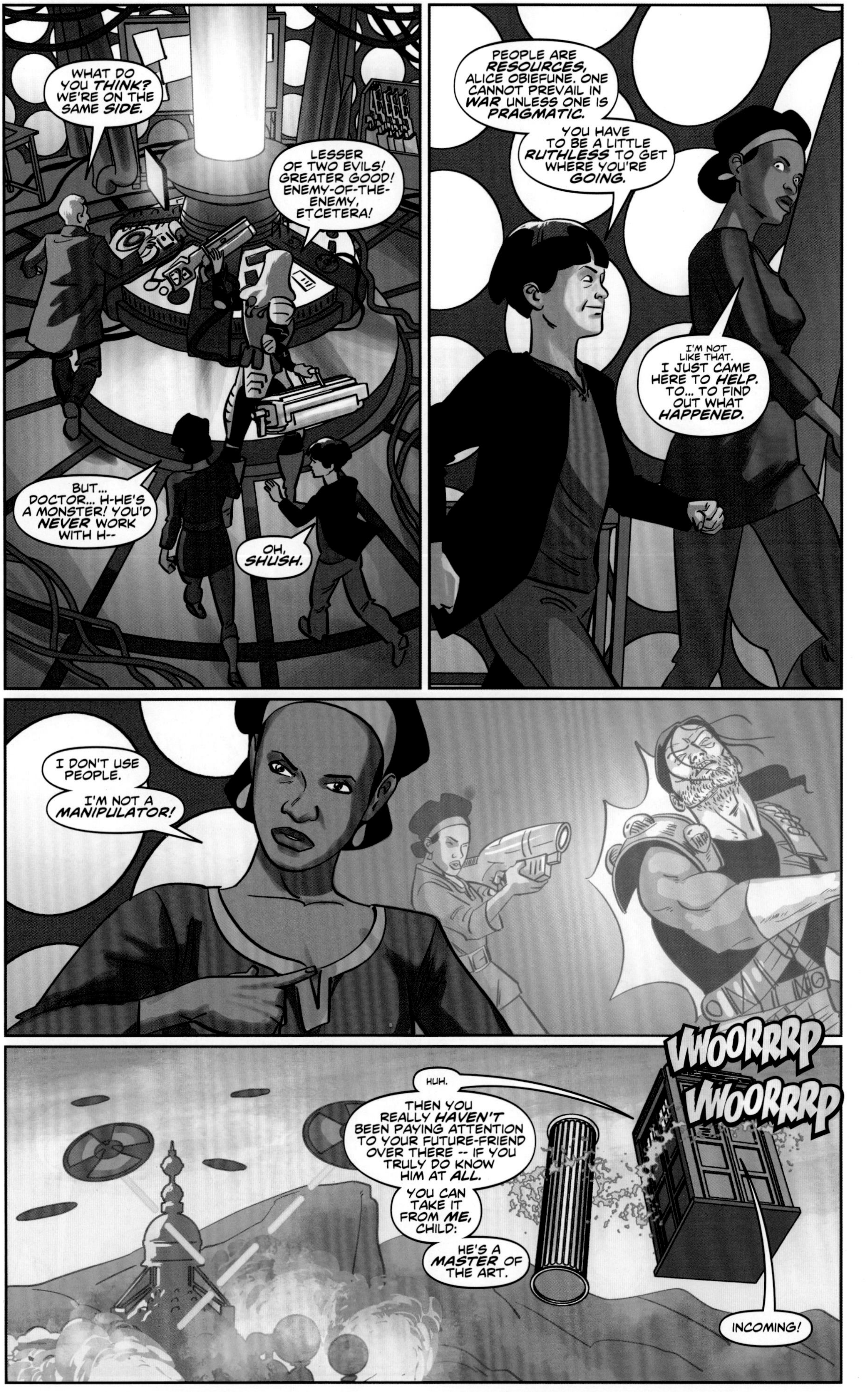
WHAT DO YOU THINK? WE'RE ON THE SAME SIDE.
LESSER OF TWO EVILS! GREATER GOOD! ENEMY-OF-THE-ENEMY, ETCETERA!
BUT... DOCTOR... H-HE'S A MONSTER! YOU'D NEVER WORK WITH H--
OH, SHUSH.
PEOPLE ARE RESOURCES, ALICE OBIEFUNE. ONE CANNOT PREVAIL IN WAR UNLESS ONE IS PRAGMATIC.
YOU HAVE TO BE A LITTLE RUTHLESS TO GET WHERE YOU'RE GOING.
I'M NOT LIKE THAT. I JUST CAME HERE TO HELP. TO... TO FIND OUT WHAT HAPPENED.
I DON'T USE PEOPLE.
I'M NOT A MANIPULATOR!
VWOORRRP
VWOORRRP
HUH.
THEN YOU REALLY HAVEN'T BEEN PAYING ATTENTION TO YOUR FUTURE-FRIEND OVER THERE -- IF YOU TRULY DO KNOW HIM AT ALL.
YOU CAN TAKE IT FROM ME, CHILD:
HE'S A MASTER OF THE ART.
INCOMING!

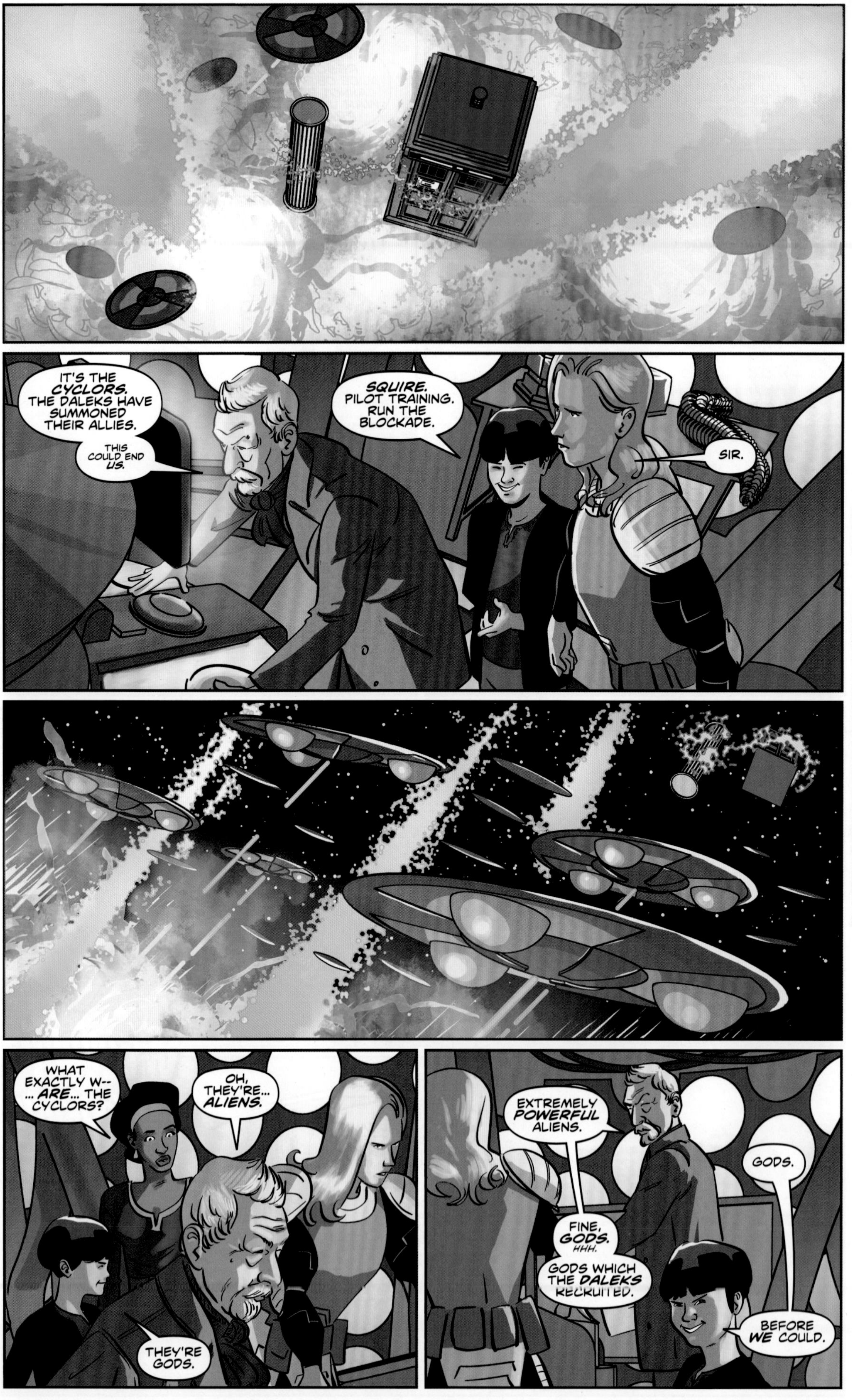
IT'S THE CYCLORS. THE DALEKS HAVE SUMMONED THEIR ALLIES.
THIS COULD END US.
SQUIRE. PILOT TRAINING. RUN THE BLOCKADE.
SIR.
WHAT EXACTLY W-- ...ARE... THE CYCLORS?
OH, THEY'RE... ALIENS.
THEY'RE GODS.
EXTREMELY POWERFUL ALIENS.
GODS.
FINE, GODS. HHH.
GODS WHICH THE DALEKS RECRUITED.
BEFORE WE COULD.

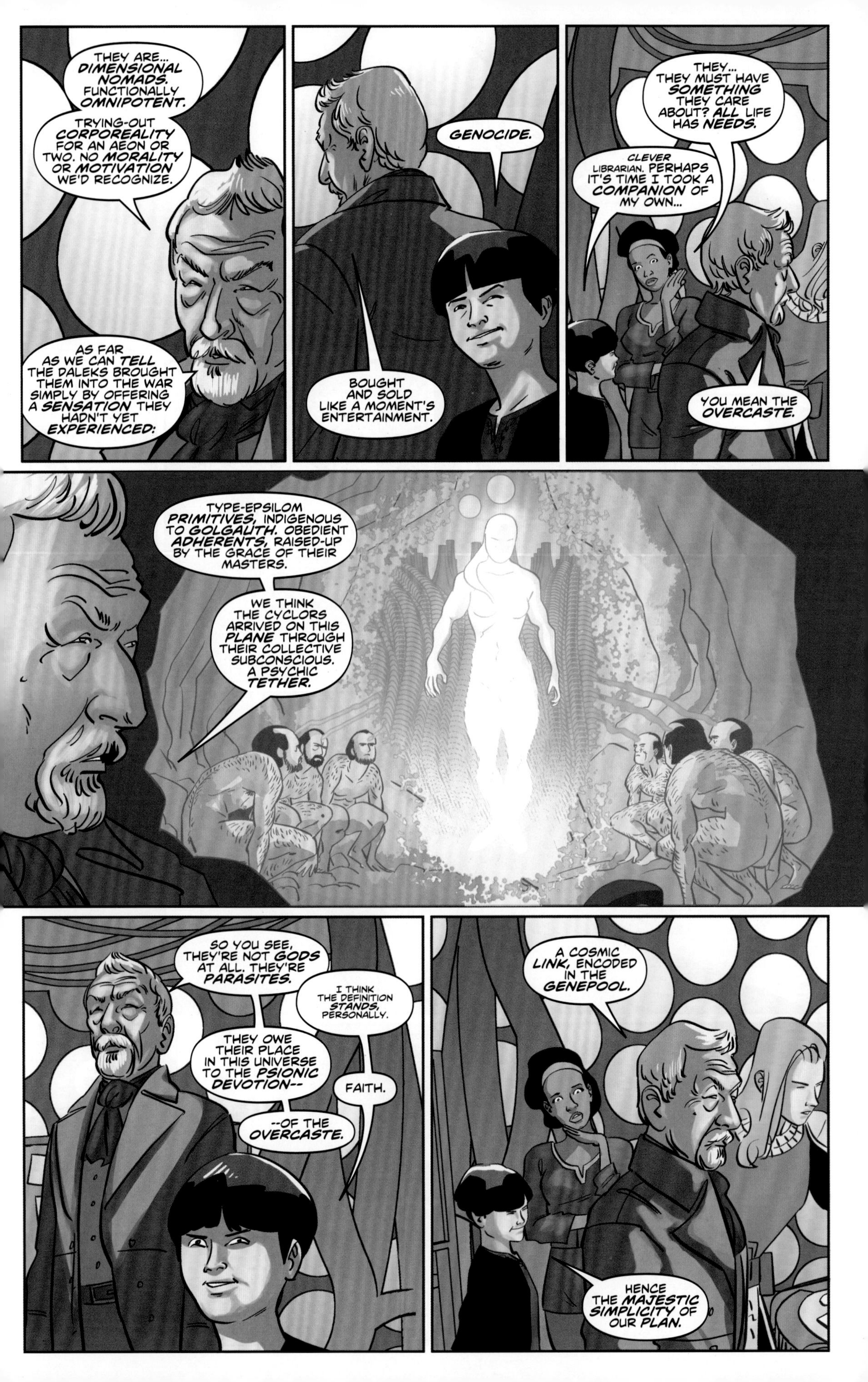
THEY ARE... DIMENSIONAL NOMADS. FUNCTIONALLY OMNIPOTENT.
TRYING-OUT CORPOREALITY FOR AN AEON OR TWO. NO MORALITY OR MOTIVATION WE'D RECOGNIZE.
AS FAR AS WE CAN TELL THE DALEKS BROUGHT THEM INTO THE WAR SIMPLY BY OFFERING A SENSATION THEY HADN'T YET EXPERIENCED:
GENOCIDE.
BOUGHT AND SOLD LIKE A MOMENT'S ENTERTAINMENT.
THEY... THEY MUST HAVE SOMETHING THEY CARE ABOUT? ALL LIFE HAS NEEDS.
CLEVER LIBRARIAN. PERHAPS IT'S TIME I TOOK A COMPANION OF MY OWN...
YOU MEAN THE OVERCASTE.
TYPE-EPSILOM PRIMITIVES, INDIGENOUS TO GOLGAUTH. OBEDIENT ADHERENTS, RAISED-UP BY THE GRACE OF THEIR MASTERS.
WE THINK THE CYCLORS ARRIVED ON THIS PLANE THROUGH THEIR COLLECTIVE SUBCONSCIOUS. A PSYCHIC TETHER.
SO YOU SEE, THEY'RE NOT GODS AT ALL. THEY'RE PARASITES.
I THINK THE DEFINITION STANDS, PERSONALLY.
THEY OWE THEIR PLACE IN THIS UNIVERSE TO THE PSIONIC DEVOTION--
FAITH.
--OF THE OVERCASTE.
A COSMIC LINK, ENCODED IN THE GENEPOOL.
HENCE THE MAJESTIC SIMPLICITY OF OUR PLAN.

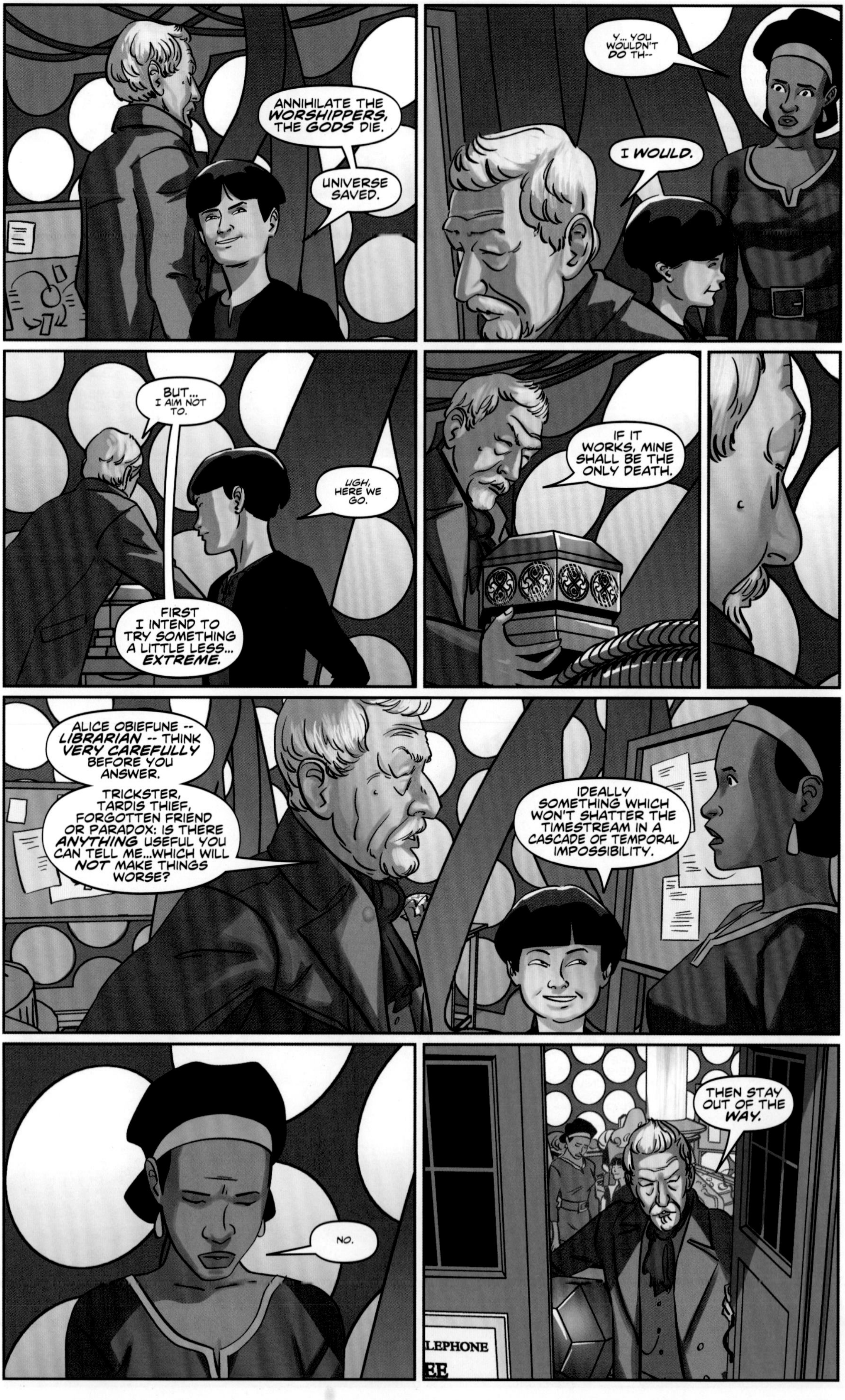
ANNIHILATE THE WORSHIPPERS, THE GODS DIE.
UNIVERSE SAVED.
Y... YOU WOULDN'T DO TH--
I WOULD.
BUT... I AIM NOT TO.
UGH, HERE WE GO.
FIRST I INTEND TO TRY SOMETHING A LITTLE LESS... EXTREME.
IF IT WORKS, MINE SHALL BE THE ONLY DEATH.
ALICE OBIEFUNE -- LIBRARIAN -- THINK VERY CAREFULLY BEFORE YOU ANSWER.
TRICKSTER, TARDIS THIEF, FORGOTTEN FRIEND OR PARADOX: IS THERE ANYTHING USEFUL YOU CAN TELL ME...WHICH WILL NOT MAKE THINGS WORSE?
IDEALLY SOMETHING WHICH WON'T SHATTER THE TIMESTREAM IN A CASCADE OF TEMPORAL IMPOSSIBILITY.
NO.
THEN STAY OUT OF THE WAY.
LEPHONE
EE

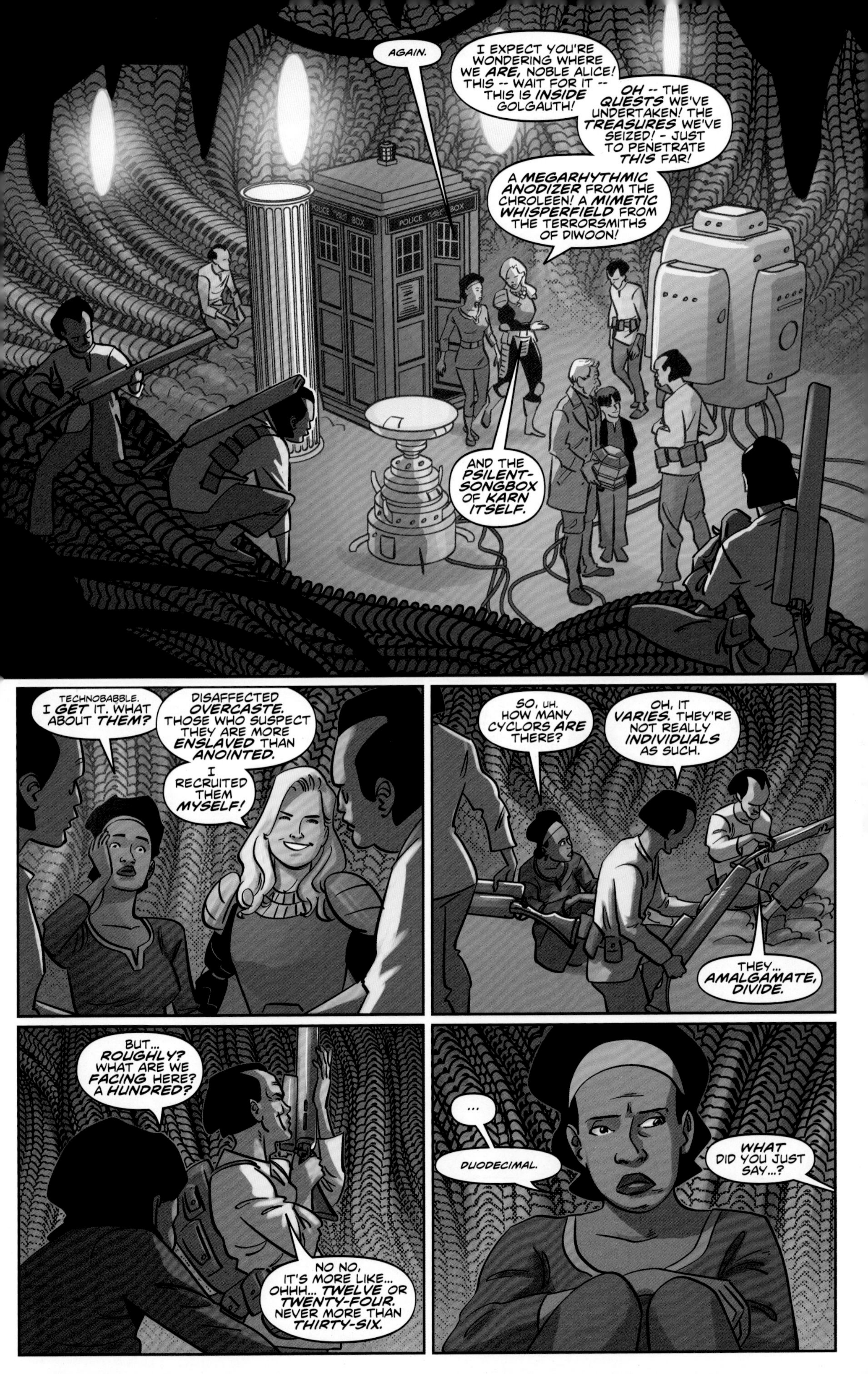
AGAIN.
I EXPECT YOU'RE WONDERING WHERE WE ARE, NOBLE ALICE! THIS -- WAIT FOR IT -- THIS IS INSIDE GOLGAUTH!
OH -- THE QUESTS WE'VE UNDERTAKEN! THE TREASURES WE'VE SEIZED! - JUST TO PENETRATE THIS FAR!
A MEGARHYTHMIC ANODIZER FROM THE CHROLEEN! A MIMETIC WHISPERFIELD FROM THE TERRORSMITHS OF DIWOON!
AND THE PSILENT-SONGBOX OF KARN ITSELF.
TECHNOBABBLE. I GET IT. WHAT ABOUT THEM?
DISAFFECTED OVERCASTE. THOSE WHO SUSPECT THEY ARE MORE ENSLAVED THAN ANOINTED.
I RECRUITED THEM MYSELF!
SO, UH. HOW MANY CYCLORS ARE THERE?
OH, IT VARIES. THEY'RE NOT REALLY INDIVIDUALS AS SUCH.
THEY... AMALGAMATE, DIVIDE.
BUT... ROUGHLY? WHAT ARE WE FACING HERE? A HUNDRED?
NO NO, IT'S MORE LIKE... OHHH... TWELVE OR TWENTY-FOUR. NEVER MORE THAN THIRTY-SIX.
...
DUODECIMAL.
WHAT DID YOU JUST SAY...?

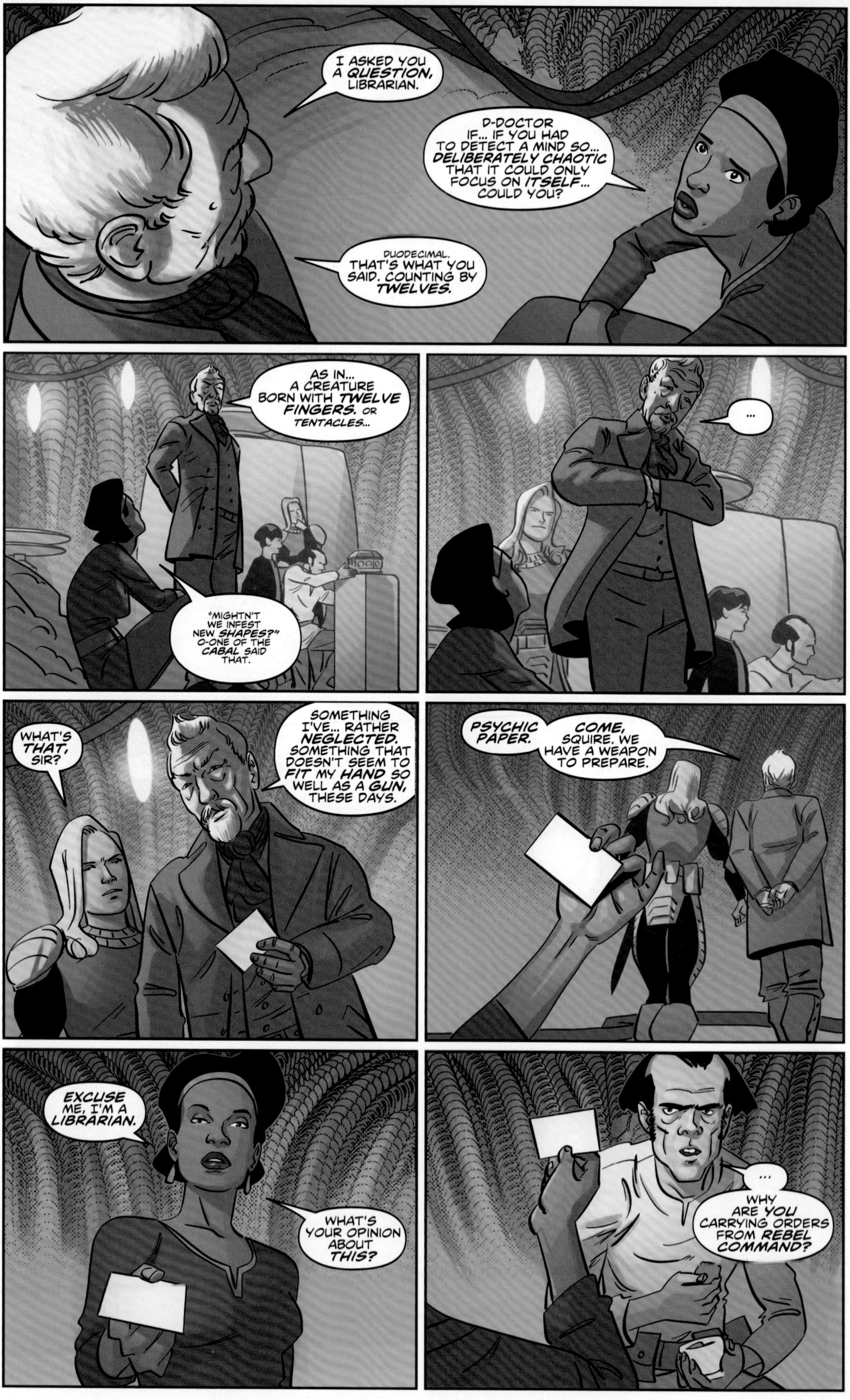
I ASKED YOU A QUESTION, LIBRARIAN.
D-DOCTOR IF... IF YOU HAD TO DETECT A MIND SO... DELIBERATELY CHAOTIC THAT IT COULD ONLY FOCUS ON ITSELF... COULD YOU?
DUODECIMAL. THAT'S WHAT YOU SAID. COUNTING BY TWELVES.
AS IN... A CREATURE BORN WITH TWELVE FINGERS. OR TENTACLES...
"MIGHTN'T WE INFEST NEW SHAPES?" O-ONE OF THE CABAL SAID THAT.
...
WHAT'S THAT, SIR?
SOMETHING I'VE... RATHER NEGLECTED. SOMETHING THAT DOESN'T SEEM TO FIT MY HAND SO WELL AS A GUN, THESE DAYS.
PSYCHIC PAPER.
COME, SQUIRE. WE HAVE A WEAPON TO PREPARE.
EXCUSE ME, I'M A LIBRARIAN.
WHAT'S YOUR OPINION ABOUT THIS?
...
WHY ARE YOU CARRYING ORDERS FROM REBEL COMMAND?

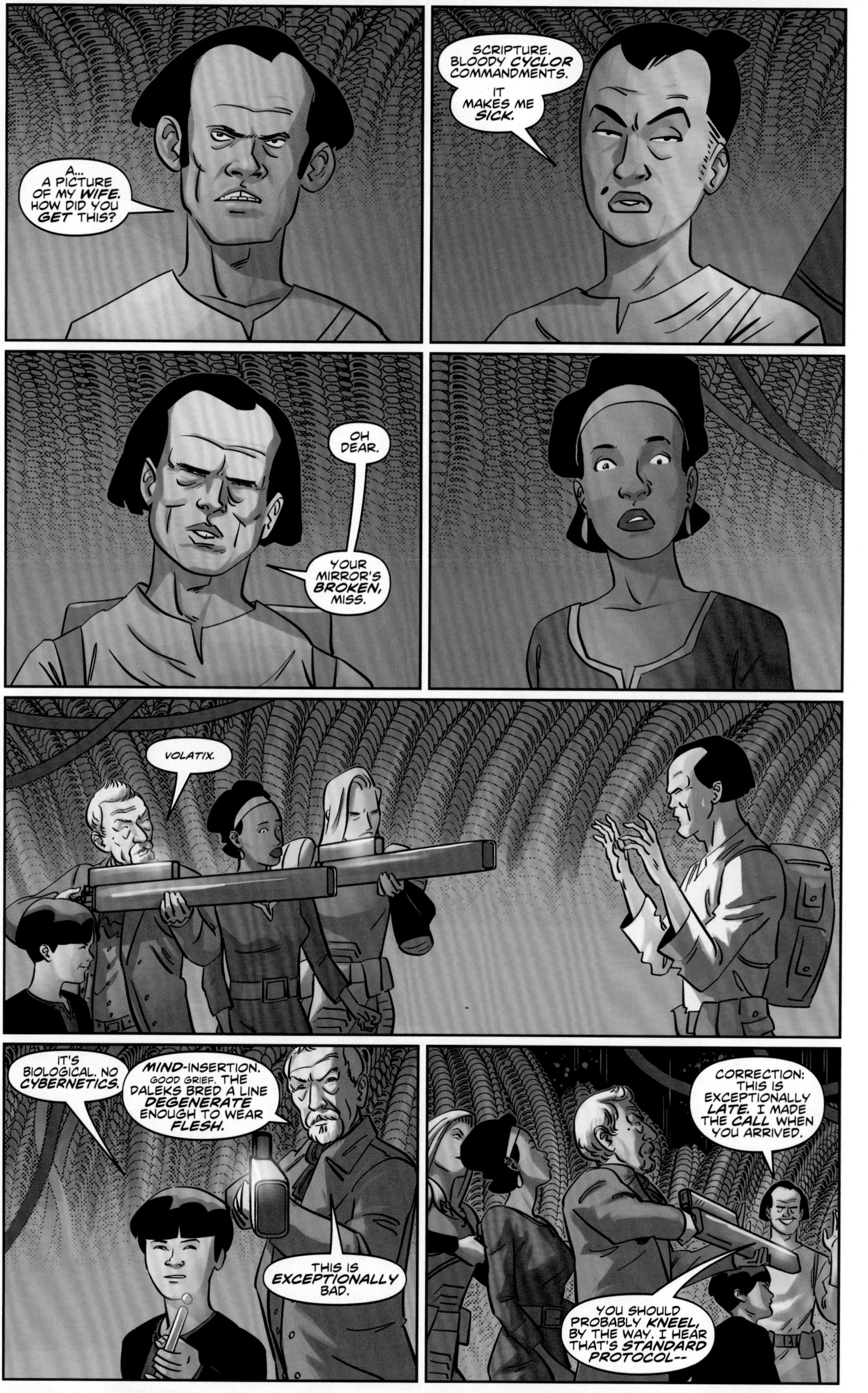
A... A PICTURE OF MY WIFE. HOW DID YOU GET THIS?
SCRIPTURE. BLOODY CYCLOR COMMANDMENTS.
IT MAKES ME SICK.
OH DEAR.
YOUR MIRROR'S BROKEN, MISS.
VOLATIX.
IT'S BIOLOGICAL. NO CYBERNETICS.
MIND-INSERTION. GOOD GRIEF. THE DALEKS BRED A LINE DEGENERATE ENOUGH TO WEAR FLESH.
THIS IS EXCEPTIONALLY BAD.
CORRECTION: THIS IS EXCEPTIONALLY LATE. I MADE THE CALL WHEN YOU ARRIVED.
YOU SHOULD PROBABLY KNEEL, BY THE WAY. I HEAR THAT'S STANDARD PROTOCOL--

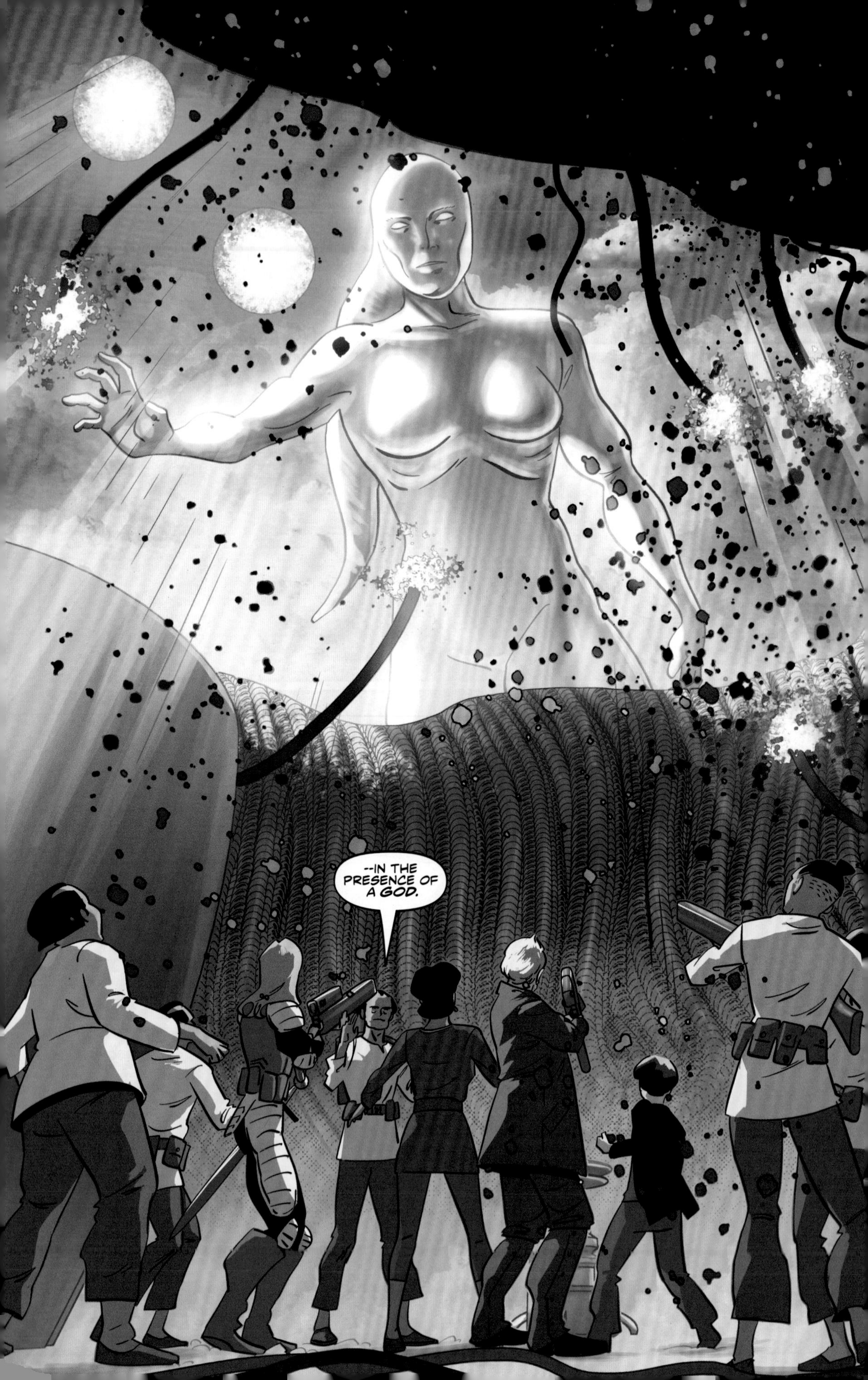
--IN THE PRESENCE OF A GOD.

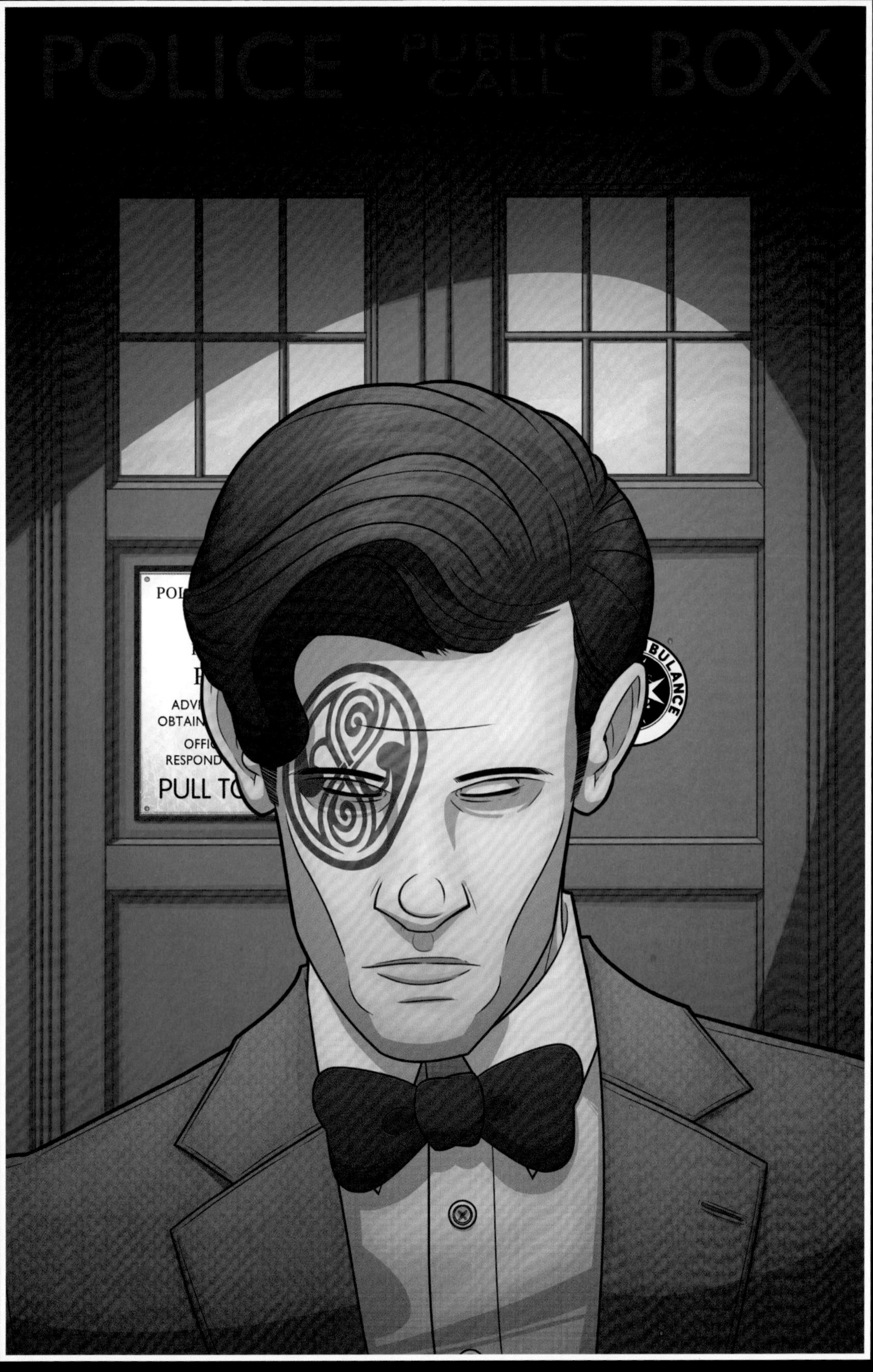
POLICE PUBLIC CALL BOX

11D #2.11 Cover A: Dan Boultwood

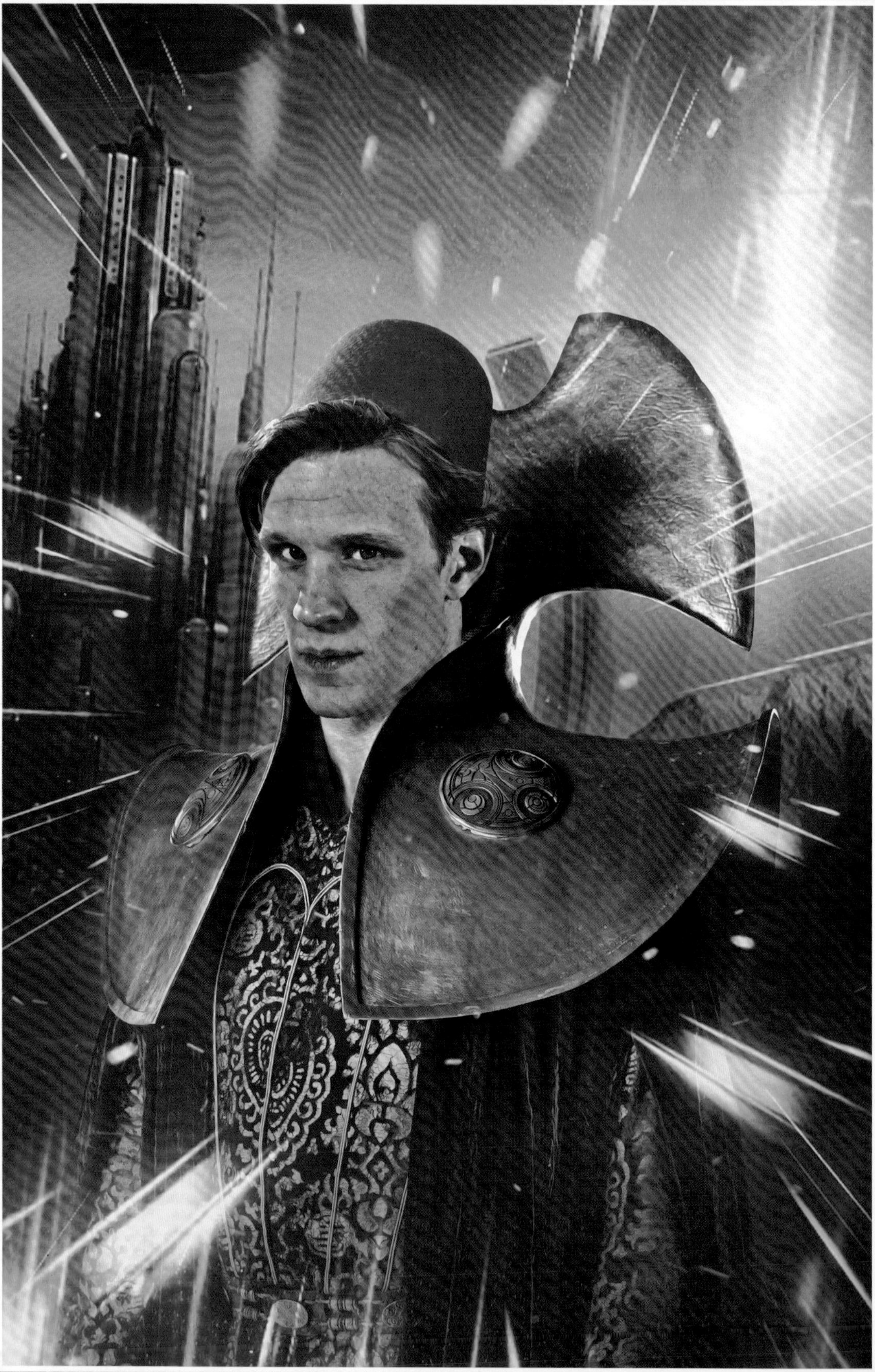

11D #2.12 Cover B: Will Brooks

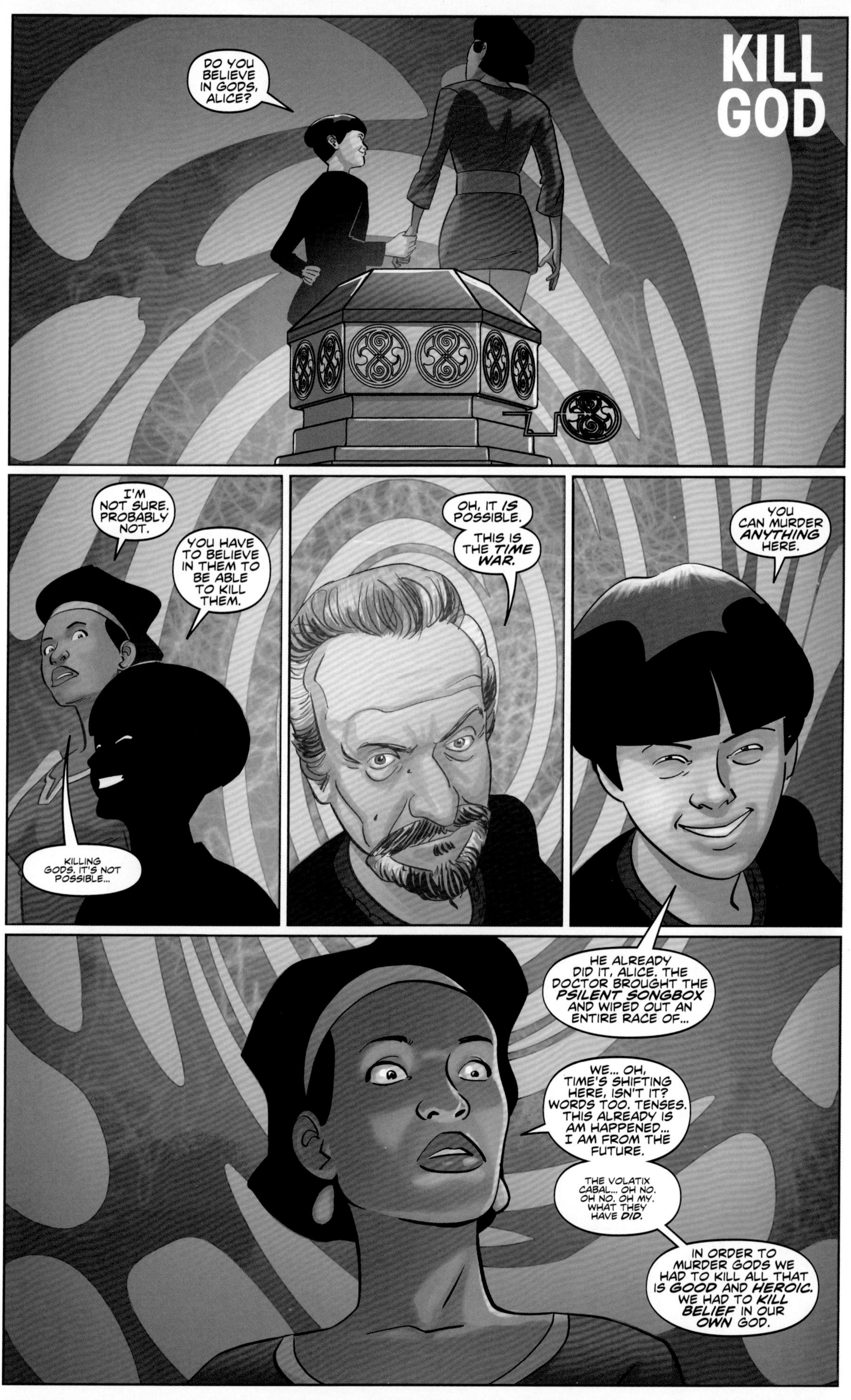
KILL GOD
DO YOU BELIEVE IN GODS, ALICE?
I'M NOT SURE. PROBABLY NOT.
YOU HAVE TO BELIEVE IN THEM TO BE ABLE TO KILL THEM.
KILLING GODS. IT'S NOT POSSIBLE...
OH, IT IS POSSIBLE.
THIS IS THE TIME WAR.
YOU CAN MURDER ANYTHING HERE.
HE ALREADY DID IT, ALICE. THE DOCTOR BROUGHT THE PSILENT SONGBOX AND WIPED OUT AN ENTIRE RACE OF...
WE... OH, TIME'S SHIFTING HERE, ISN'T IT? WORDS TOO. TENSES. THIS ALREADY IS AM HAPPENED... I AM FROM THE FUTURE.
THE VOLATIX CABAL... OH NO. OH NO. OH MY. WHAT THEY HAVE DID.
IN ORDER TO MURDER GODS WE HAD TO KILL ALL THAT IS GOOD AND HEROIC. WE HAD TO KILL BELIEF IN OUR OWN GOD.

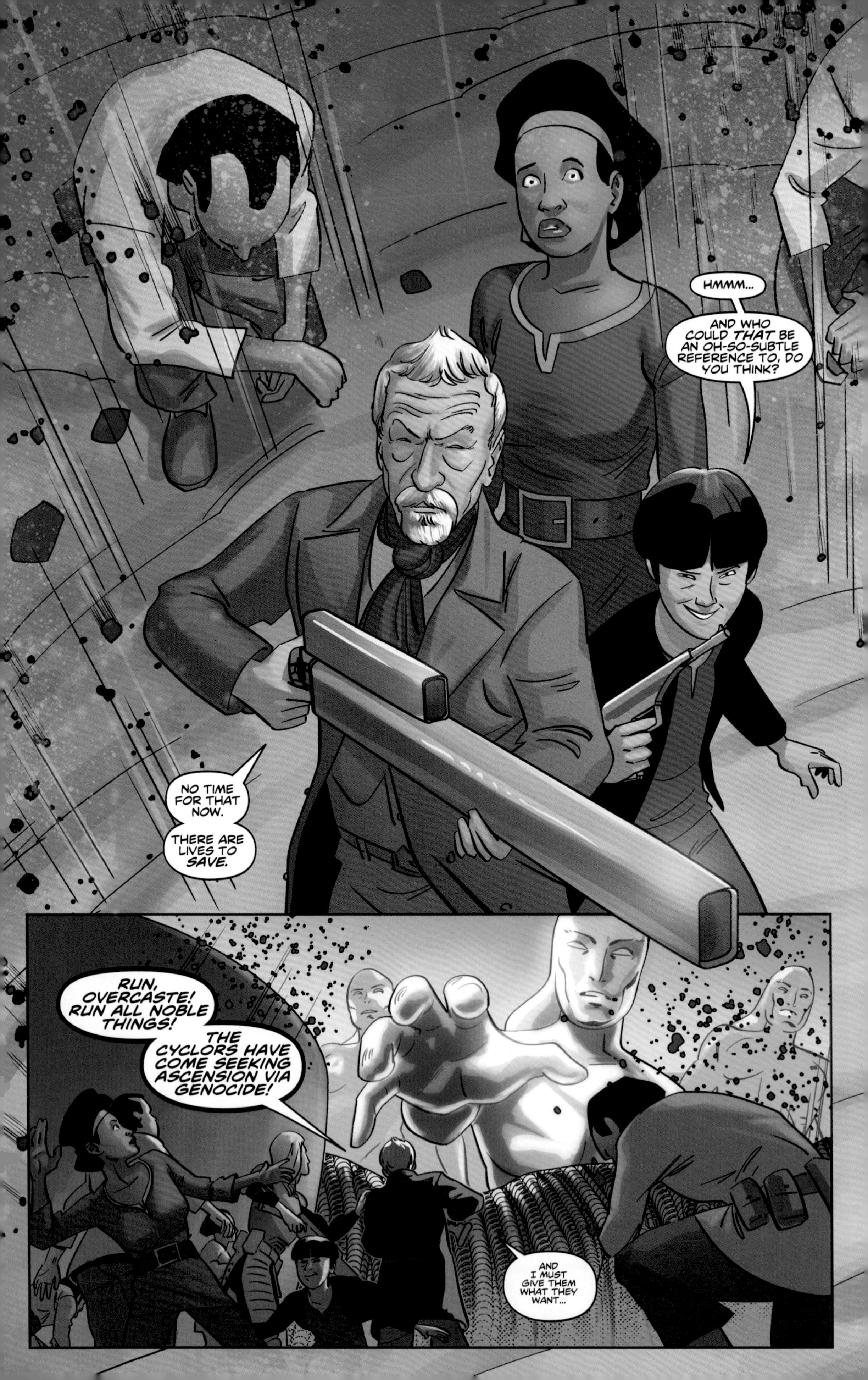
HMMM...
AND WHO COULD THAT BE AN OH-SO-SUBTLE REFERENCE TO, DO YOU THINK?
NO TIME FOR THAT NOW.
THERE ARE LIVES TO SAVE.
RUN, OVERCASTE! RUN ALL NOBLE THINGS!
THE CYCLORS HAVE COME SEEKING ASCENSION VIA GENOCIDE!
AND I MUST GIVE THEM WHAT THEY WANT...

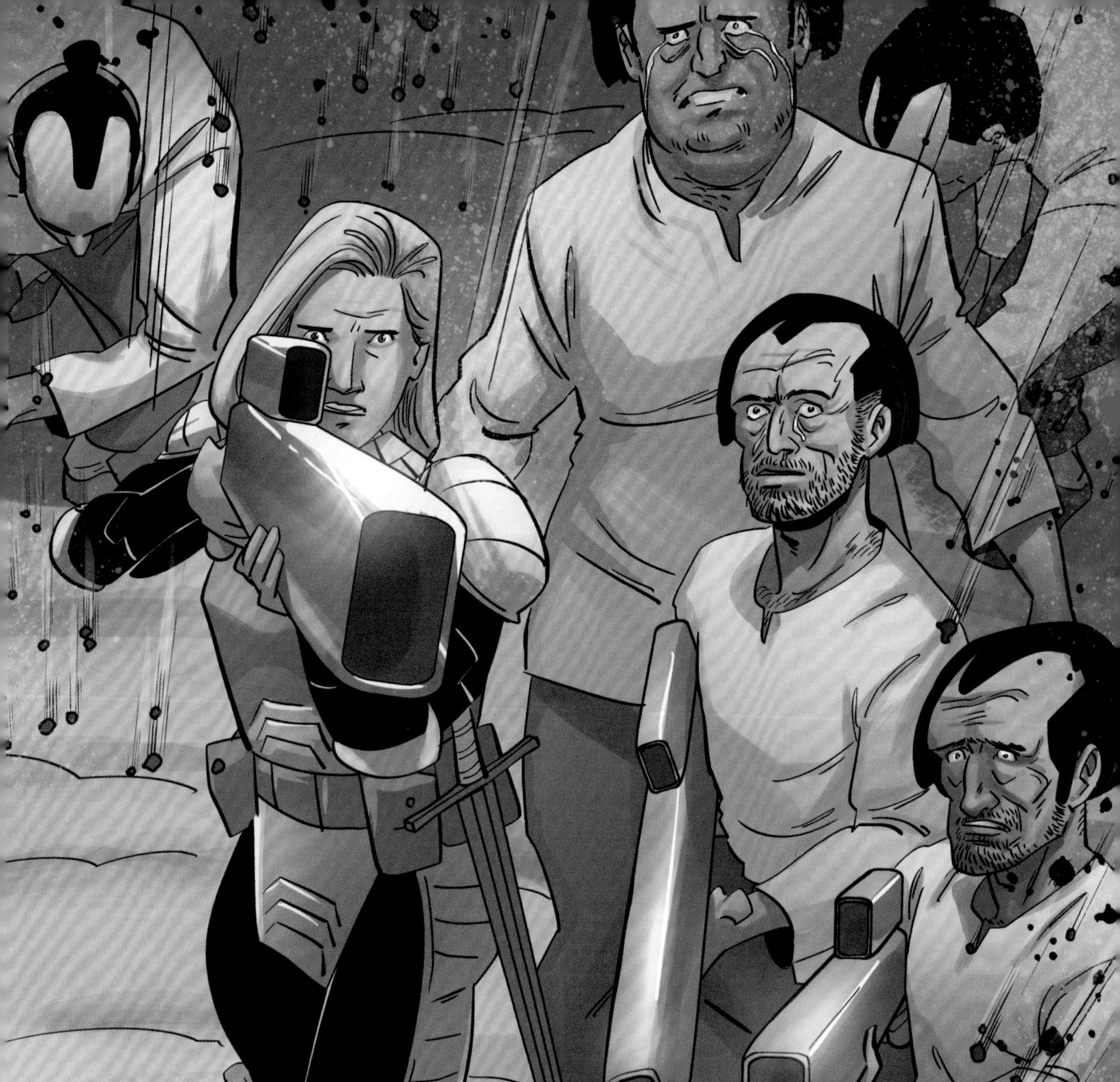

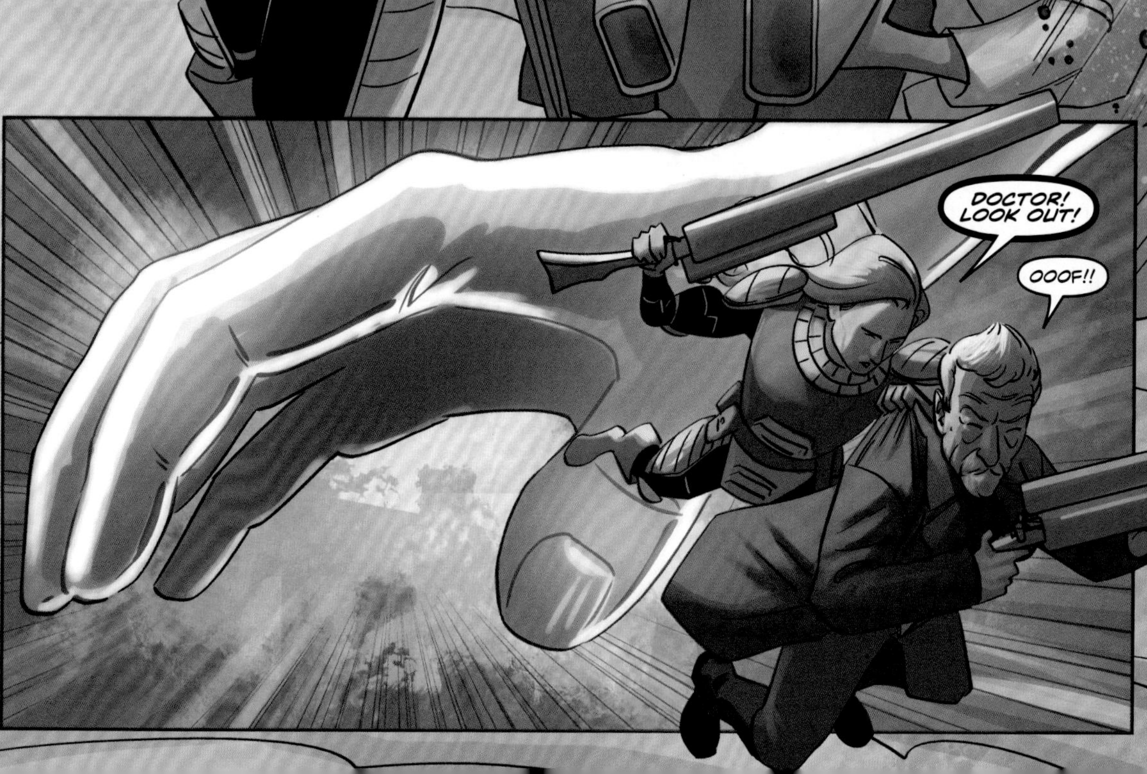
DOCTOR! LOOK OUT!
OOOF!!

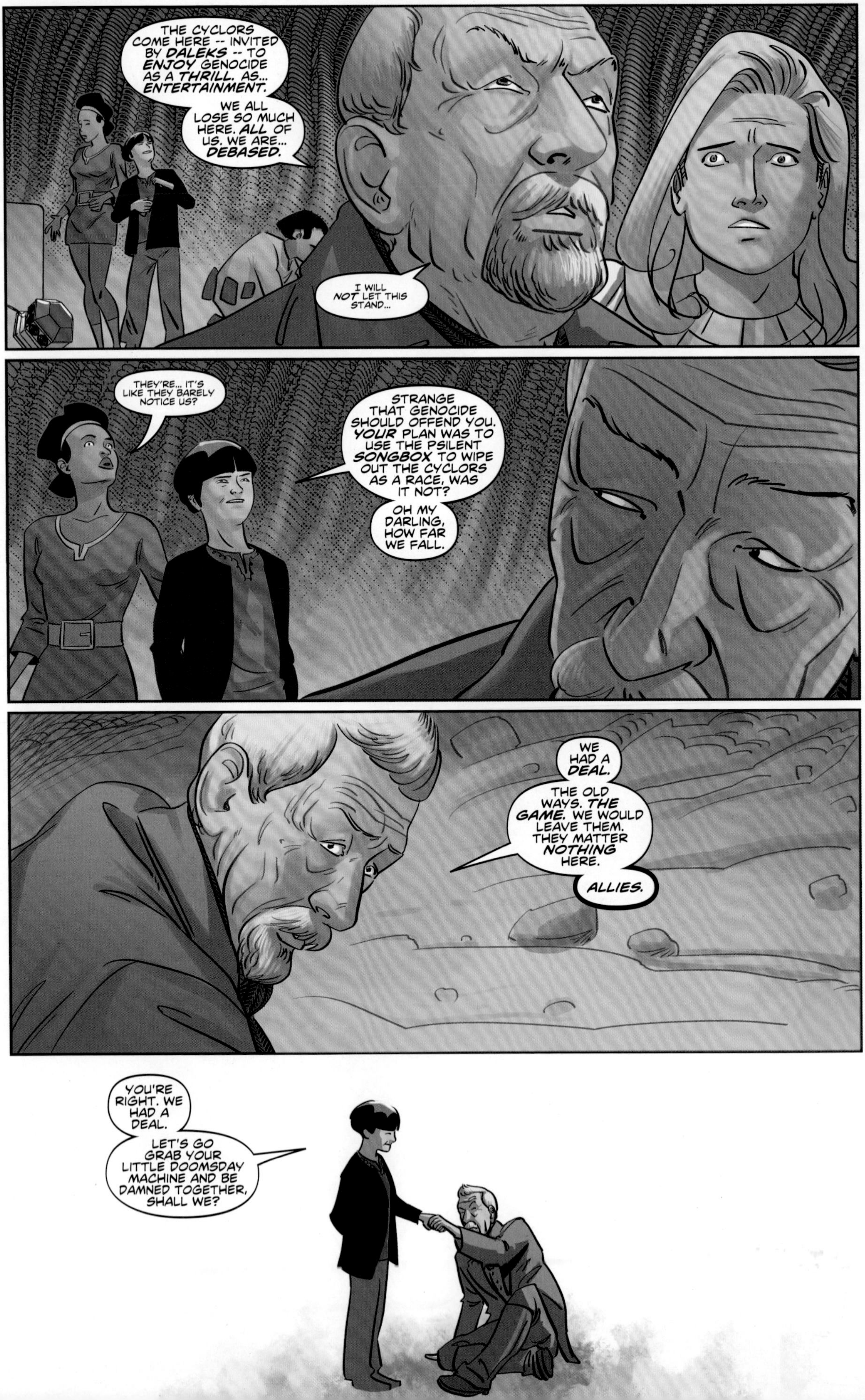
THE CYCLORS COME HERE -- INVITED BY DALEKS -- TO ENJOY GENOCIDE AS A THRILL. AS... ENTERTAINMENT.
WE ALL LOSE SO MUCH HERE. ALL OF US. WE ARE... DEBASED.
I WILL NOT LET THIS STAND...
THEY'RE... IT'S LIKE THEY BARELY NOTICE US?
STRANGE THAT GENOCIDE SHOULD OFFEND YOU. YOUR PLAN WAS TO USE THE PSILENT SONGBOX TO WIPE OUT THE CYCLORS AS A RACE, WAS IT NOT?
OH MY DARLING, HOW FAR WE FALL.
WE HAD A DEAL.
THE OLD WAYS. THE GAME. WE WOULD LEAVE THEM. THEY MATTER NOTHING HERE.
ALLIES.
YOU'RE RIGHT. WE HAD A DEAL.
LET'S GO GRAB YOUR LITTLE DOOMSDAY MACHINE AND BE DAMNED TOGETHER, SHALL WE?

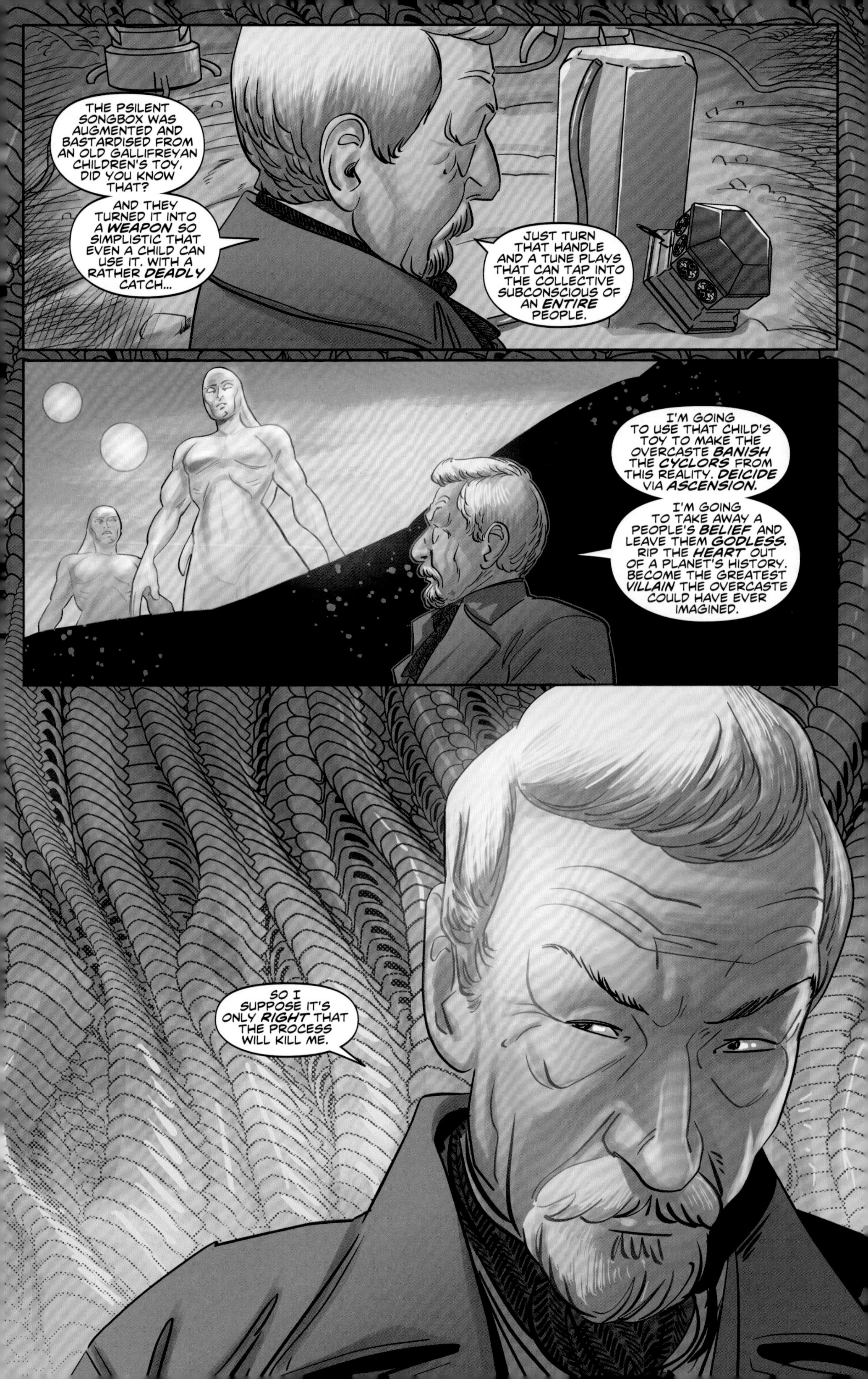
THE PSILENT SONGBOX WAS AUGMENTED AND BASTARDISED FROM AN OLD GALLIFREYAN CHILDREN'S TOY, DID YOU KNOW THAT?
AND THEY TURNED IT INTO A WEAPON SO SIMPLISTIC THAT EVEN A CHILD CAN USE IT. WITH A RATHER DEADLY CATCH...
JUST TURN THAT HANDLE AND A TUNE PLAYS THAT CAN TAP INTO THE COLLECTIVE SUBCONSCIOUS OF AN ENTIRE PEOPLE.
I'M GOING TO USE THAT CHILD'S TOY TO MAKE THE OVERCASTE BANISH THE CYCLORS FROM THIS REALITY. DEICIDE VIA ASCENSION.
I'M GOING TO TAKE AWAY A PEOPLE'S BELIEF AND LEAVE THEM GODLESS. RIP THE HEART OUT OF A PLANET'S HISTORY. BECOME THE GREATEST VILLAIN THE OVERCASTE COULD HAVE EVER IMAGINED.
SO I SUPPOSE IT'S ONLY RIGHT THAT THE PROCESS WILL KILL ME.

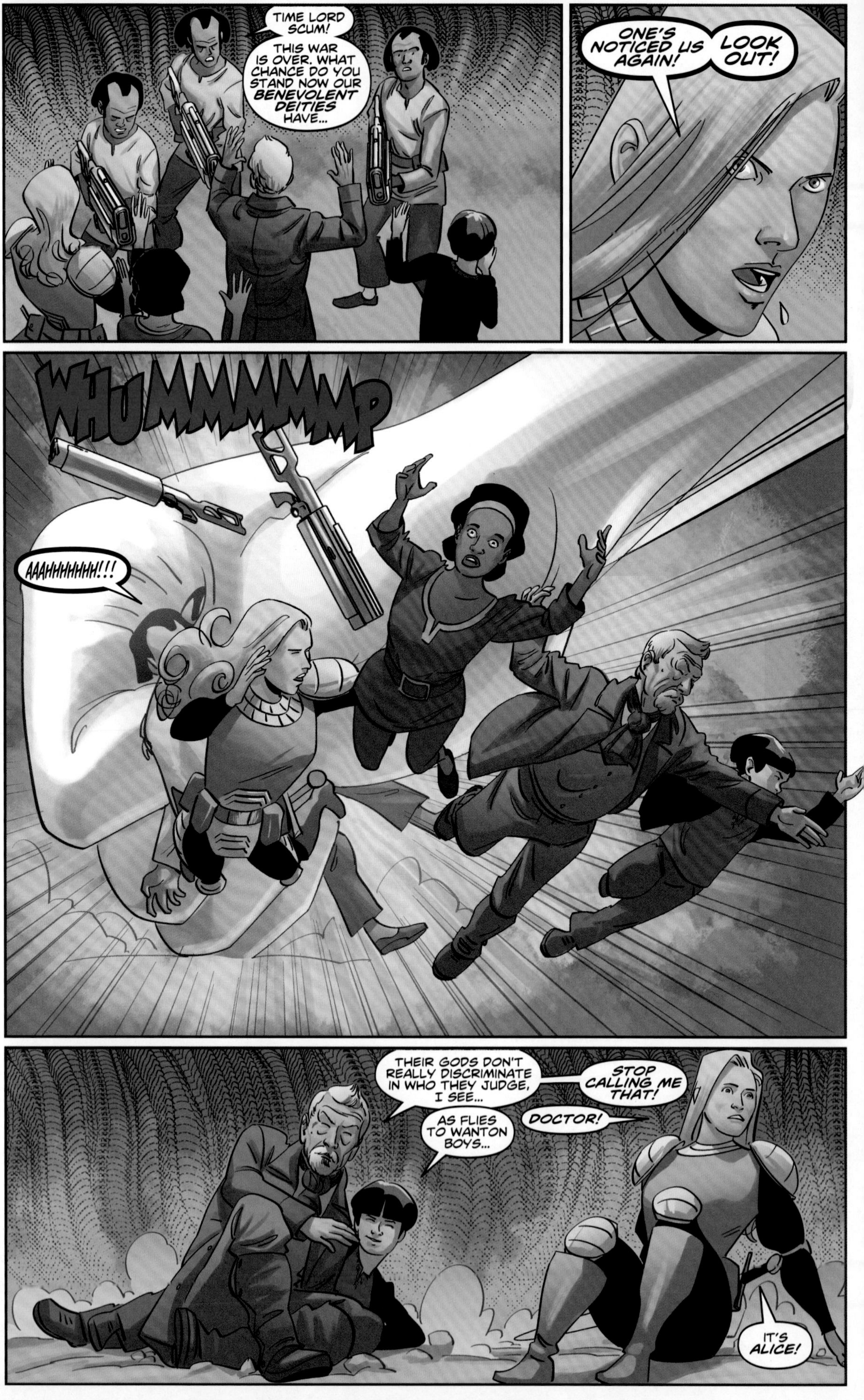
TIME LORD SCUM!
THIS WAR IS OVER. WHAT CHANCE DO YOU STAND NOW OUR BENEVOLENT DEITIES HAVE...
ONE'S NOTICED US AGAIN!
LOOK OUT!
WHUMMMMMMP
AAAHHHHHHH!!!
THEIR GODS DON'T REALLY DISCRIMINATE IN WHO THEY JUDGE, I SEE...
AS FLIES TO WANTON BOYS...
DOCTOR!
STOP CALLING ME THAT!
IT'S ALICE!

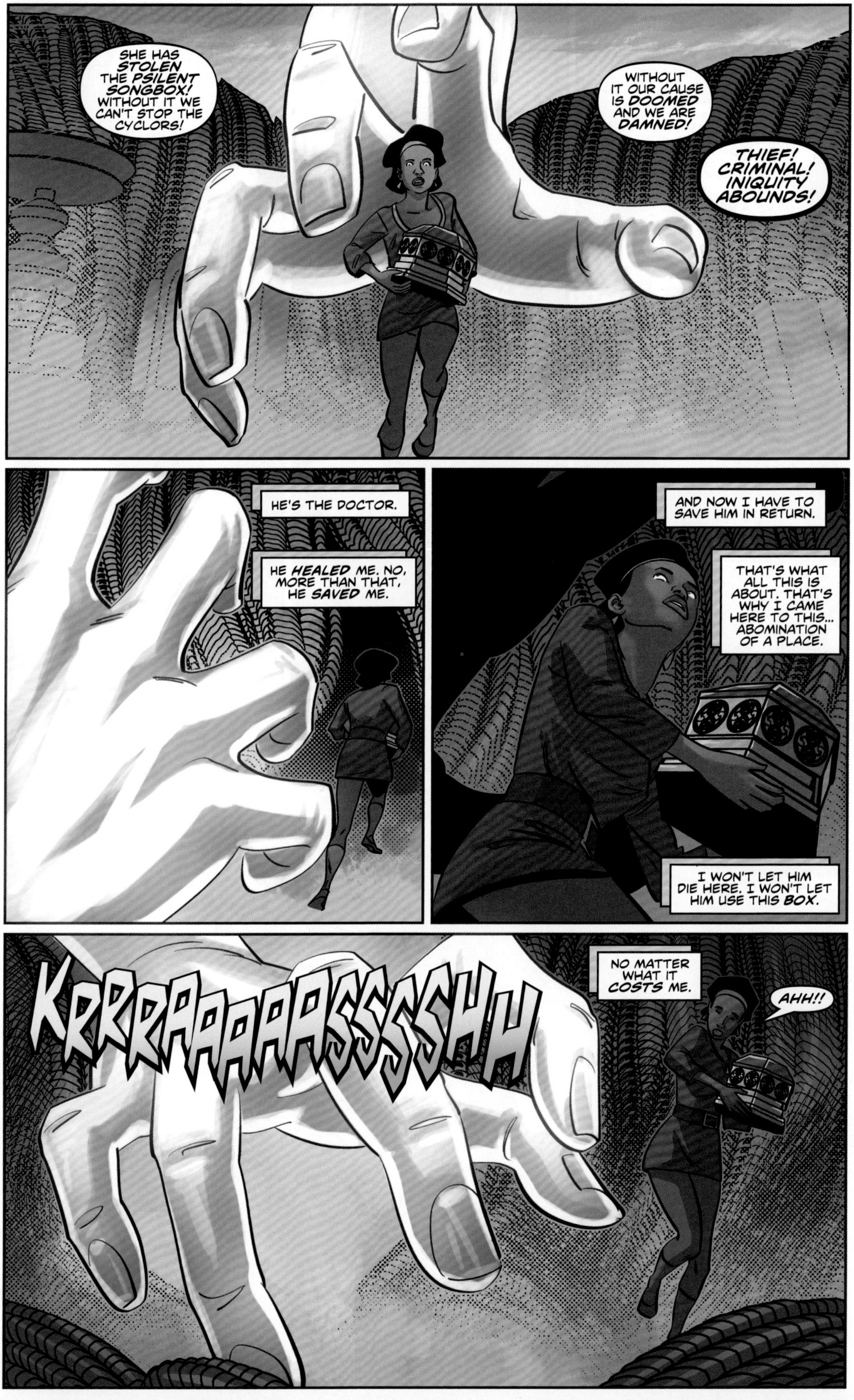
SHE HAS STOLEN THE PSILENT SONGBOX! WITHOUT IT WE CAN'T STOP THE CYCLORS!
WITHOUT IT OUR CAUSE IS DOOMED AND WE ARE DAMNED!
THIEF! CRIMINAL! INIQUITY ABOUNDS!
HE'S THE DOCTOR.
HE HEALED ME. NO, MORE THAN THAT, HE SAVED ME.
AND NOW I HAVE TO SAVE HIM IN RETURN.
THAT'S WHAT ALL THIS IS ABOUT. THAT'S WHY I CAME HERE TO THIS... ABOMINATION OF A PLACE.
I WON'T LET HIM DIE HERE. I WON'T LET HIM USE THIS BOX.
KRRRAAAAAASSSSHH
NO MATTER WHAT IT COSTS ME.
AHH!!

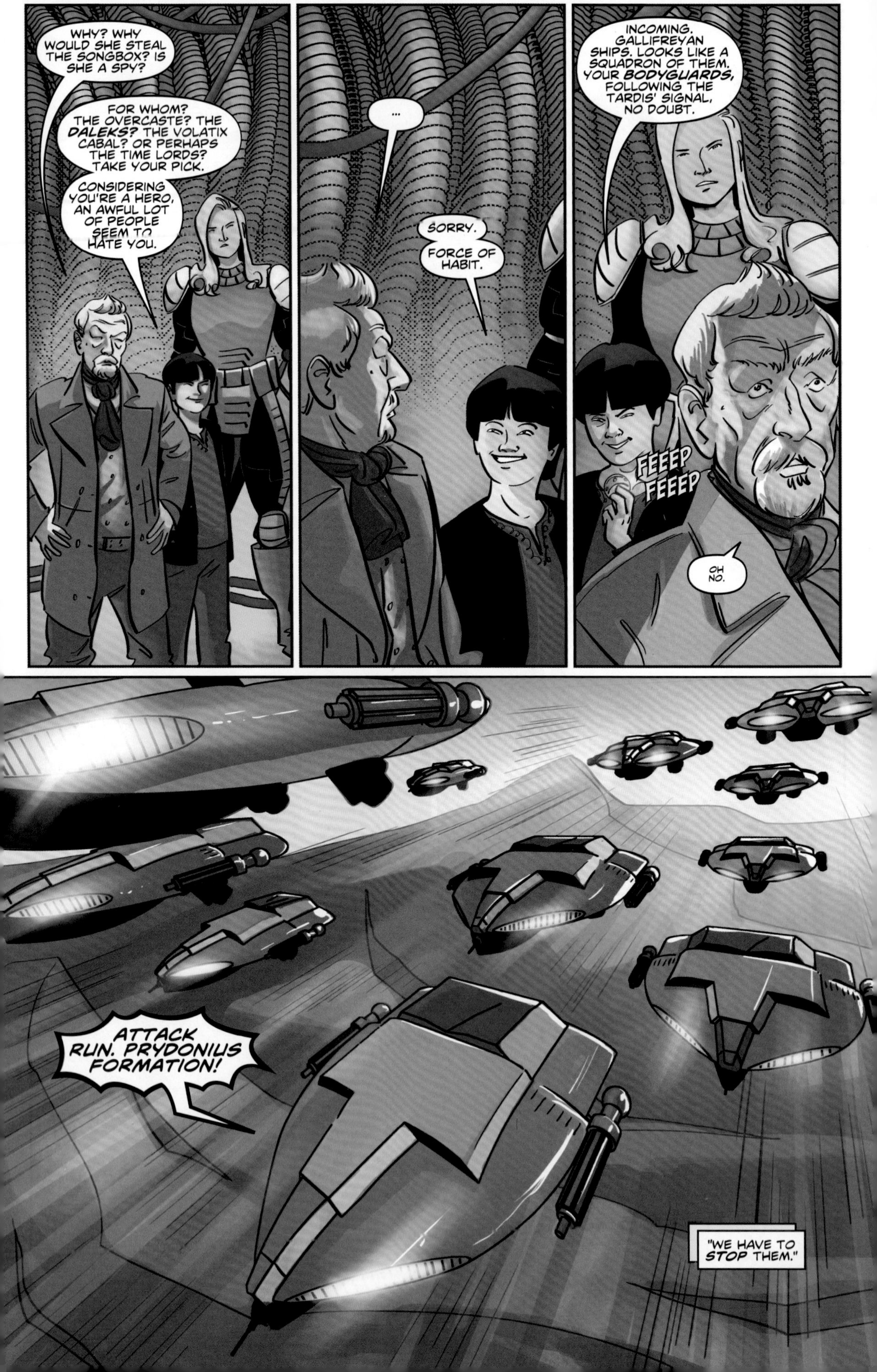
WHY? WHY WOULD SHE STEAL THE SONGBOX? IS SHE A SPY?
FOR WHOM? THE OVERCASTE? THE DALEKS? THE VOLATIX CABAL? OR PERHAPS THE TIME LORDS? TAKE YOUR PICK.
CONSIDERING YOU'RE A HERO, AN AWFUL LOT OF PEOPLE SEEM TO HATE YOU.
...
SORRY.
FORCE OF HABIT.
INCOMING. GALLIFREYAN SHIPS. LOOKS LIKE A SQUADRON OF THEM. YOUR BODYGUARDS, FOLLOWING THE TARDIS' SIGNAL, NO DOUBT.
FEEEP FEEEP
OH NO.
ATTACK RUN. PRYDONIUS FORMATION!
"WE HAVE TO STOP THEM."

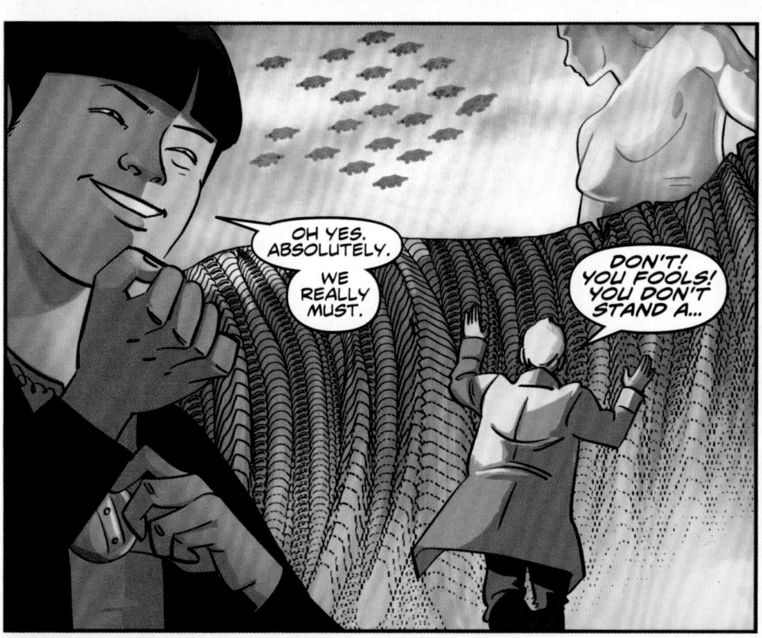
OH YES. ABSOLUTELY.
WE REALLY MUST.
DON'T! YOU FOOLS! YOU DON'T STAND A...

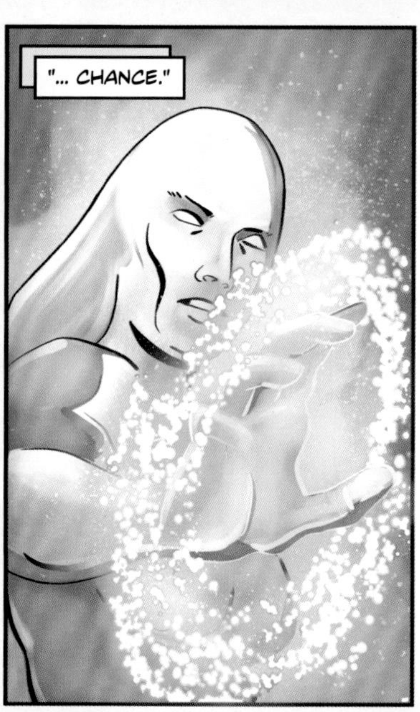
"... CHANCE."

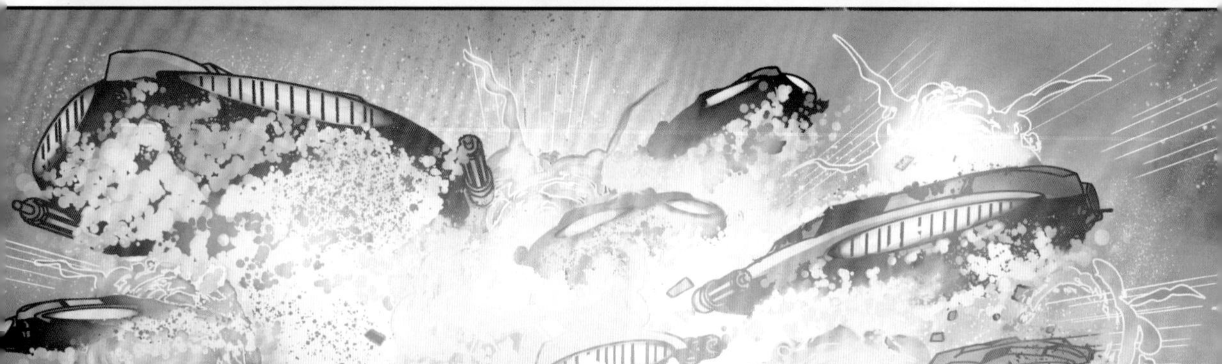

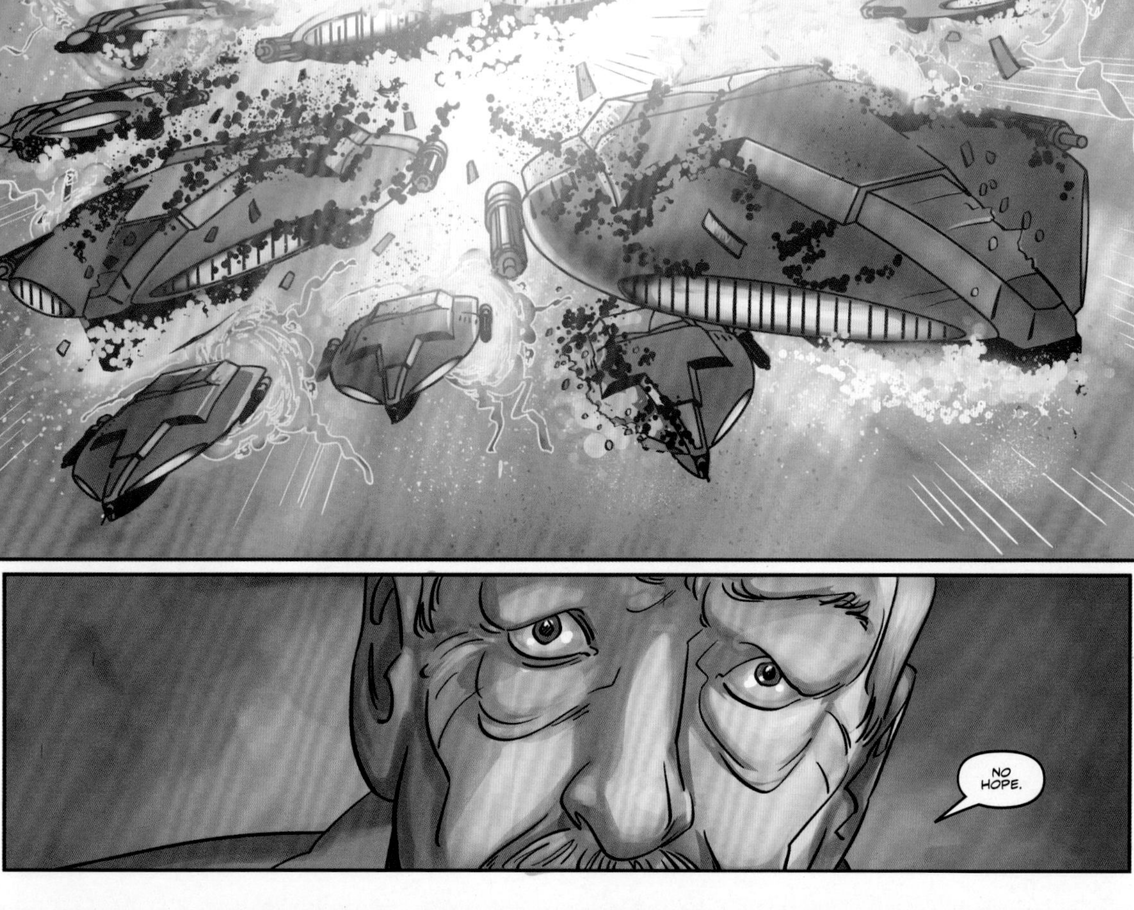
NO HOPE.

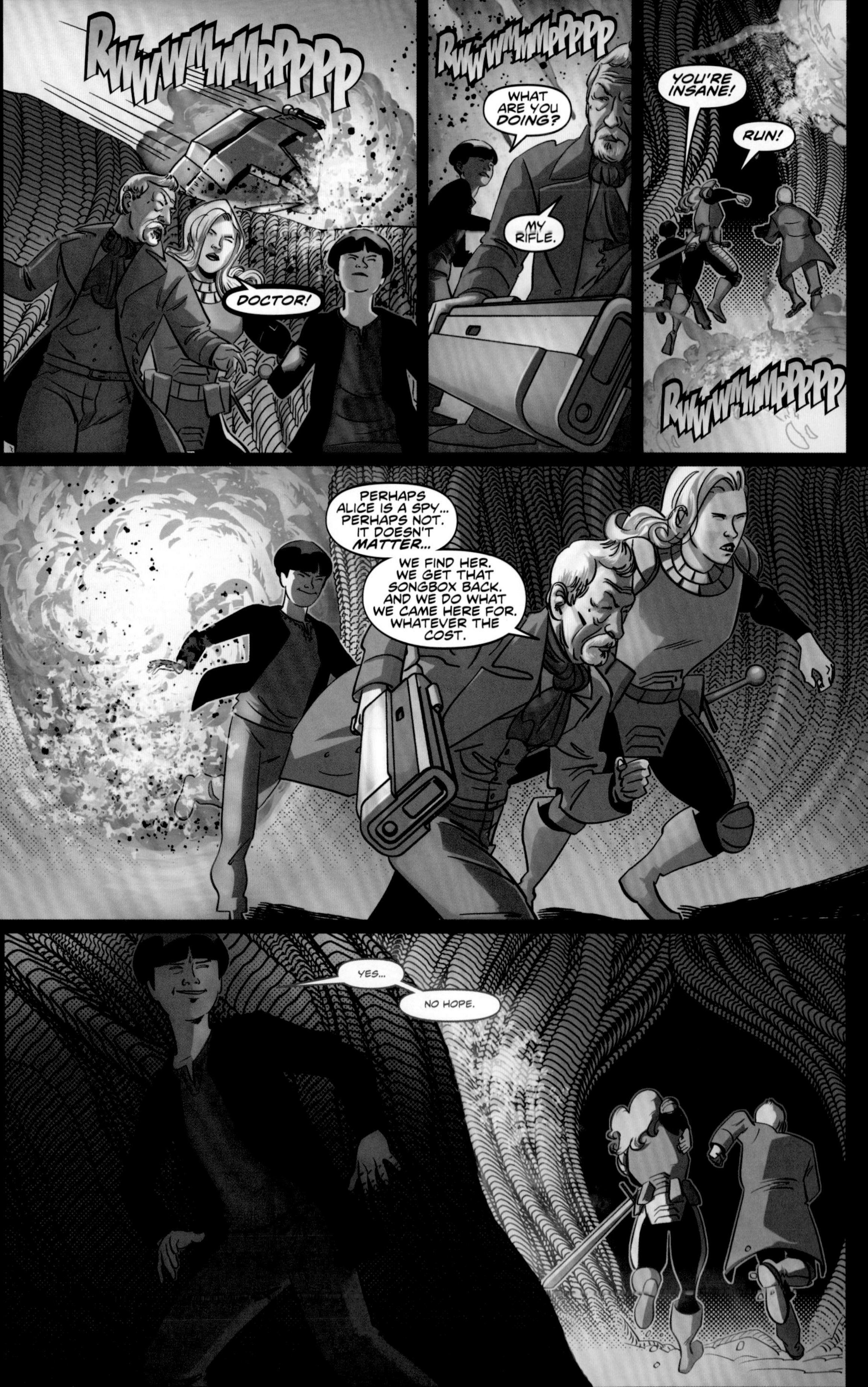
RWWWMMMPPPPP
DOCTOR!
RWWWMMMPPPP
WHAT ARE YOU DOING?
MY RIFLE.
YOU'RE INSANE!
RUN!
RWWWMMMPPPP
PERHAPS ALICE IS A SPY... PERHAPS NOT. IT DOESN'T MATTER...
WE FIND HER. WE GET THAT SONGBOX BACK. AND WE DO WHAT WE CAME HERE FOR. WHATEVER THE COST.
YES...
NO HOPE.

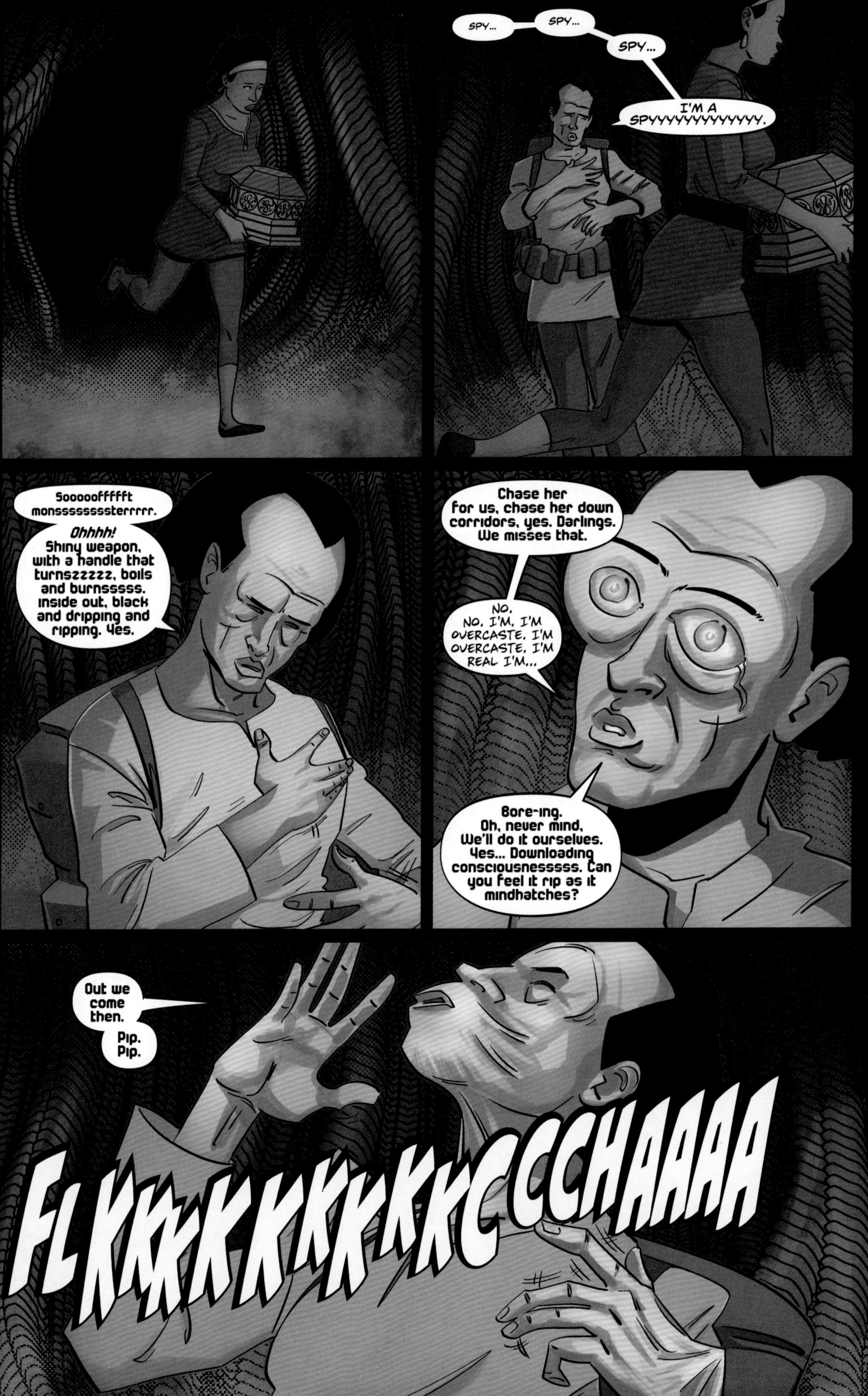
SPY...
SPY...
SPY...
I'M A SPYYYYYYYYYYYYYY.
Soooooffffft monssssssssterrrrr.
Ohhhh! Shiny weapon, with a handle that turnszzzzz, boils and burnsssss. Inside out, black and dripping and ripping. Yes.
Chase her for us, chase her down corridors, yes. Darlings. We misses that.
NO. NO. I'M. I'M OVERCASTE. I'M OVERCASTE. I'M REAL I'M...
Bore-ing. Oh, never mind, We'll do it ourselves. Yes... Downloading consciousnesssss. Can you feel it rip as it mindhatches?
Out we come then.
Pip. Pip.
FLKKKKKKKKKKCCCHAAAA

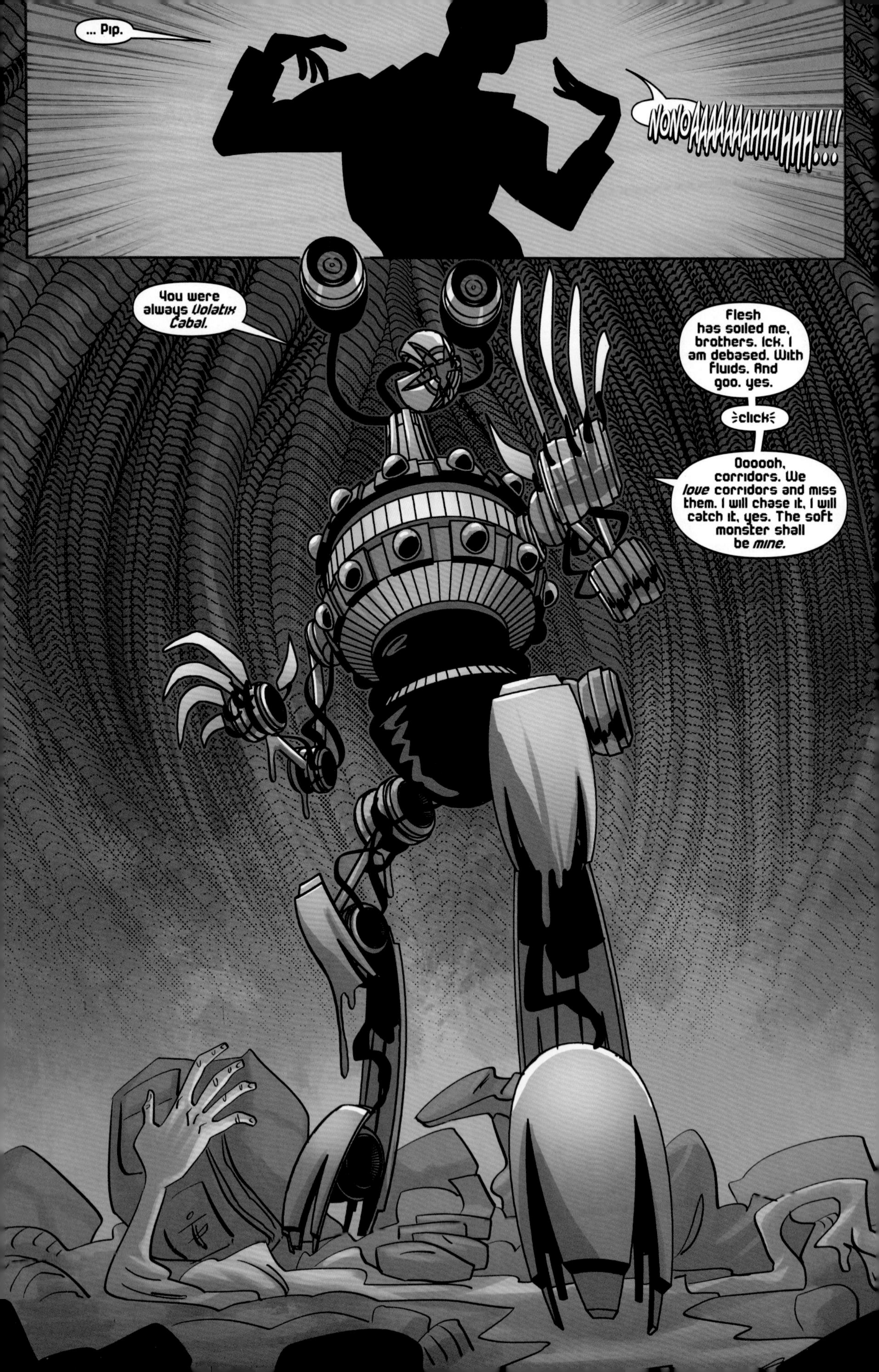
... Pip.
NONOAAAAAAAHHHHHH!!!
You were always Volatix Cabal.
Flesh has soiled me, brothers. Ick. I am debased. With fluids. And goo. yes.
click
Oooooh, corridors. We love corridors and miss them. I will chase it, I will catch it, yes. The soft monster shall be mine.

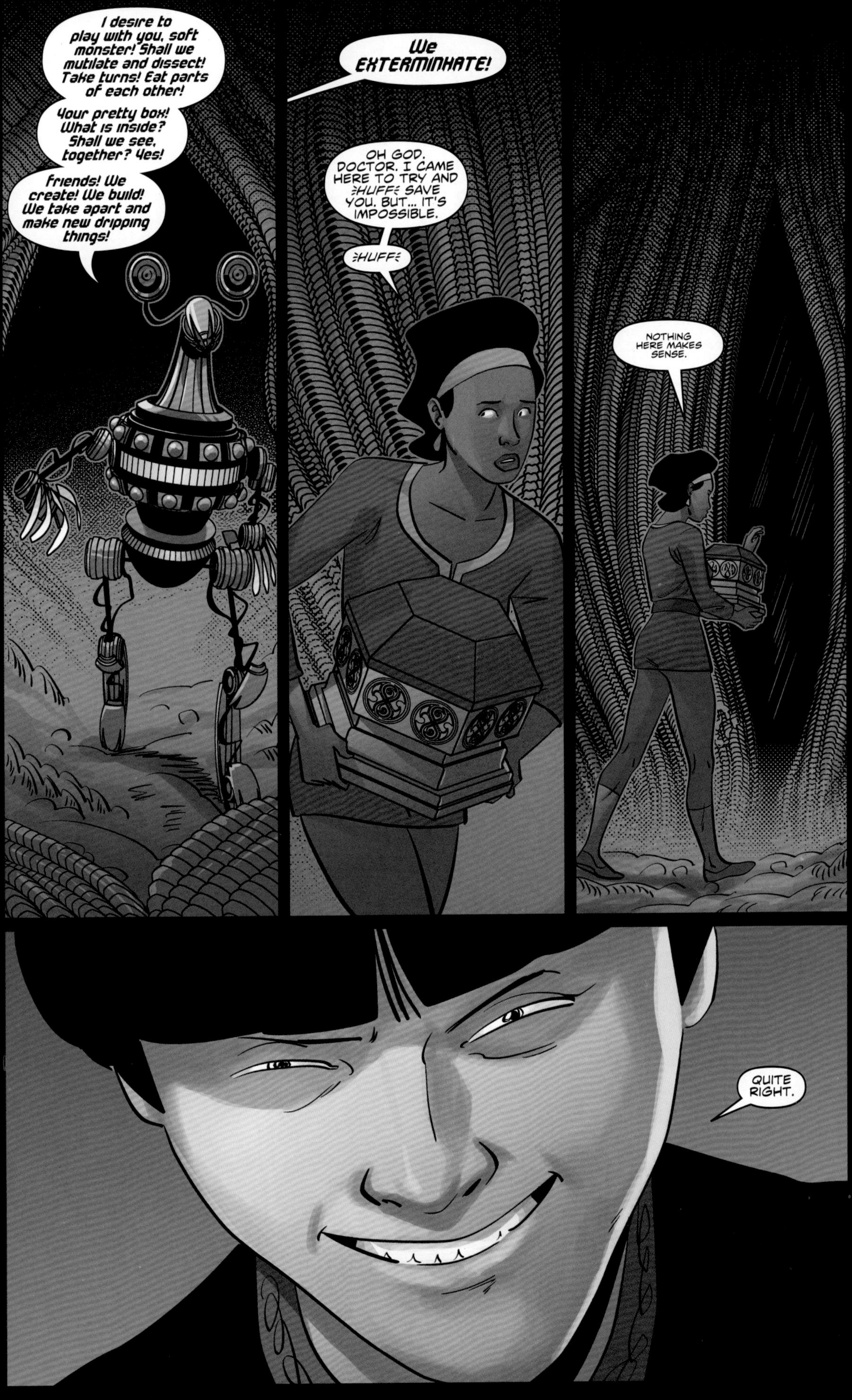
I desire to play with you, soft monster! Shall we mutilate and dissect! Take turns! Eat parts of each other!
Your pretty box! What is inside? Shall we see, together? Yes!
Friends! We create! We build! We take apart and make new dripping things!
We EXTERMINHATE!
OH GOD. DOCTOR. I CAME HERE TO TRY AND *HUFF* SAVE YOU. BUT... IT'S IMPOSSIBLE.
HUFF
NOTHING HERE MAKES SENSE.
QUITE RIGHT.

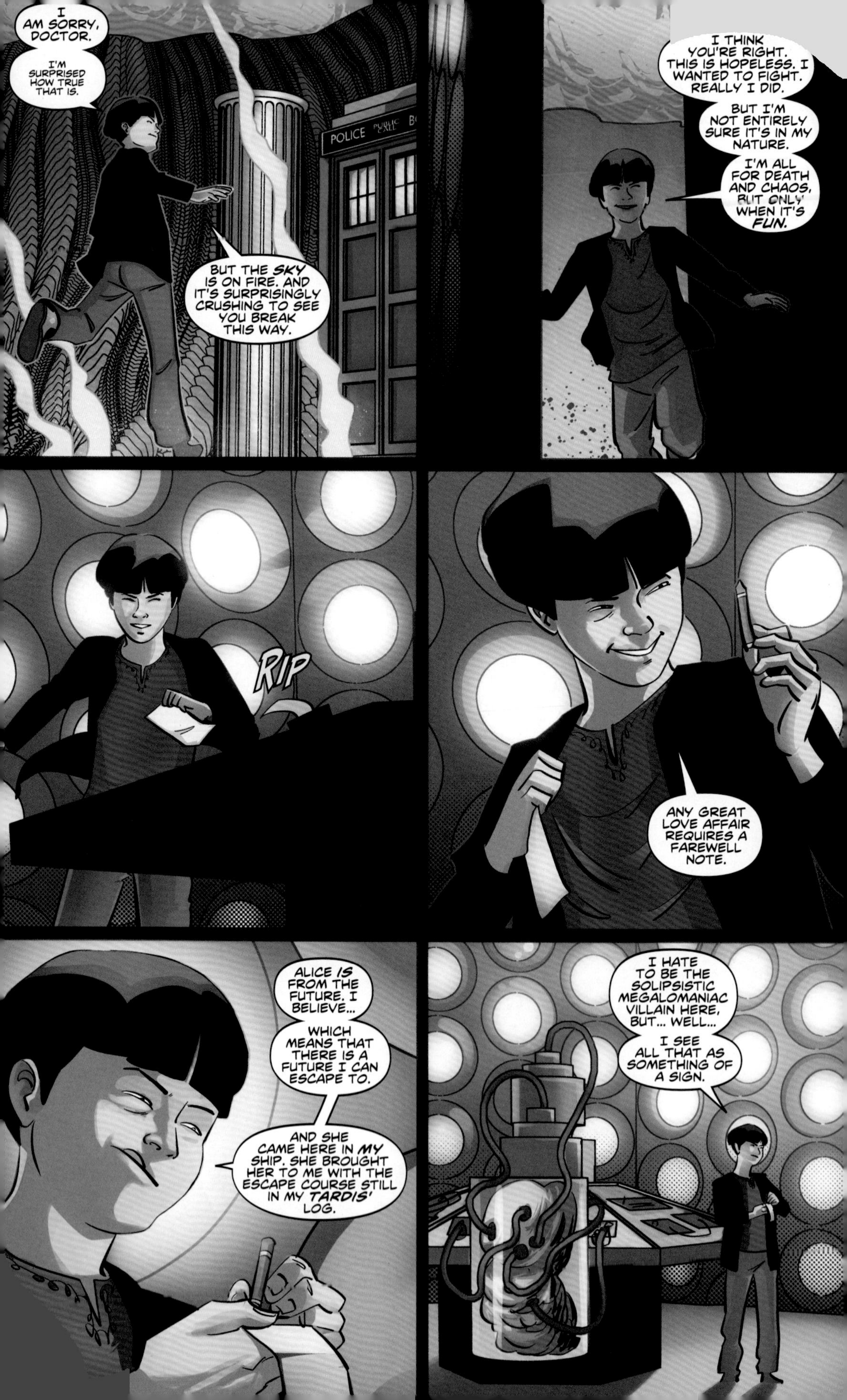
I AM SORRY, DOCTOR.
I'M SURPRISED HOW TRUE THAT IS.
BUT THE SKY IS ON FIRE. AND IT'S SURPRISINGLY CRUSHING TO SEE YOU BREAK THIS WAY.
POLICE PUBLIC CALL BO
I THINK YOU'RE RIGHT. THIS IS HOPELESS. I WANTED TO FIGHT. REALLY I DID.
BUT I'M NOT ENTIRELY SURE IT'S IN MY NATURE.
I'M ALL FOR DEATH AND CHAOS, BUT ONLY WHEN IT'S FUN.
RIP
ANY GREAT LOVE AFFAIR REQUIRES A FAREWELL NOTE.
ALICE IS FROM THE FUTURE. I BELIEVE...
WHICH MEANS THAT THERE IS A FUTURE I CAN ESCAPE TO.
AND SHE CAME HERE IN MY SHIP. SHE BROUGHT HER TO ME WITH THE ESCAPE COURSE STILL IN MY TARDIS' LOG.
I HATE TO BE THE SOLIPSISTIC MEGALOMANIAC VILLAIN HERE, BUT... WELL...
I SEE ALL THAT AS SOMETHING OF A SIGN.

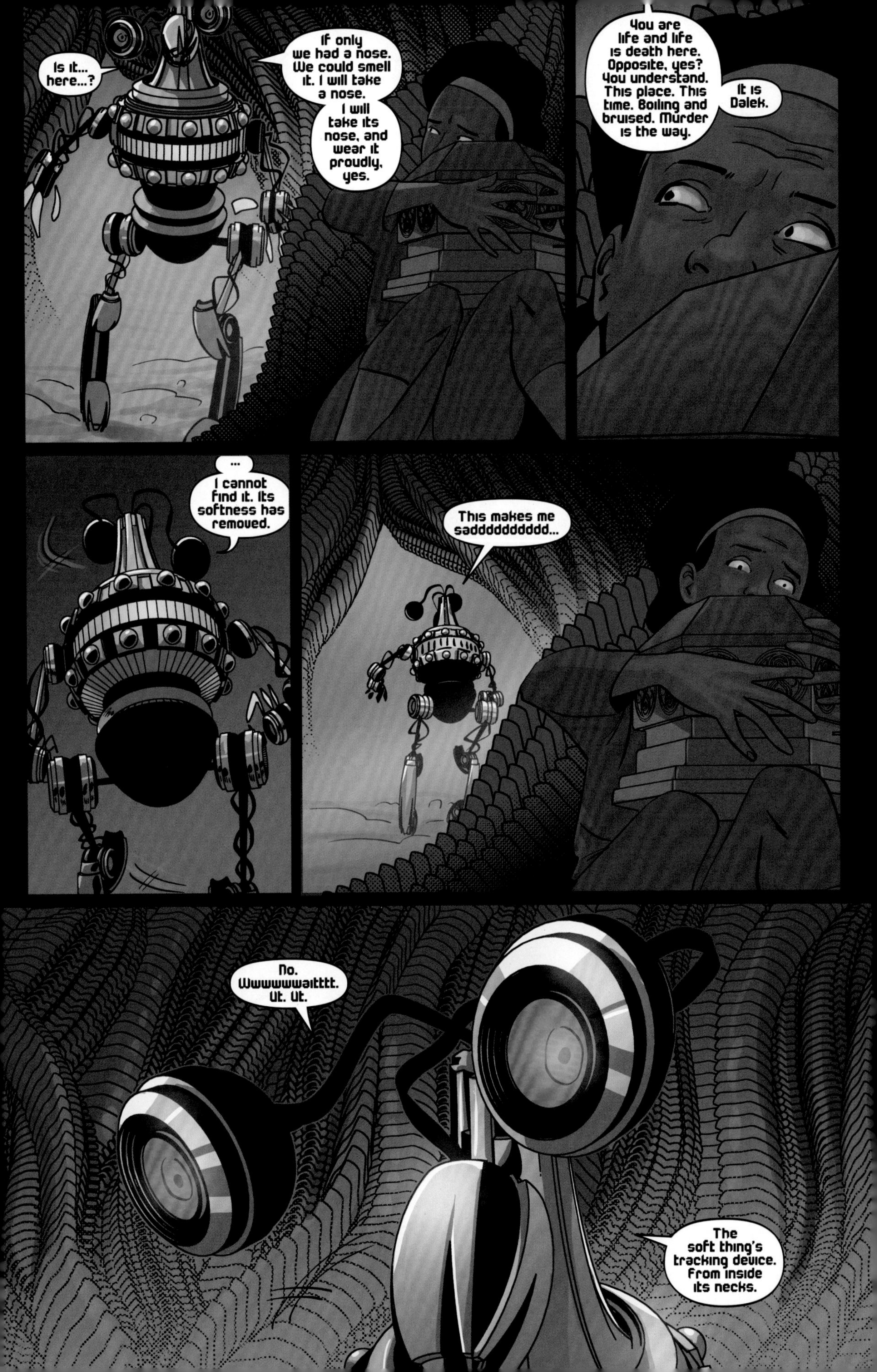
Is it... here...?
If only we had a nose. We could smell it. I will take a nose.
I will take its nose, and wear it proudly, yes.
You are life and life is death here. Opposite, yes? You understand. This place. This time. Boiling and bruised. Murder is the way.
It is Dalek.
... I cannot find it. Its softness has removed.
This makes me sadddddddddd...
No. Wwwwwwaitttt. Ut. Ut.
The soft thing's tracking device. From inside its necks.

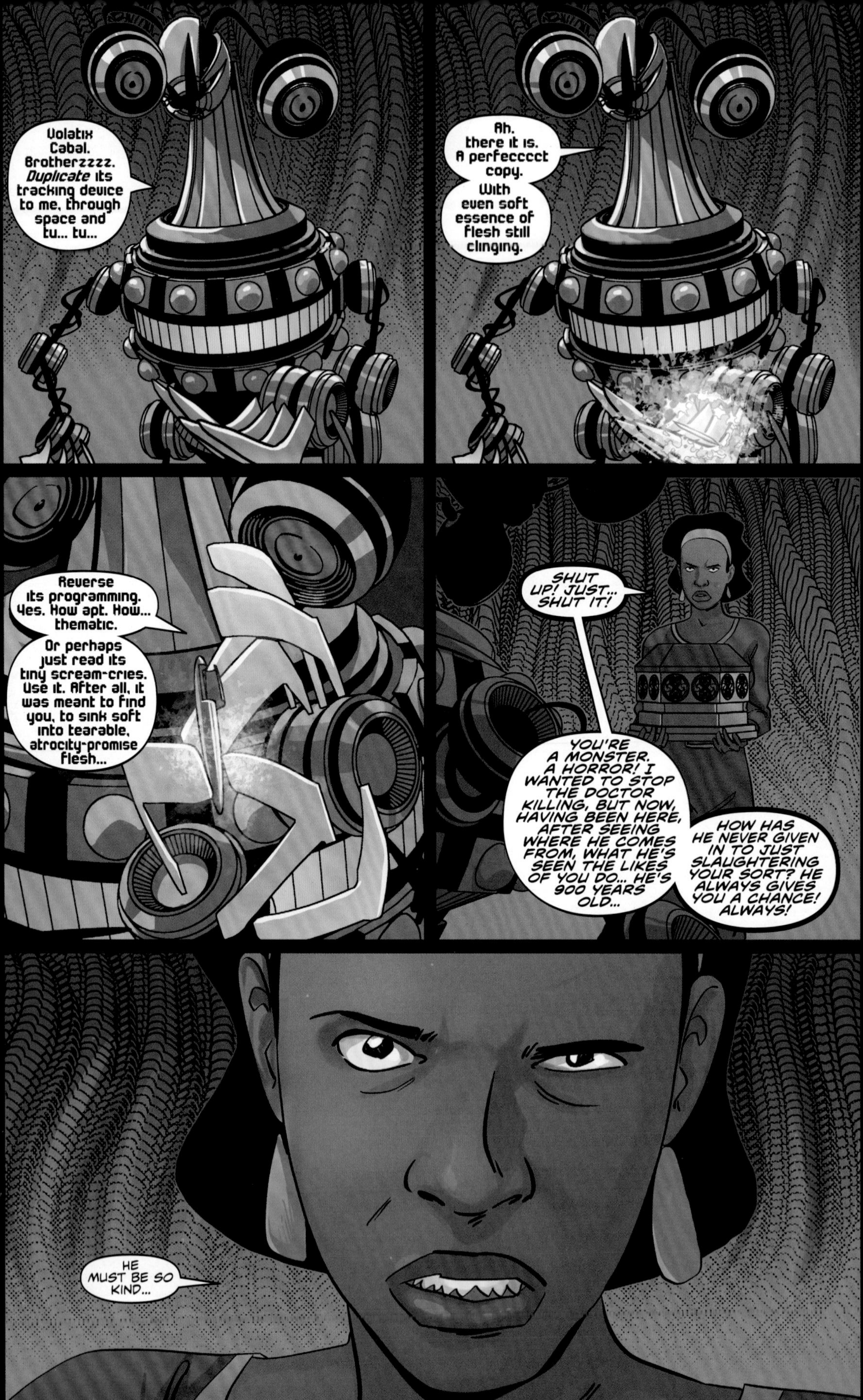

Volatix Cabal. Brotherzzzz. *Duplicate* its tracking device to me, through space and tu... tu...
Ah. there it is. A perfecccct copy.
With even soft essence of flesh still clinging.
Reverse its programming. Yes. How apt. How... thematic.
Or perhaps just read its tiny scream-cries. Use it. After all, it was meant to find you, to sink soft into tearable, atrocity-promise flesh...
SHUT UP! JUST... SHUT IT!
YOU'RE A MONSTER. A HORROR! I WANTED TO STOP THE DOCTOR KILLING, BUT NOW, HAVING BEEN HERE, AFTER SEEING WHERE HE COMES FROM, WHAT HE'S SEEN THE LIKES OF YOU DO... HE'S 900 YEARS OLD...
HOW HAS HE NEVER GIVEN IN TO JUST SLAUGHTERING YOUR SORT? HE ALWAYS GIVES YOU A CHANCE! ALWAYS!
HE MUST BE SO KIND...

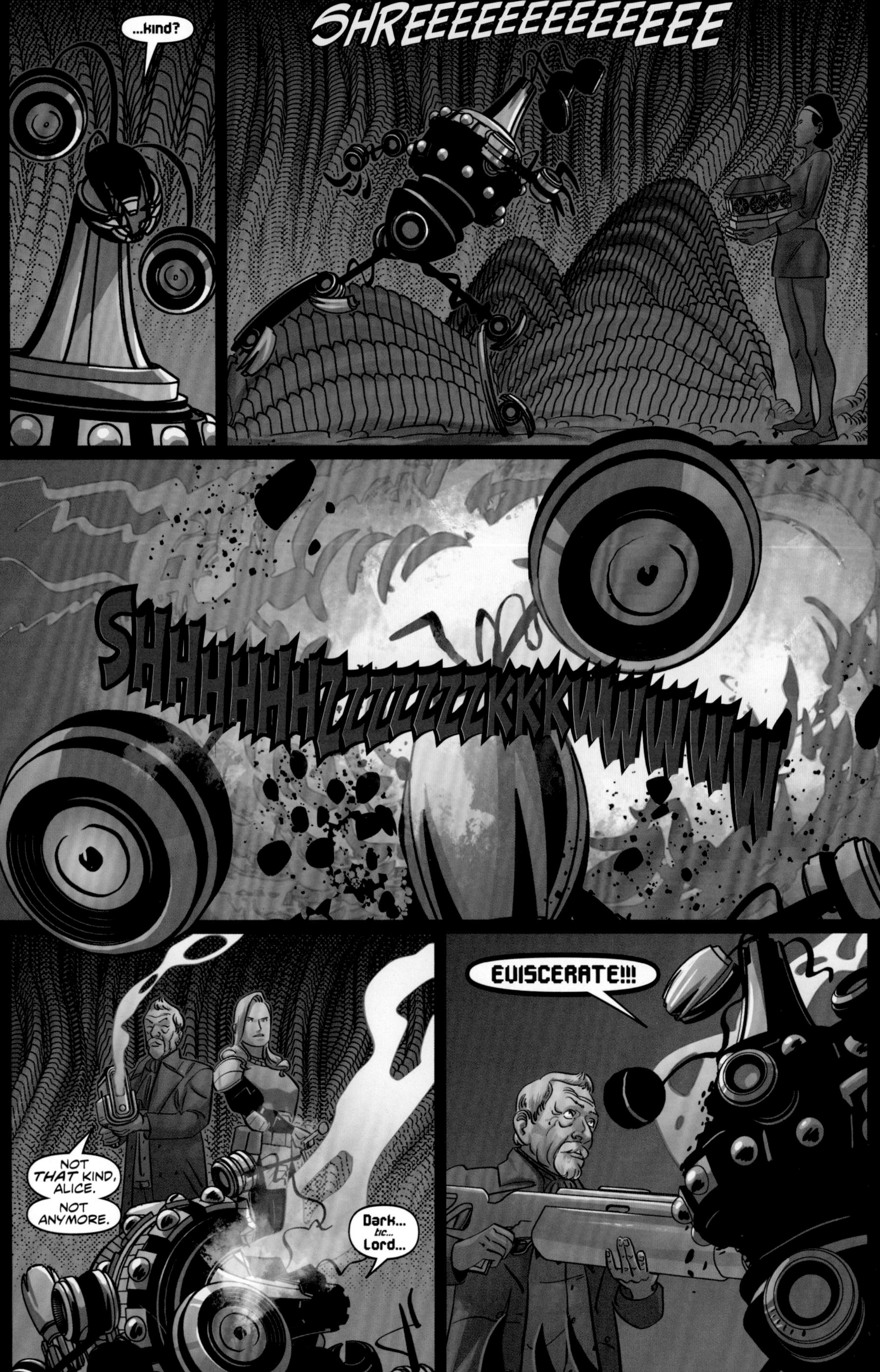
...kind?
SHREEEEEEEEEEEEE
SHHHHHHZZZZZZZKKKWWWWWW
NOT THAT KIND, ALICE.
NOT ANYMORE.
Dark... tic... Lord...
EVISCERATE!!!

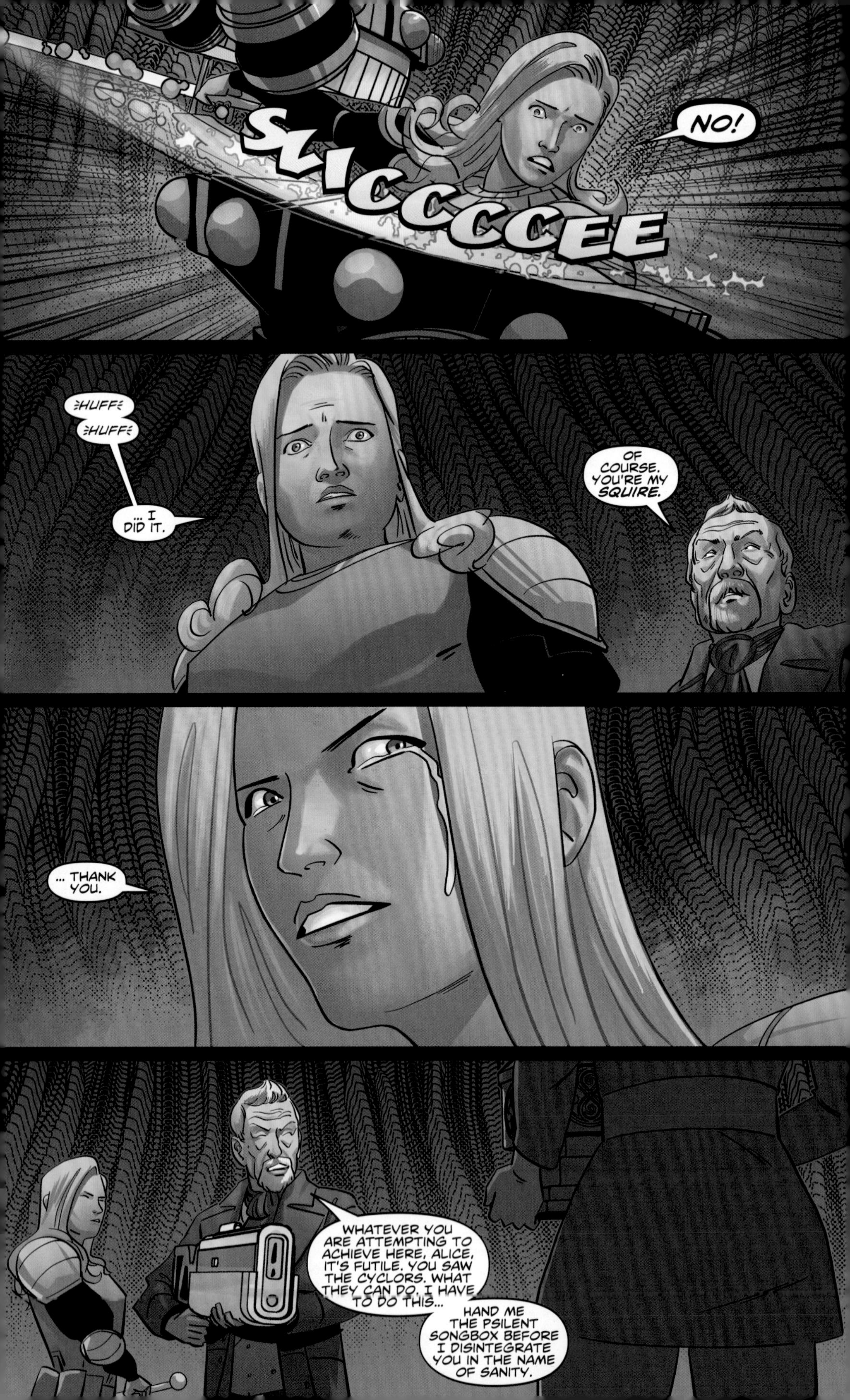
SLICCCCEE
NO!
HUFF
HUFF
... I DID IT.
OF COURSE. YOU'RE MY SQUIRE.
... THANK YOU.
WHATEVER YOU ARE ATTEMPTING TO ACHIEVE HERE, ALICE, IT'S FUTILE. YOU SAW THE CYCLORS. WHAT THEY CAN DO. I HAVE TO DO THIS...
HAND ME THE PSILENT SONGBOX BEFORE I DISINTEGRATE YOU IN THE NAME OF SANITY.

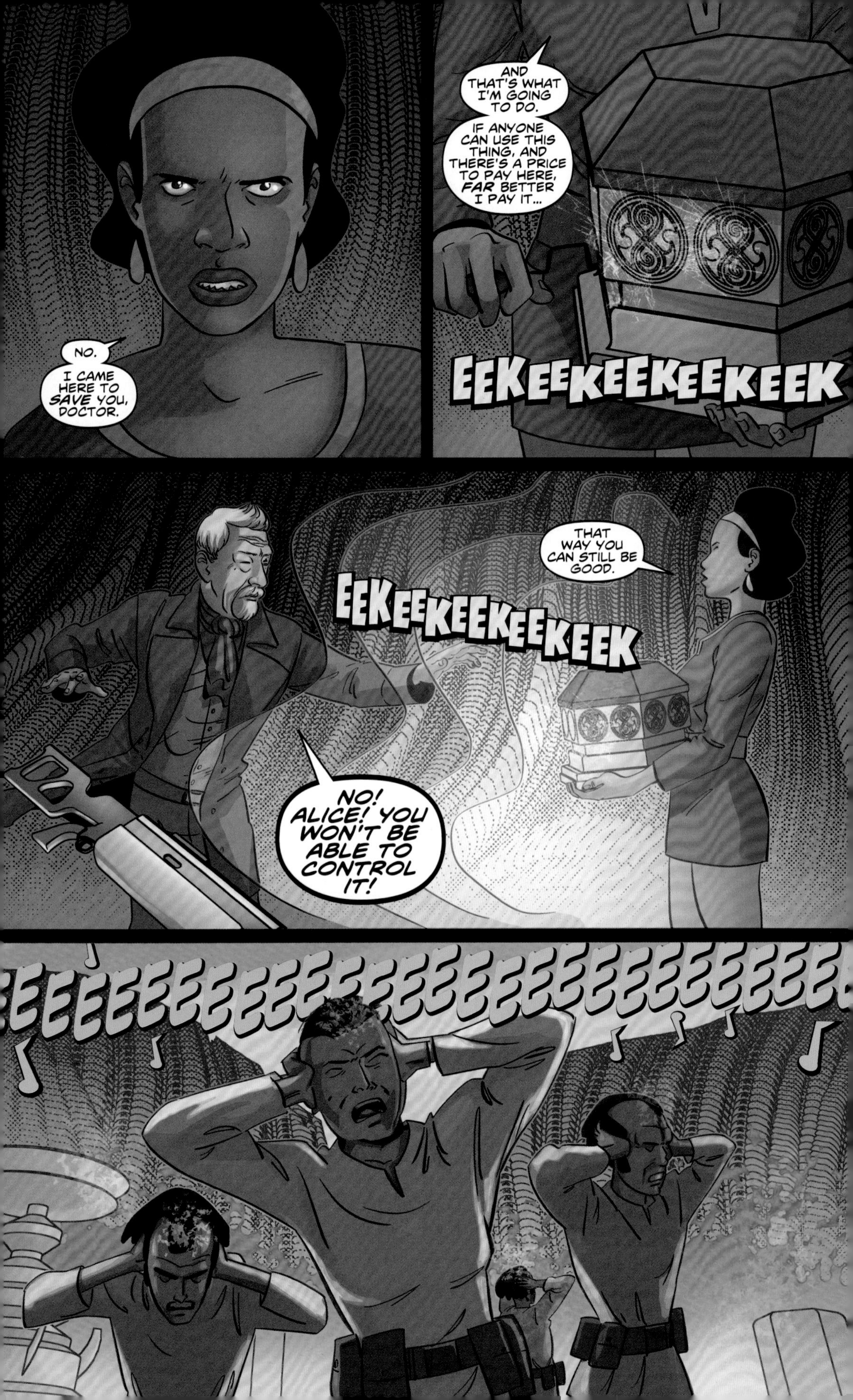
NO.
I CAME HERE TO SAVE YOU, DOCTOR.
AND THAT'S WHAT I'M GOING TO DO.
IF ANYONE CAN USE THIS THING, AND THERE'S A PRICE TO PAY HERE, FAR BETTER I PAY IT...
EEKEEKEEKEEKEEK
THAT WAY YOU CAN STILL BE GOOD.
EEKEEKEEKEEKEEK
NO! ALICE! YOU WON'T BE ABLE TO CONTROL IT!
EEEEEEEEEEEEEEEEEEEEEEEEEEEEEEE

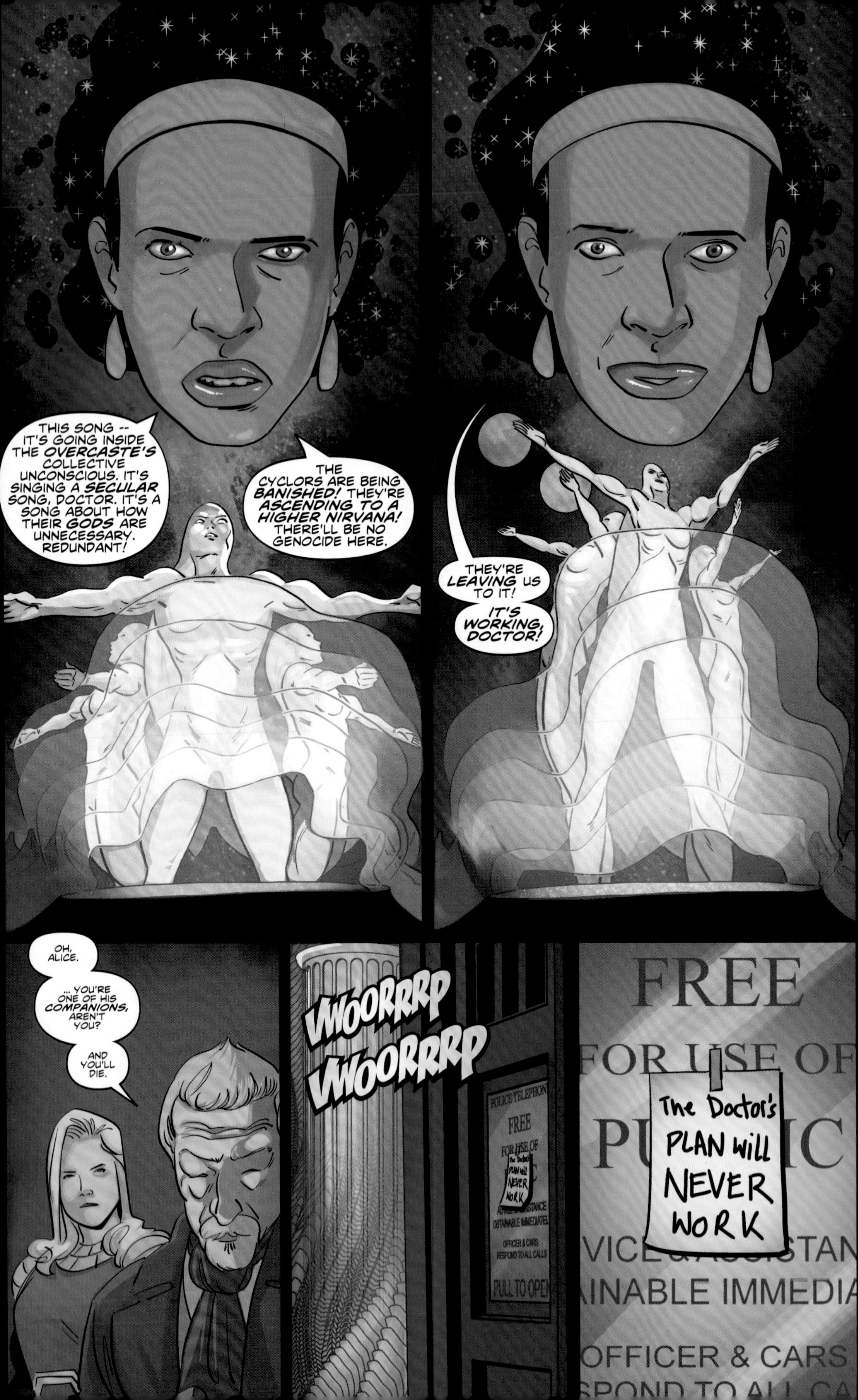

THIS SONG -- IT'S GOING INSIDE THE OVERCASTE'S COLLECTIVE UNCONSCIOUS. IT'S SINGING A SECULAR SONG, DOCTOR. IT'S A SONG ABOUT HOW THEIR GODS ARE UNNECESSARY. REDUNDANT!
THE CYCLORS ARE BEING BANISHED! THEY'RE ASCENDING TO A HIGHER NIRVANA! THERE'LL BE NO GENOCIDE HERE.
THEY'RE LEAVING US TO IT!
IT'S WORKING, DOCTOR!
OH, ALICE.
... YOU'RE ONE OF HIS COMPANIONS, AREN'T YOU?
AND YOU'LL DIE.
VWOORRRP
VWOORRRP
FREE
FOR USE OF
PUBLIC
The Doctor's PLAN WILL NEVER WORK
VICE & ASSISTAN
AINABLE IMMEDIA
OFFICER & CARS

YES!

IT'S WORKING! WHOEVER YOU WERE, ALICE. HOWEVER YOU CREATED THIS HORROR, THIS... CHRONAL TUMOR, YOU HAVE MY ETERNAL THANK--

AHHH!

FLLLLLSSSWWWWWILLL

YOU DIDN'T CREATE IT, DID YOU?

I DID. IN A FUTURE I WILL NEVER SEE.

SKREEEEEEEEEEEE

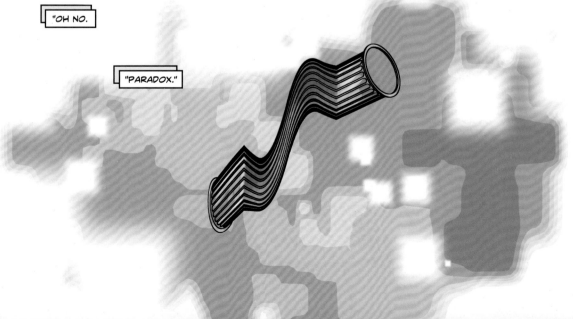

"OH NO.

"PARADOX."

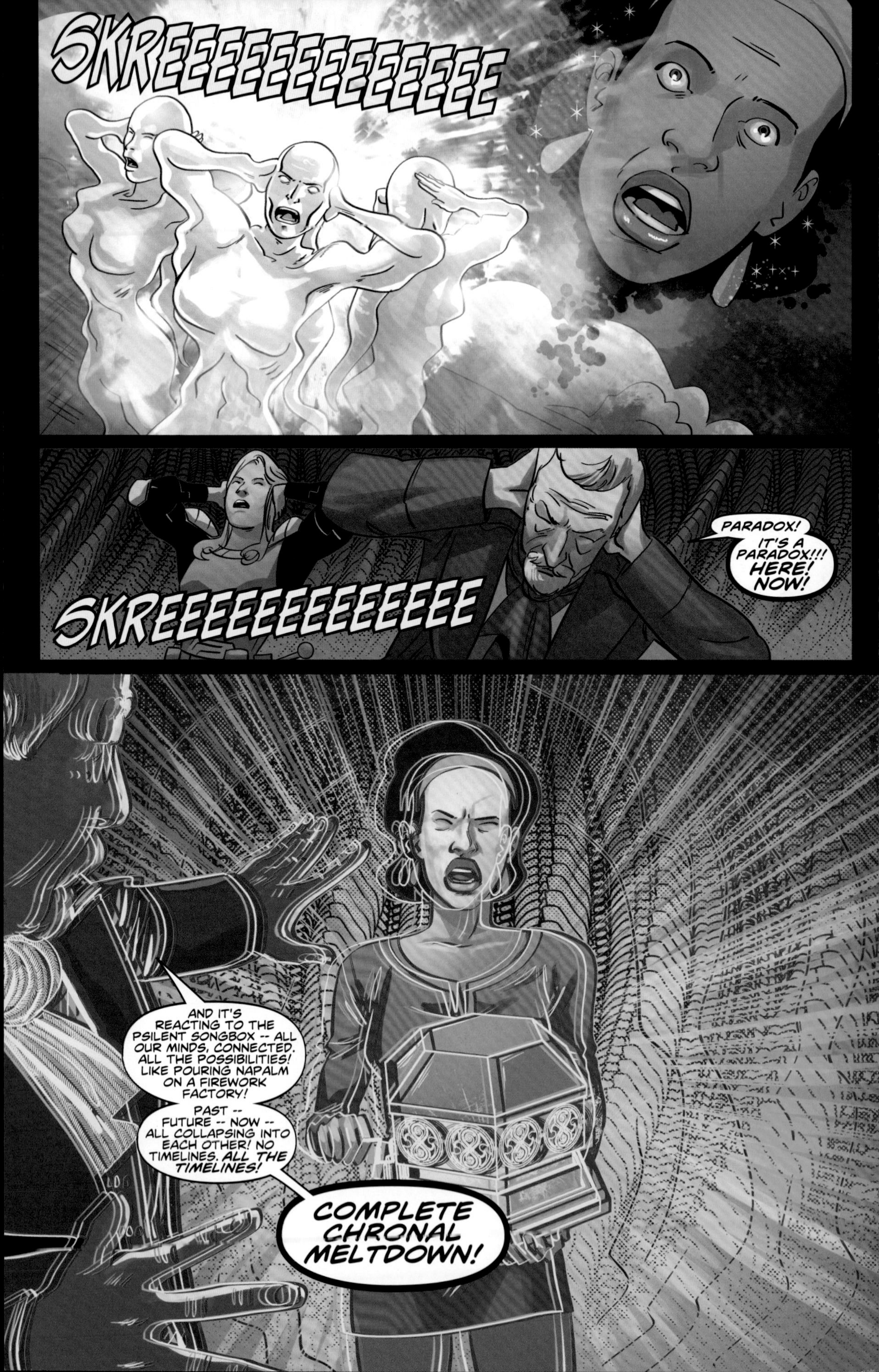
SKREEEEEEEEEEEEEE
PARADOX! IT'S A PARADOX!!! HERE! NOW!
SKREEEEEEEEEEEEEE
AND IT'S REACTING TO THE PSILENT SONGBOX -- ALL OUR MINDS, CONNECTED. ALL THE POSSIBILITIES! LIKE POURING NAPALM ON A FIREWORK FACTORY!
PAST -- FUTURE -- NOW -- ALL COLLAPSING INTO EACH OTHER! NO TIMELINES. ALL THE TIMELINES!
COMPLETE CHRONAL MELTDOWN!

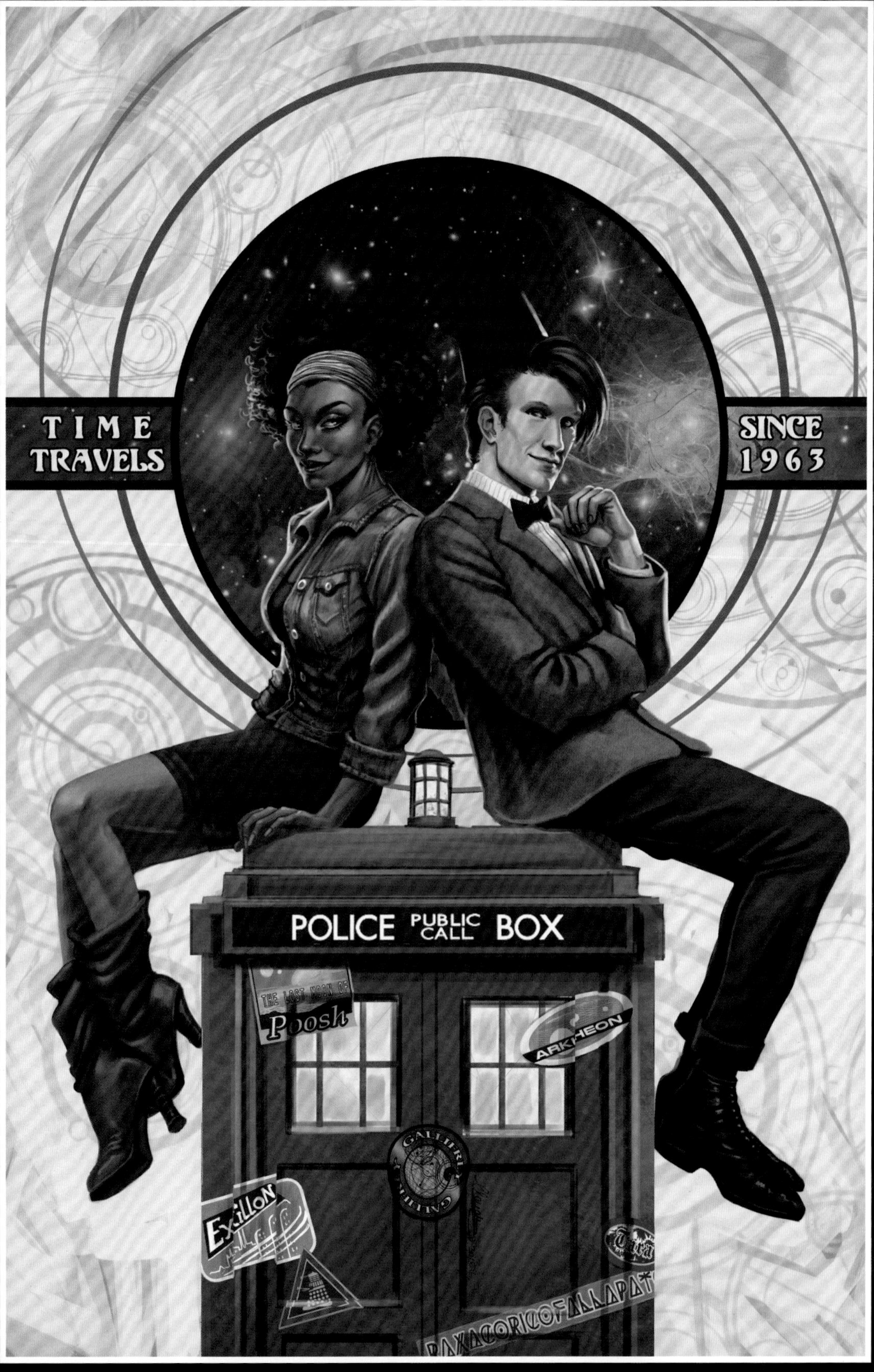
TIME TRAVELS
SINCE 1963
POLICE PUBLIC CALL BOX
THE LOST MOON OF
Poosh
ARKHEON
Exillon

11D #2.12 Cover A: Claudia Ianniciello

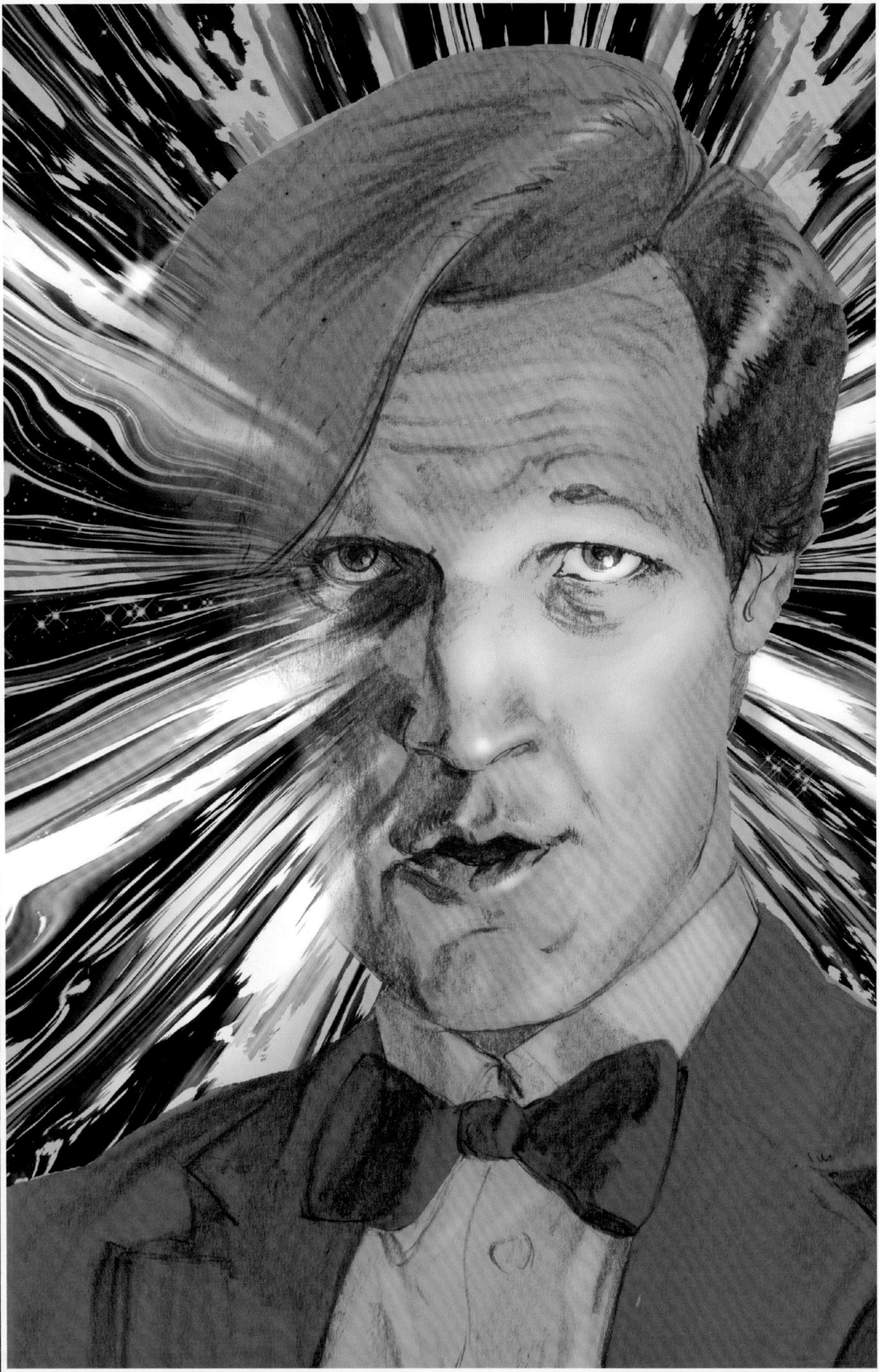

11D #2.13 Cover A: Simon Fraser

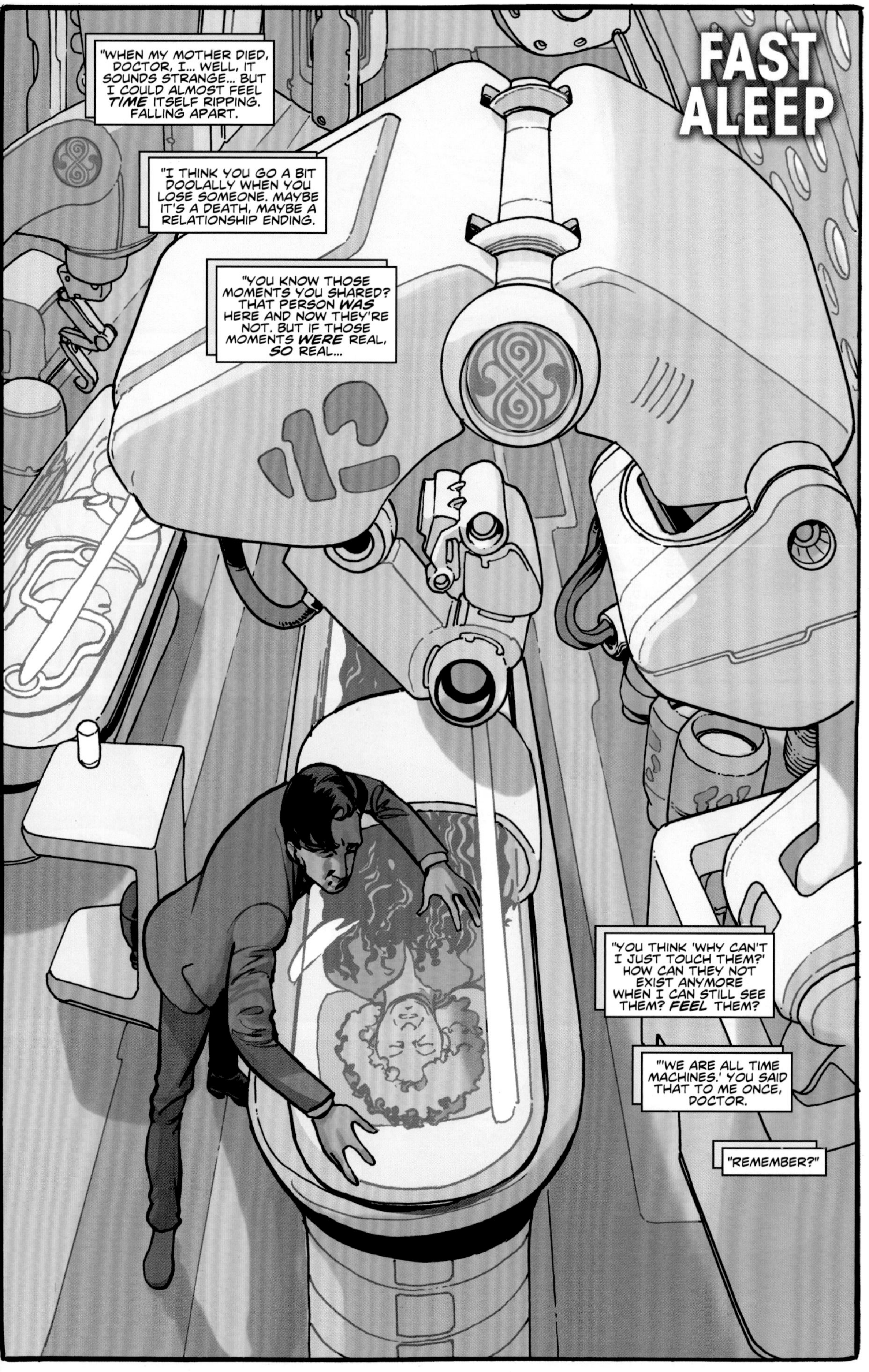
FAST ALEEP
"WHEN MY MOTHER DIED, DOCTOR, I... WELL, IT SOUNDS STRANGE... BUT I COULD ALMOST FEEL TIME ITSELF RIPPING. FALLING APART.
"I THINK YOU GO A BIT DOOLALLY WHEN YOU LOSE SOMEONE. MAYBE IT'S A DEATH, MAYBE A RELATIONSHIP ENDING.
"YOU KNOW THOSE MOMENTS YOU SHARED? THAT PERSON WAS HERE AND NOW THEY'RE NOT. BUT IF THOSE MOMENTS WERE REAL, SO REAL...
"YOU THINK 'WHY CAN'T I JUST TOUCH THEM?' HOW CAN THEY NOT EXIST ANYMORE WHEN I CAN STILL SEE THEM? FEEL THEM?
"'WE ARE ALL TIME MACHINES.' YOU SAID THAT TO ME ONCE, DOCTOR.
"REMEMBER?"

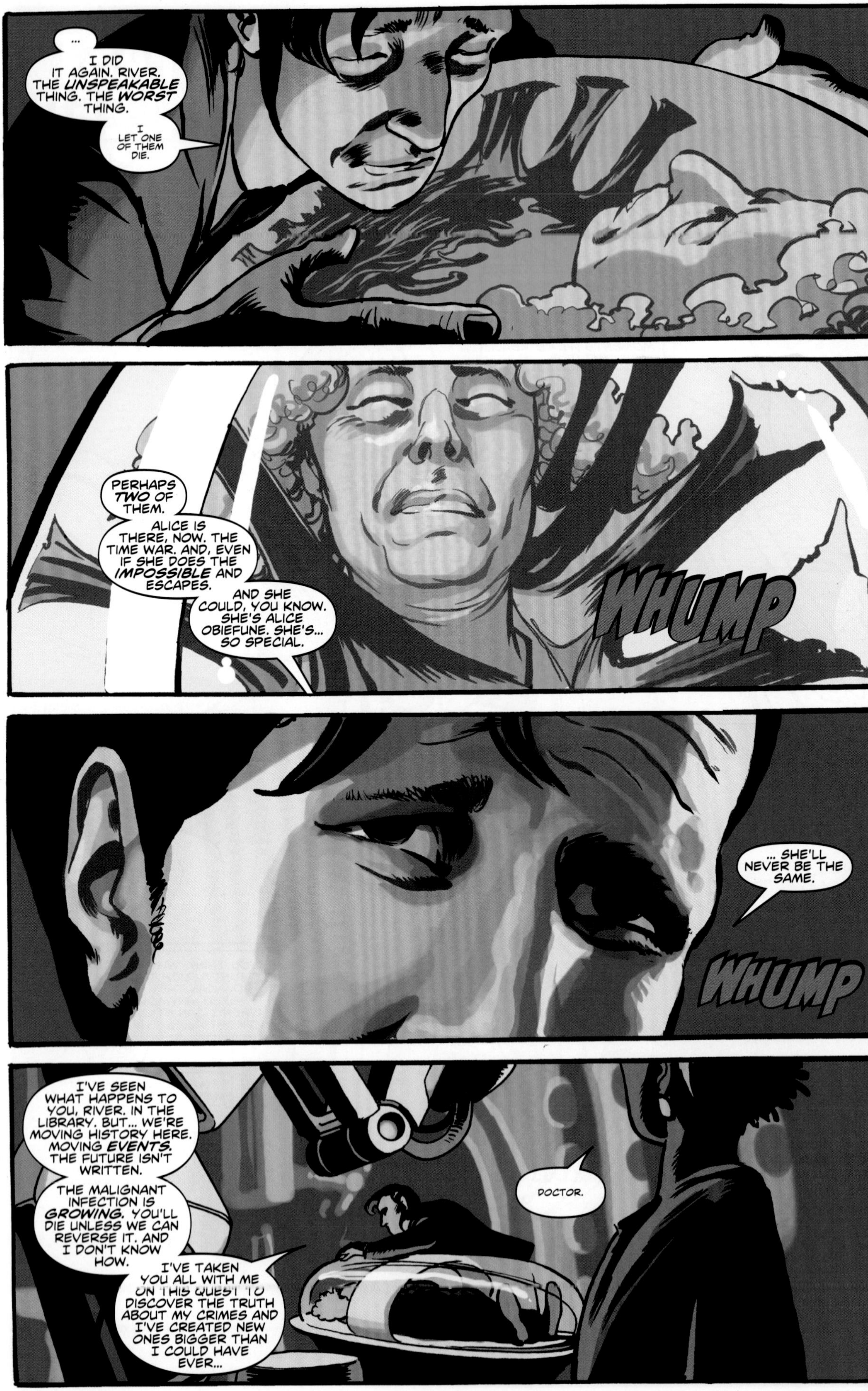
...
I DID IT AGAIN. RIVER. THE UNSPEAKABLE THING. THE WORST THING.
I LET ONE OF THEM DIE.
PERHAPS TWO OF THEM.
ALICE IS THERE, NOW. THE TIME WAR. AND, EVEN IF SHE DOES THE IMPOSSIBLE AND ESCAPES.
AND SHE COULD, YOU KNOW. SHE'S ALICE OBIEFUNE. SHE'S... SO SPECIAL.
WHUMP
... SHE'LL NEVER BE THE SAME.
WHUMP
I'VE SEEN WHAT HAPPENS TO YOU, RIVER. IN THE LIBRARY. BUT... WE'RE MOVING HISTORY HERE. MOVING EVENTS. THE FUTURE ISN'T WRITTEN.
THE MALIGNANT INFECTION IS GROWING. YOU'LL DIE UNLESS WE CAN REVERSE IT. AND I DON'T KNOW HOW.
I'VE TAKEN YOU ALL WITH ME ON THIS QUEST TO DISCOVER THE TRUTH ABOUT MY CRIMES AND I'VE CREATED NEW ONES BIGGER THAN I COULD HAVE EVER...
DOCTOR.

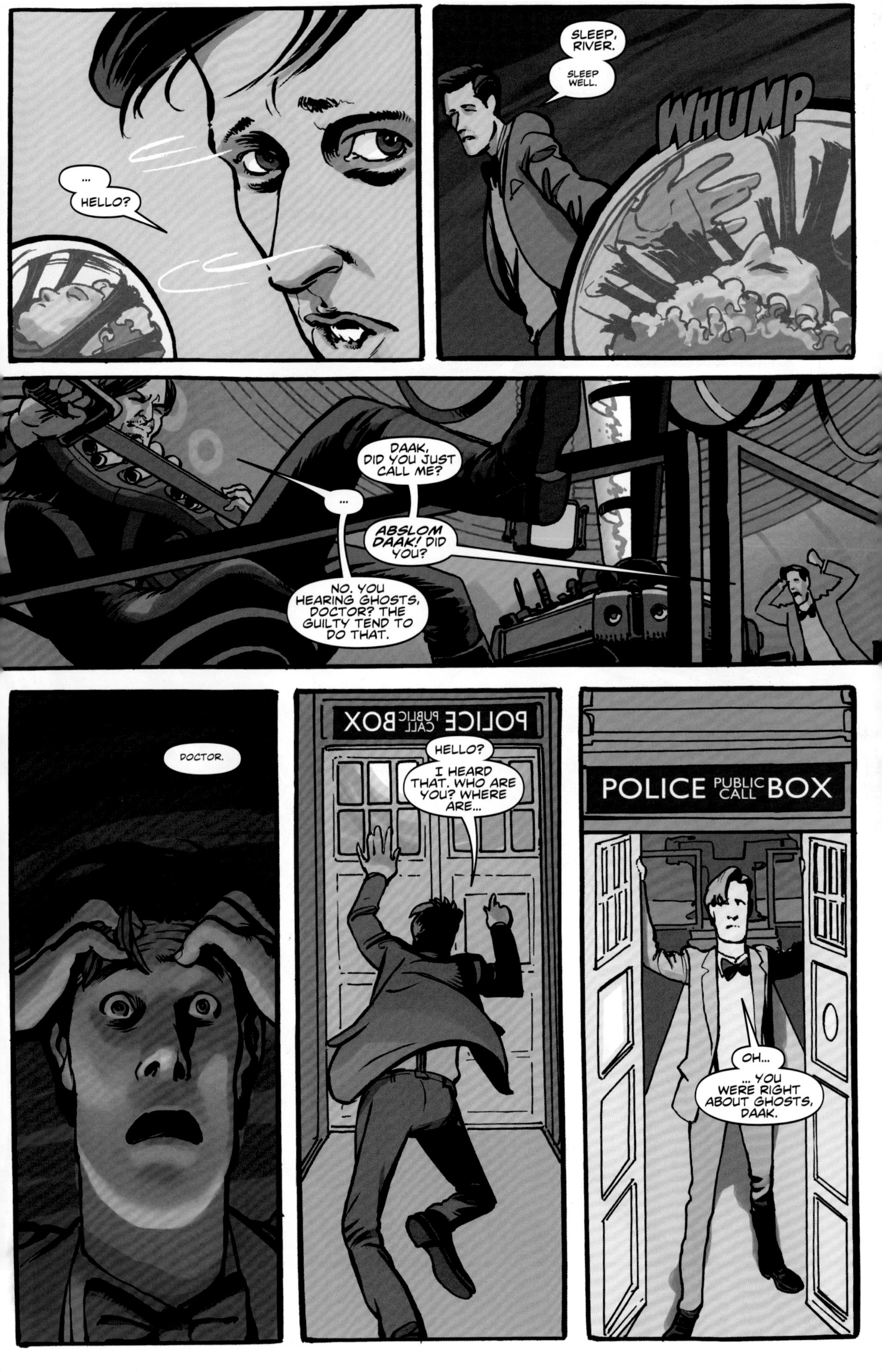
...
HELLO?
SLEEP, RIVER.
SLEEP WELL.
WHUMP
DAAK, DID YOU JUST CALL ME?
...
ABSLOM DAAK! DID YOU?
NO. YOU HEARING GHOSTS, DOCTOR? THE GUILTY TEND TO DO THAT.
DOCTOR.
POLICE PUBLIC CALL BOX
HELLO?
I HEARD THAT. WHO ARE YOU? WHERE ARE...
POLICE PUBLIC CALL BOX
OH...
... YOU WERE RIGHT ABOUT GHOSTS, DAAK.

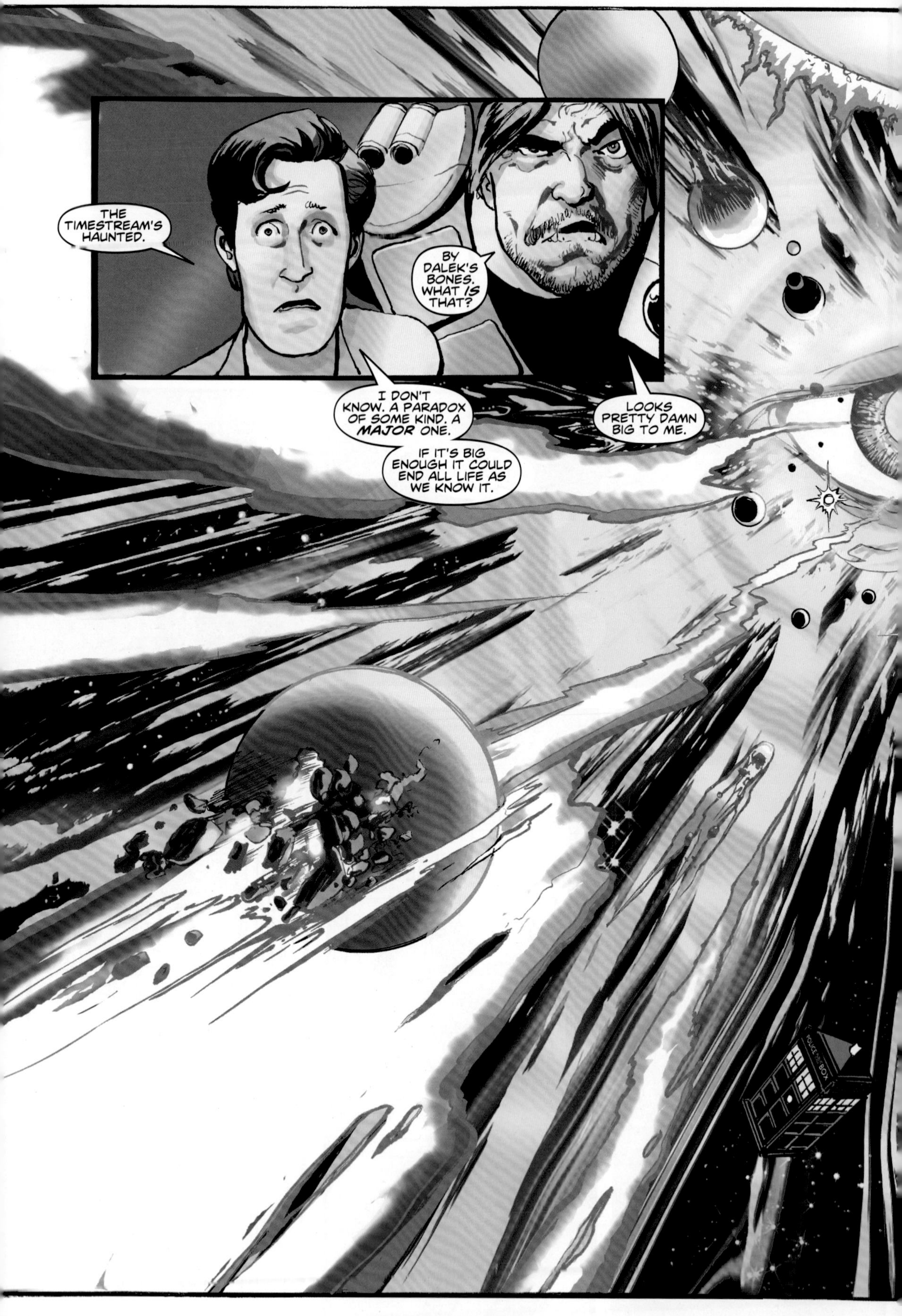
THE TIMESTREAM'S HAUNTED.
BY DALEK'S BONES. WHAT IS THAT?
I DON'T KNOW. A PARADOX OF SOME KIND. A MAJOR ONE.
IF IT'S BIG ENOUGH IT COULD END ALL LIFE AS WE KNOW IT.
LOOKS PRETTY DAMN BIG TO ME.
POLICE BOX

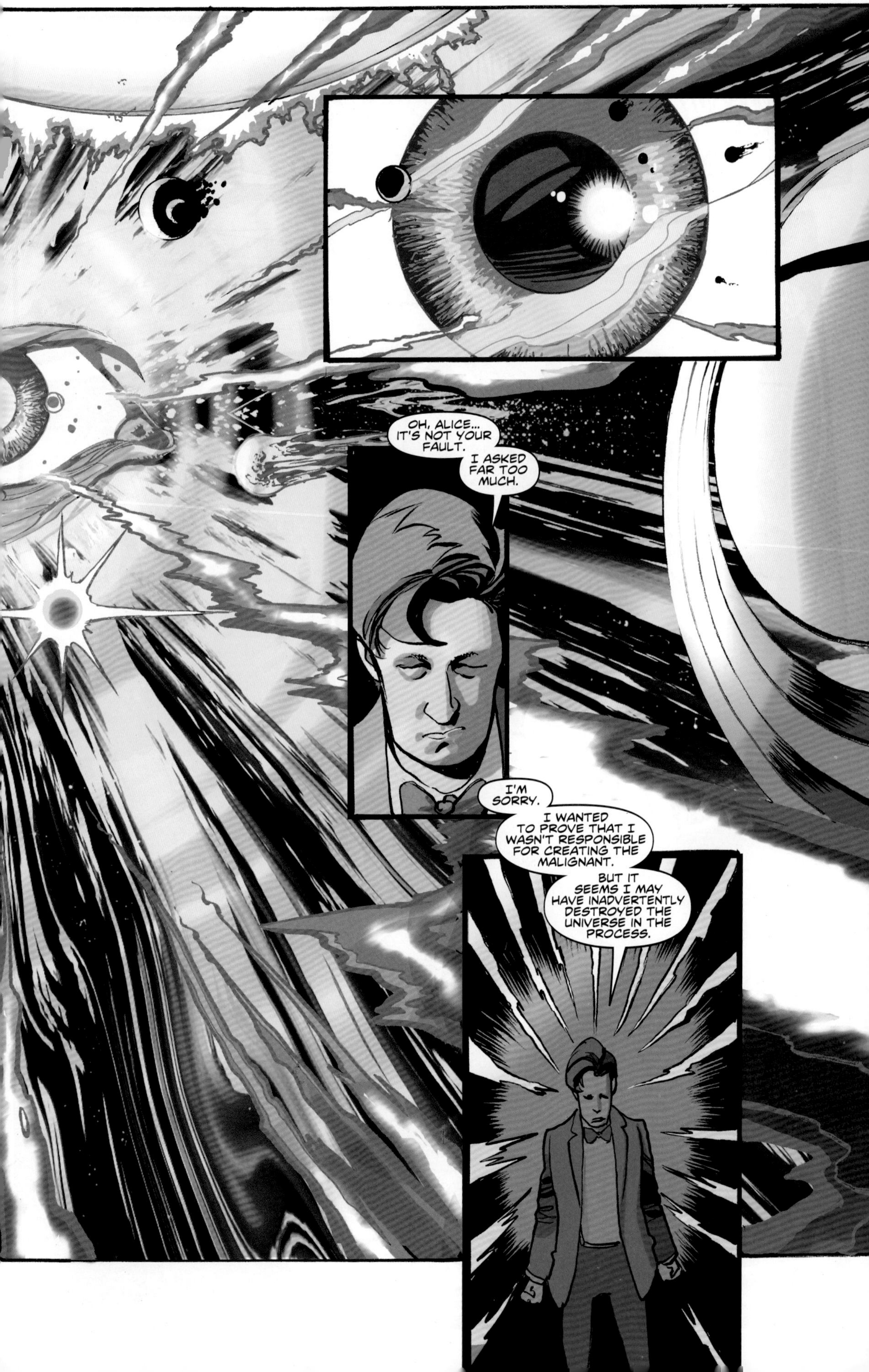
OH, ALICE... IT'S NOT YOUR FAULT.
I ASKED FAR TOO MUCH.
I'M SORRY.
I WANTED TO PROVE THAT I WASN'T RESPONSIBLE FOR CREATING THE MALIGNANT.
BUT IT SEEMS I MAY HAVE INADVERTENTLY DESTROYED THE UNIVERSE IN THE PROCESS.

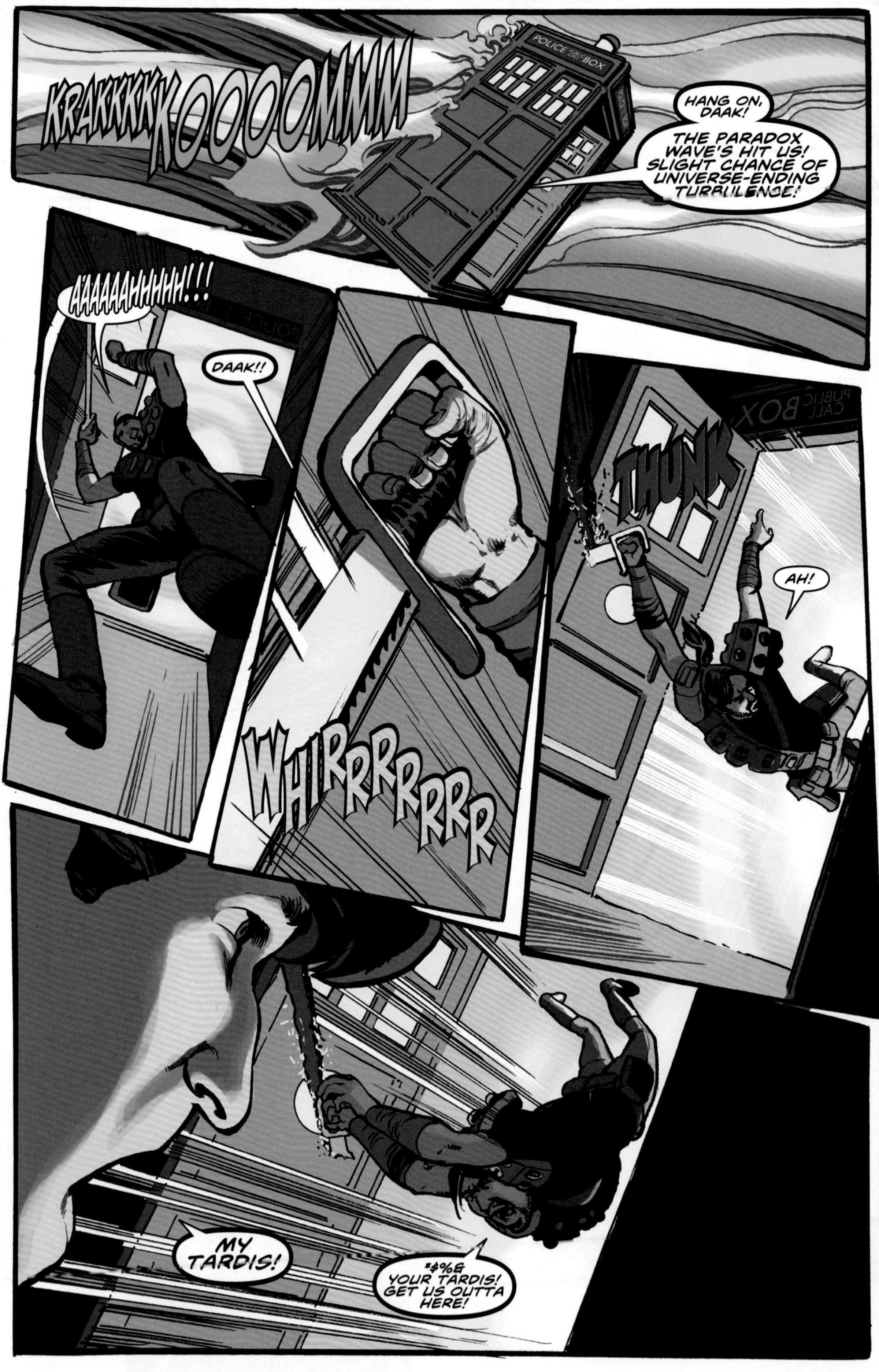
KRAKKKKKOOOOOMMM
HANG ON, DAAK!
THE PARADOX WAVE'S HIT US! SLIGHT CHANCE OF UNIVERSE-ENDING TURBULENCE!
POLICE PUBLIC CALL BOX
AAAAAAHHHHH!!!
DAAK!!
WHIRRRRRRR
THUNK
PUBLIC CALL BOX
AH!
MY TARDIS!
*$%& YOUR TARDIS! GET US OUTTA HERE!

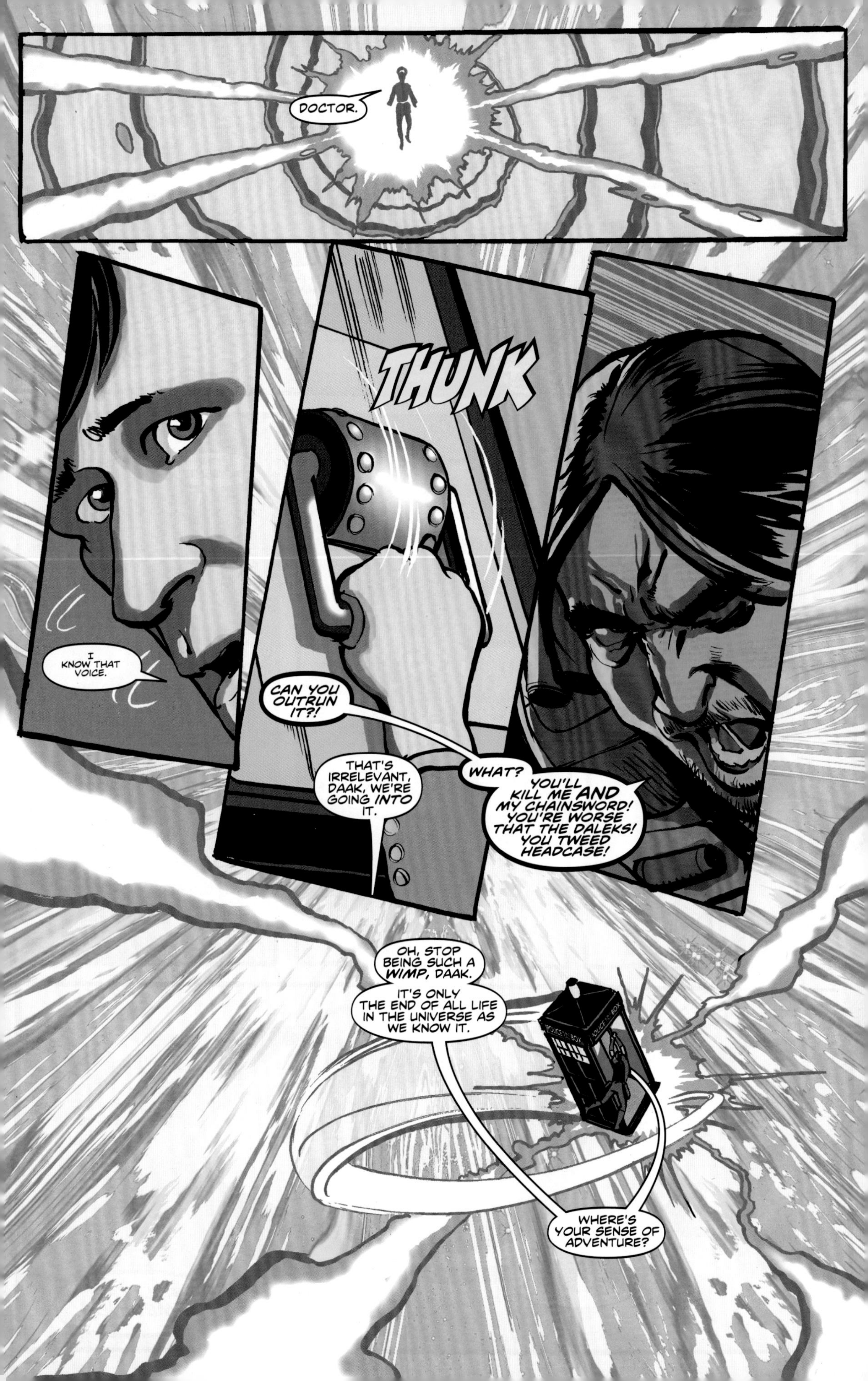
DOCTOR.
I KNOW THAT VOICE.
THUNK
CAN YOU OUTRUN IT?!
THAT'S IRRELEVANT, DAAK, WE'RE GOING INTO IT.
WHAT?
YOU'LL KILL ME AND MY CHAINSWORD! YOU'RE WORSE THAT THE DALEKS! YOU TWEED HEADCASE!
OH, STOP BEING SUCH A WIMP, DAAK.
IT'S ONLY THE END OF ALL LIFE IN THE UNIVERSE AS WE KNOW IT.
WHERE'S YOUR SENSE OF ADVENTURE?

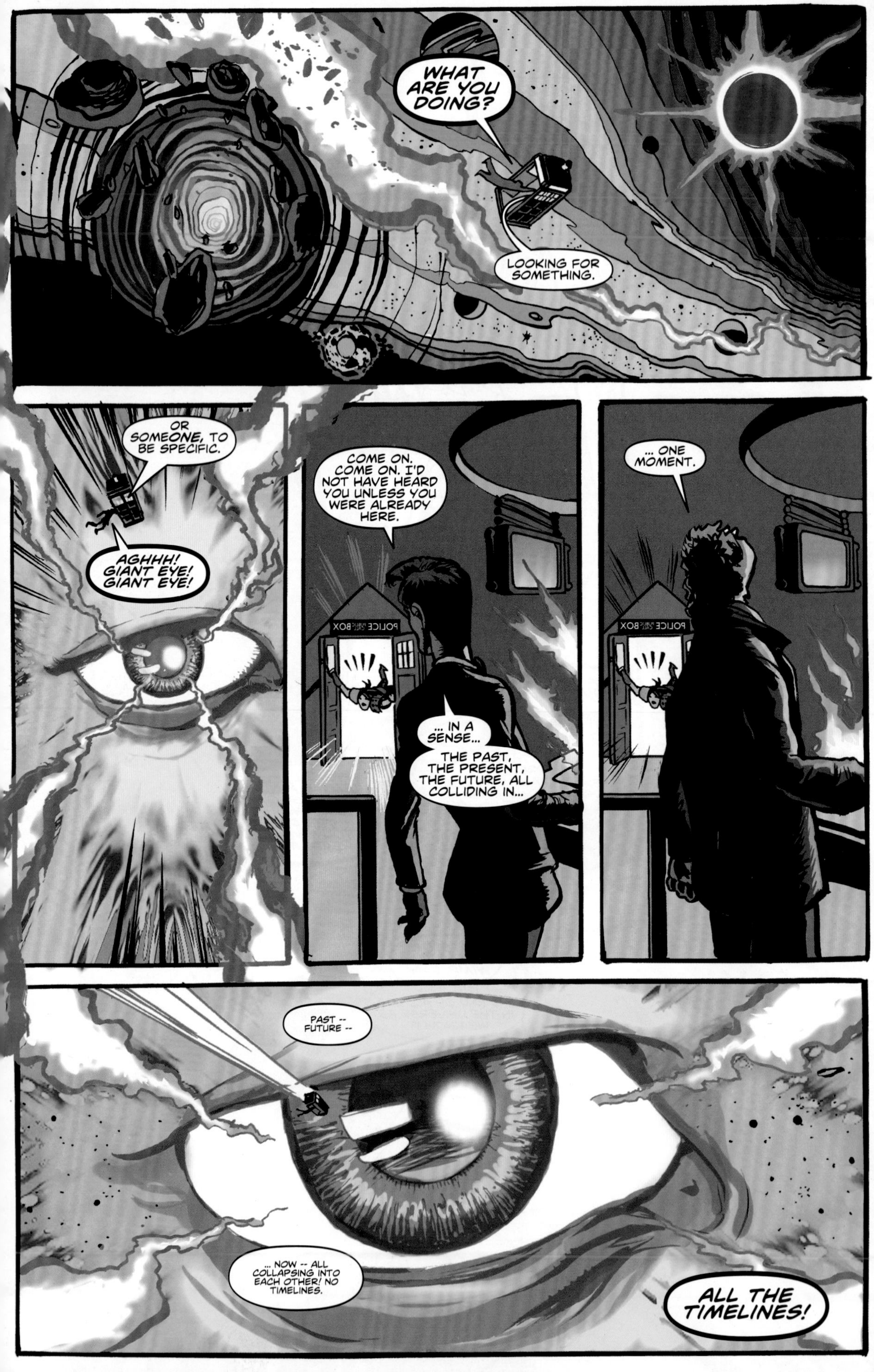
WHAT ARE YOU DOING?
LOOKING FOR SOMETHING.
OR SOMEONE, TO BE SPECIFIC.
AGHHH! GIANT EYE! GIANT EYE!
COME ON. COME ON. I'D NOT HAVE HEARD YOU UNLESS YOU WERE ALREADY HERE.
... IN A SENSE...
THE PAST, THE PRESENT, THE FUTURE, ALL COLLIDING IN...
... ONE MOMENT.
PAST -- FUTURE --
... NOW -- ALL COLLAPSING INTO EACH OTHER! NO TIMELINES.
ALL THE TIMELINES!

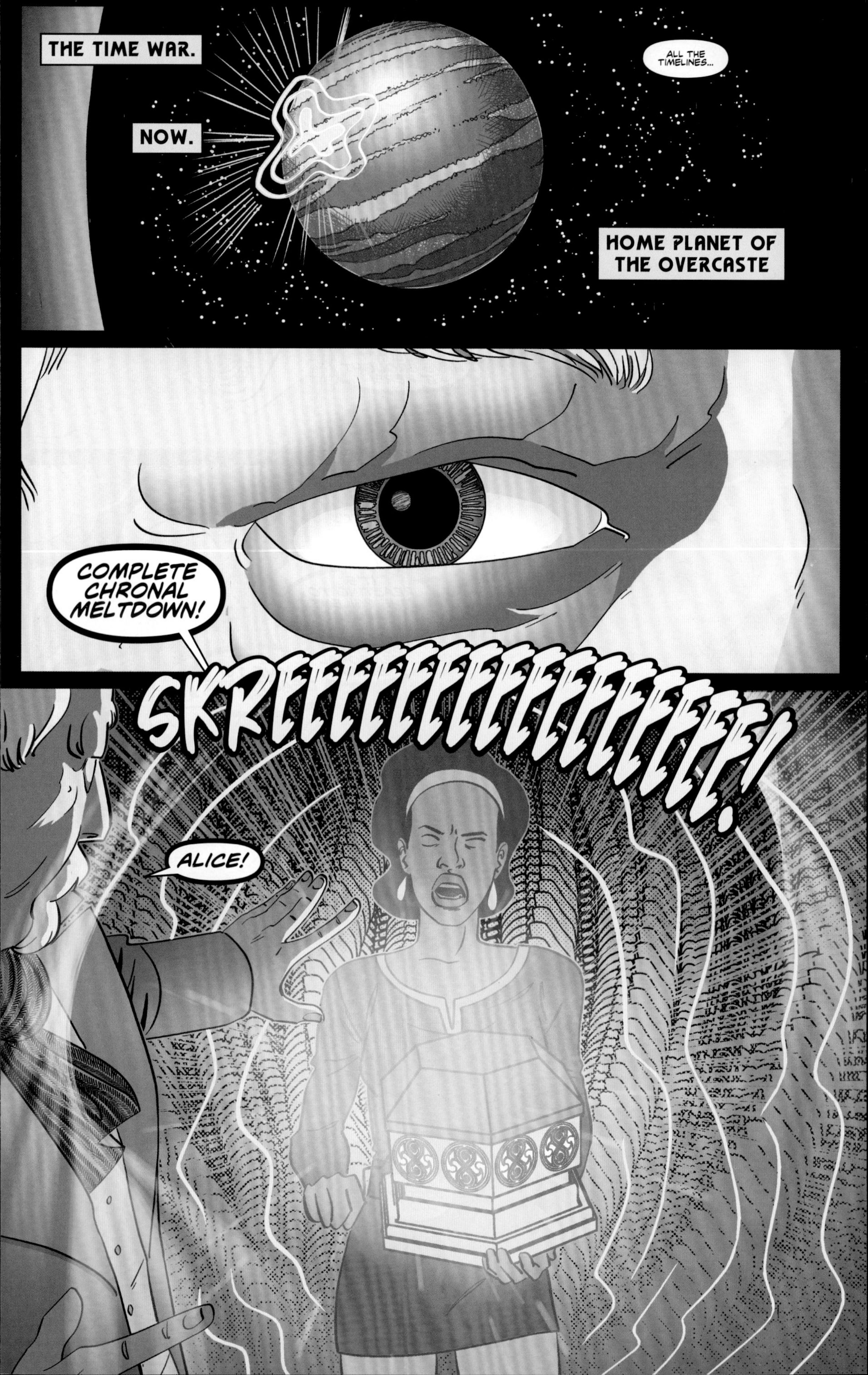
THE TIME WAR.
NOW.
ALL THE TIMELINES...
HOME PLANET OF THE OVERCASTE
COMPLETE CHRONAL MELTDOWN!
SKREEEEEEEEEEEEEEEEEEEEE!
ALICE!

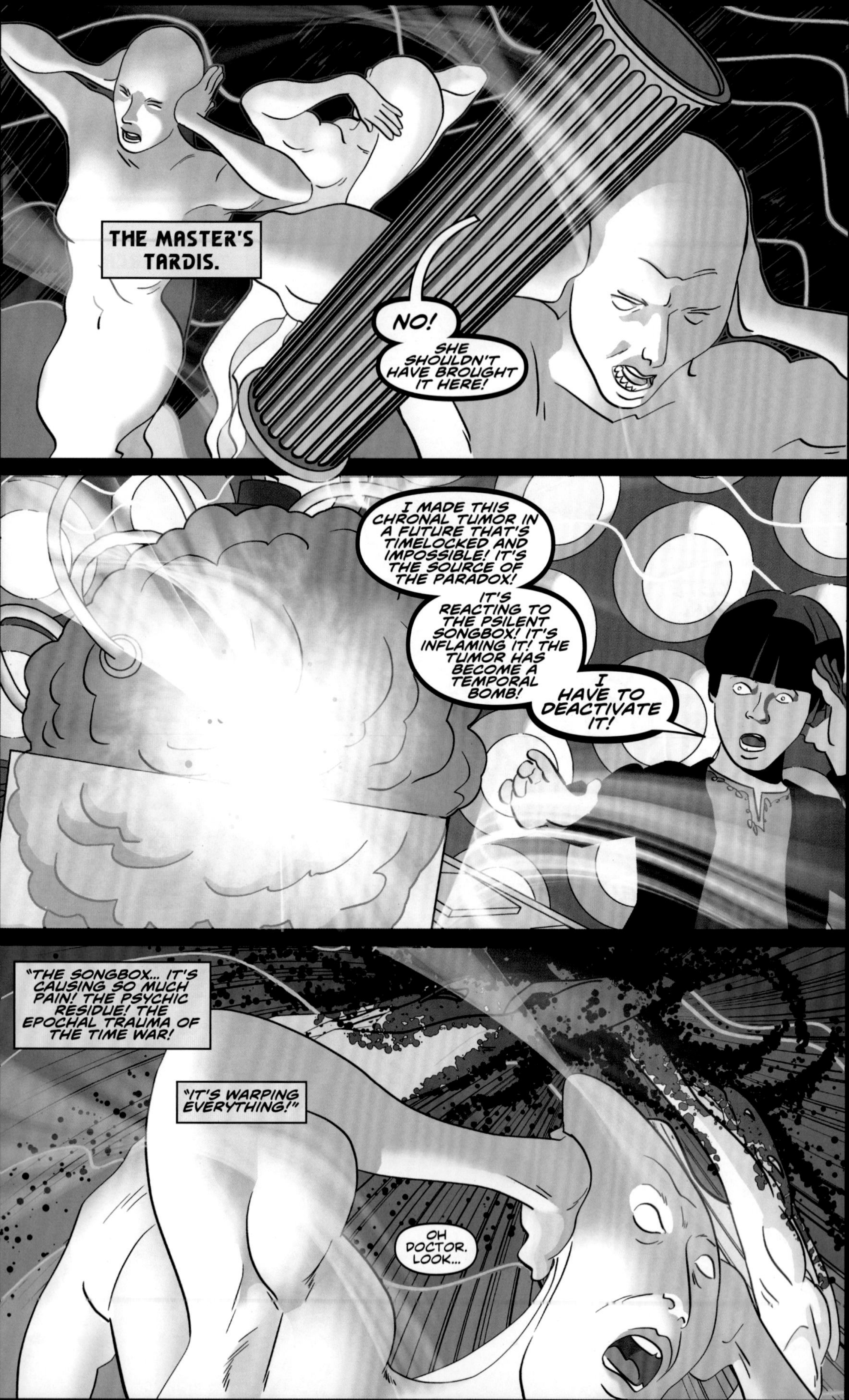
THE MASTER'S TARDIS.
NO!
SHE SHOULDN'T HAVE BROUGHT IT HERE!
I MADE THIS CHRONAL TUMOR IN A FUTURE THAT'S TIMELOCKED AND IMPOSSIBLE! IT'S THE SOURCE OF THE PARADOX!
IT'S REACTING TO THE PSILENT SONGBOX! IT'S INFLAMING IT! THE TUMOR HAS BECOME A TEMPORAL BOMB!
I HAVE TO DEACTIVATE IT!
"THE SONGBOX... IT'S CAUSING SO MUCH PAIN! THE PSYCHIC RESIDUE! THE EPOCHAL TRAUMA OF THE TIME WAR!
"IT'S WARPING EVERYTHING!"
OH DOCTOR. LOOK...

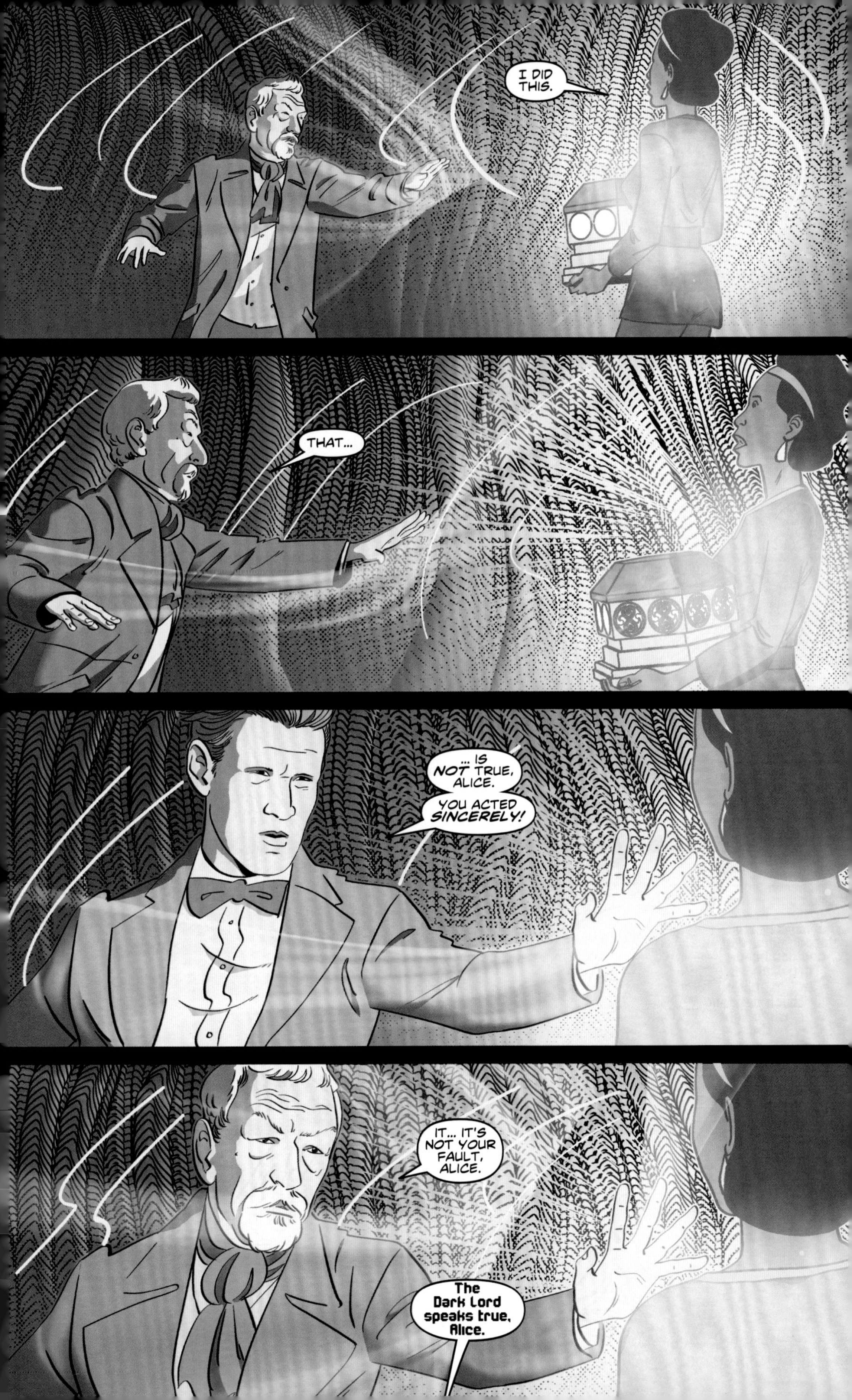
I DID THIS.
THAT...
... IS NOT TRUE, ALICE.
YOU ACTED SINCERELY!
IT... IT'S NOT YOUR FAULT, ALICE.
The Dark Lord speaks true, Alice.

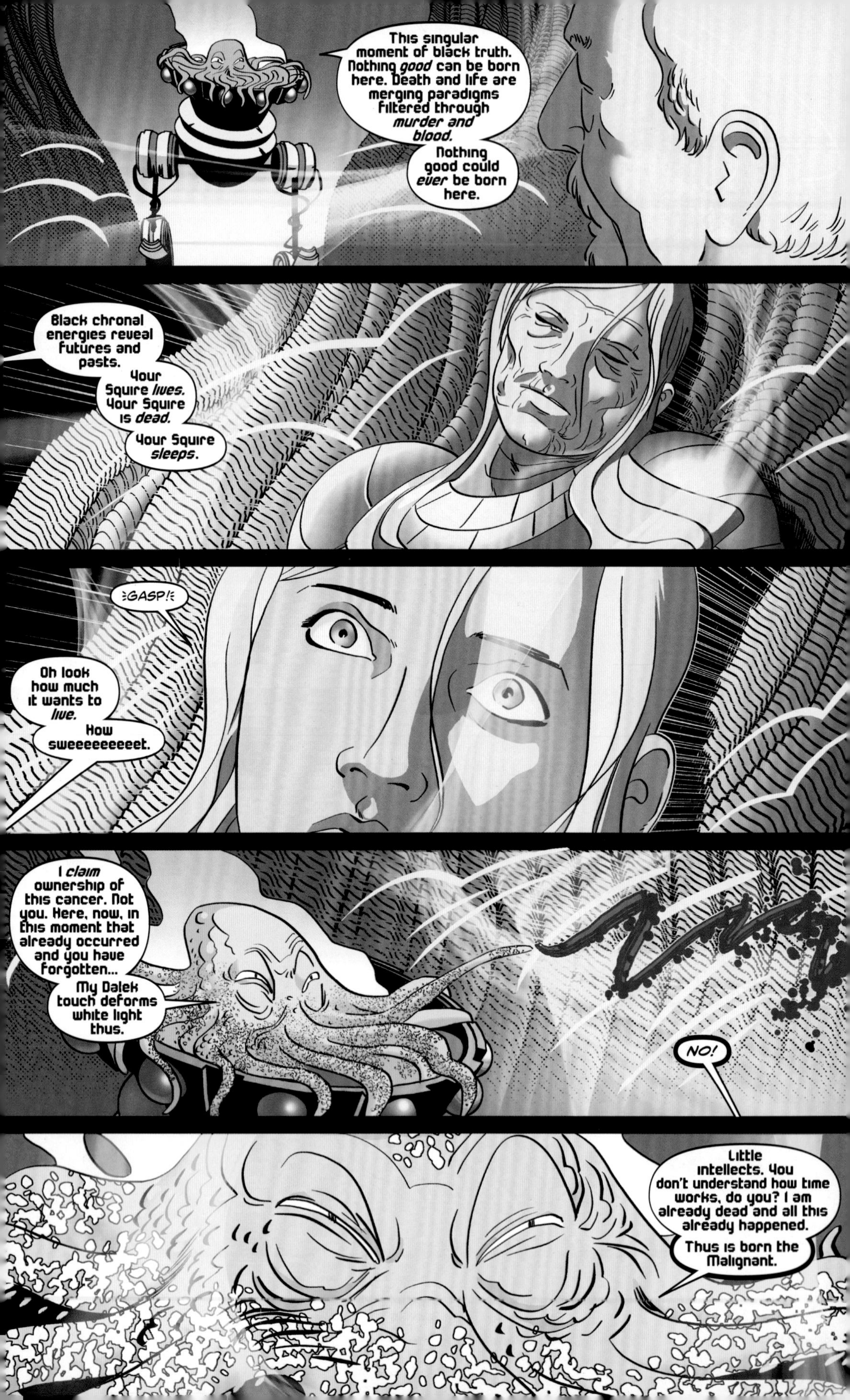
This singular moment of black truth. Nothing *good* can be born here. Death and life are merging paradigms filtered through *murder and blood.*
Nothing good could *ever* be born here.
Black chronal energies reveal futures and pasts.
Your Squire *lives.* Your Squire is *dead.*
Your Squire *sleeps.*
GASP!
Oh look how much it wants to *live.*
How sweeeeeeeeet.
I *claim* ownership of this cancer. Not you. Here, now, in this moment that already occurred and you have forgotten...
My Dalek touch deforms white light thus.
NO!
Little intellects. You don't understand how time works, do you? I am already dead and all this already happened.
Thus is born the Malignant.

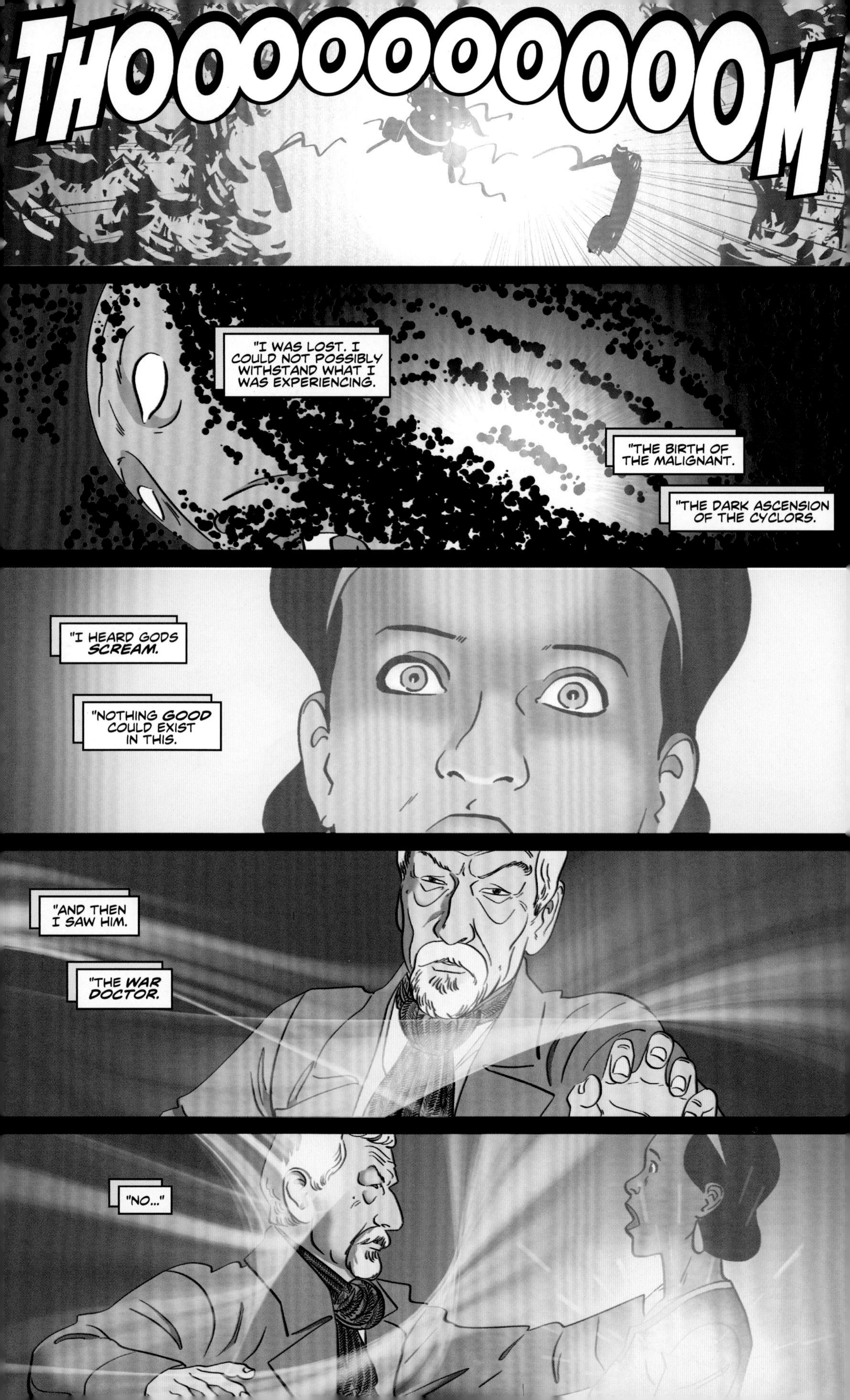
THOOOOOOOOOOOM
"I WAS LOST. I COULD NOT POSSIBLY WITHSTAND WHAT I WAS EXPERIENCING.
"THE BIRTH OF THE MALIGNANT.
"THE DARK ASCENSION OF THE CYCLORS.
"I HEARD GODS *SCREAM*.
"NOTHING *GOOD* COULD EXIST IN THIS.
"AND THEN I SAW HIM.
"THE *WAR DOCTOR*.
"NO..."

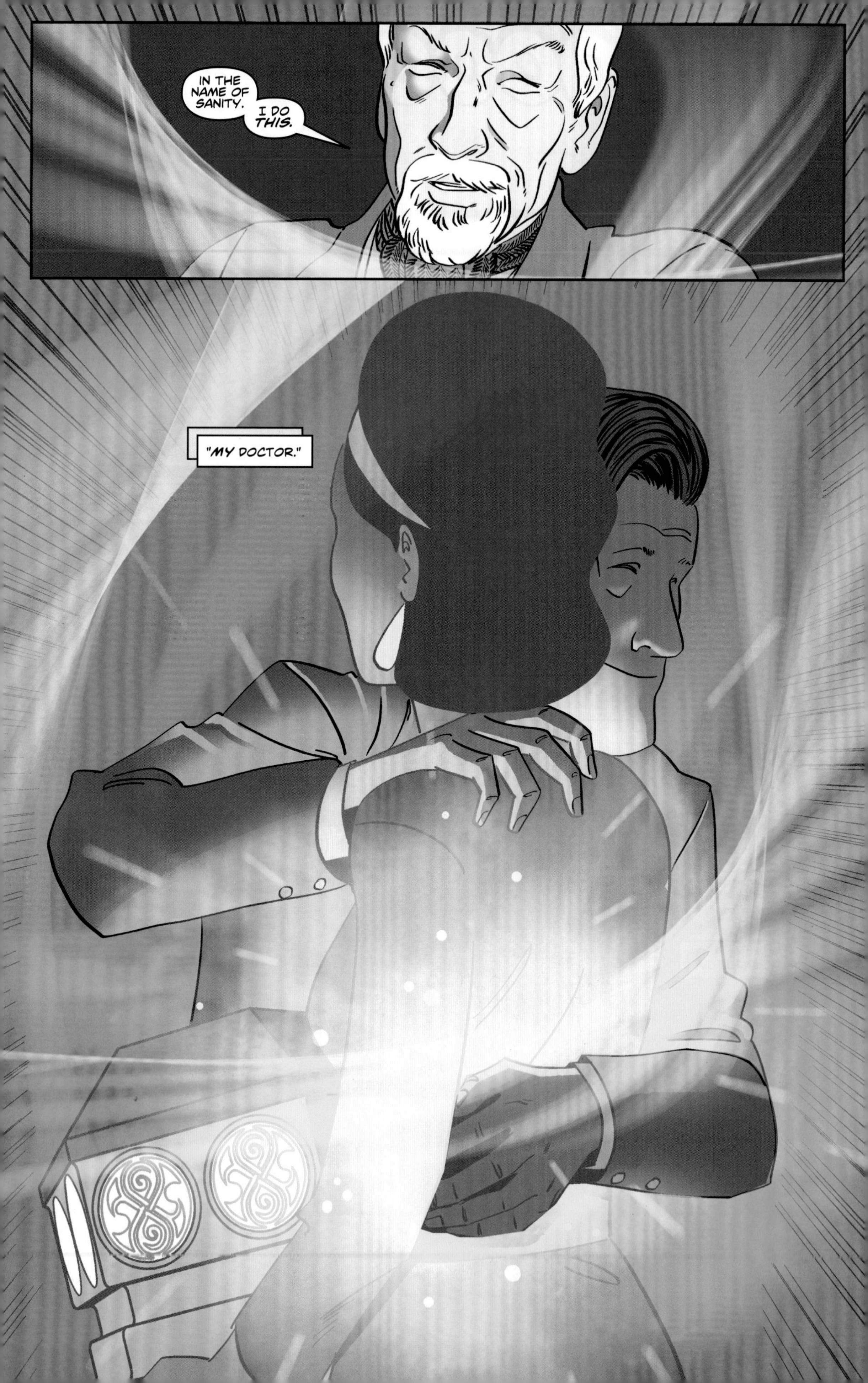
IN THE NAME OF SANITY.
I DO THIS.
"MY DOCTOR."

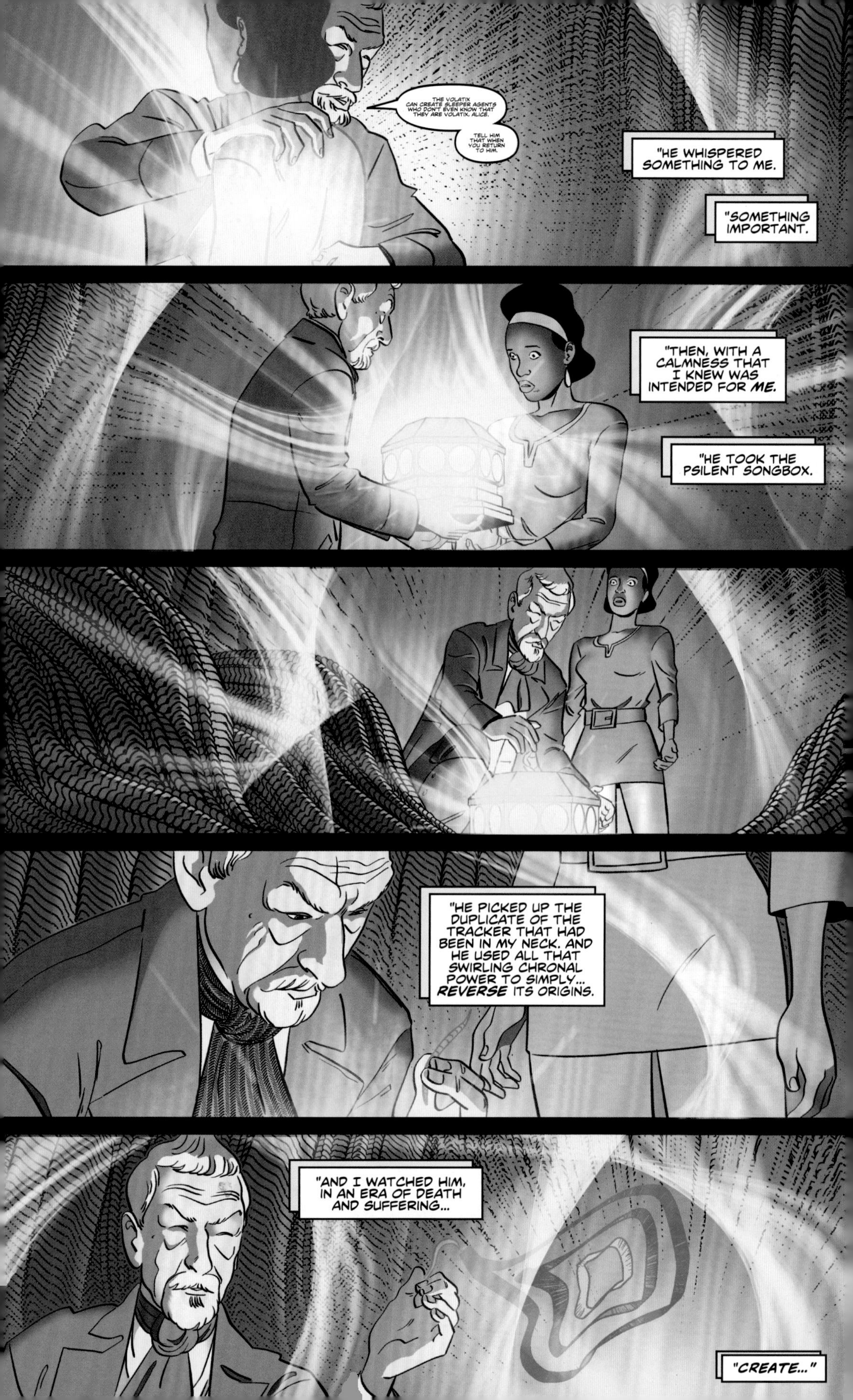
THE VOLATIX CAN CREATE SLEEPER AGENTS WHO DON'T EVEN KNOW THAT THEY ARE VOLATIX, ALICE.
TELL HIM THAT WHEN YOU RETURN TO HIM.
"HE WHISPERED SOMETHING TO ME.
"SOMETHING IMPORTANT.
"THEN, WITH A CALMNESS THAT I KNEW WAS INTENDED FOR *ME*.
"HE TOOK THE PSILENT SONGBOX.
"HE PICKED UP THE DUPLICATE OF THE TRACKER THAT HAD BEEN IN MY NECK. AND HE USED ALL THAT SWIRLING CHRONAL POWER TO SIMPLY... ***REVERSE*** ITS ORIGINS.
"AND I WATCHED HIM, IN AN ERA OF DEATH AND SUFFERING...
"*CREATE...*"

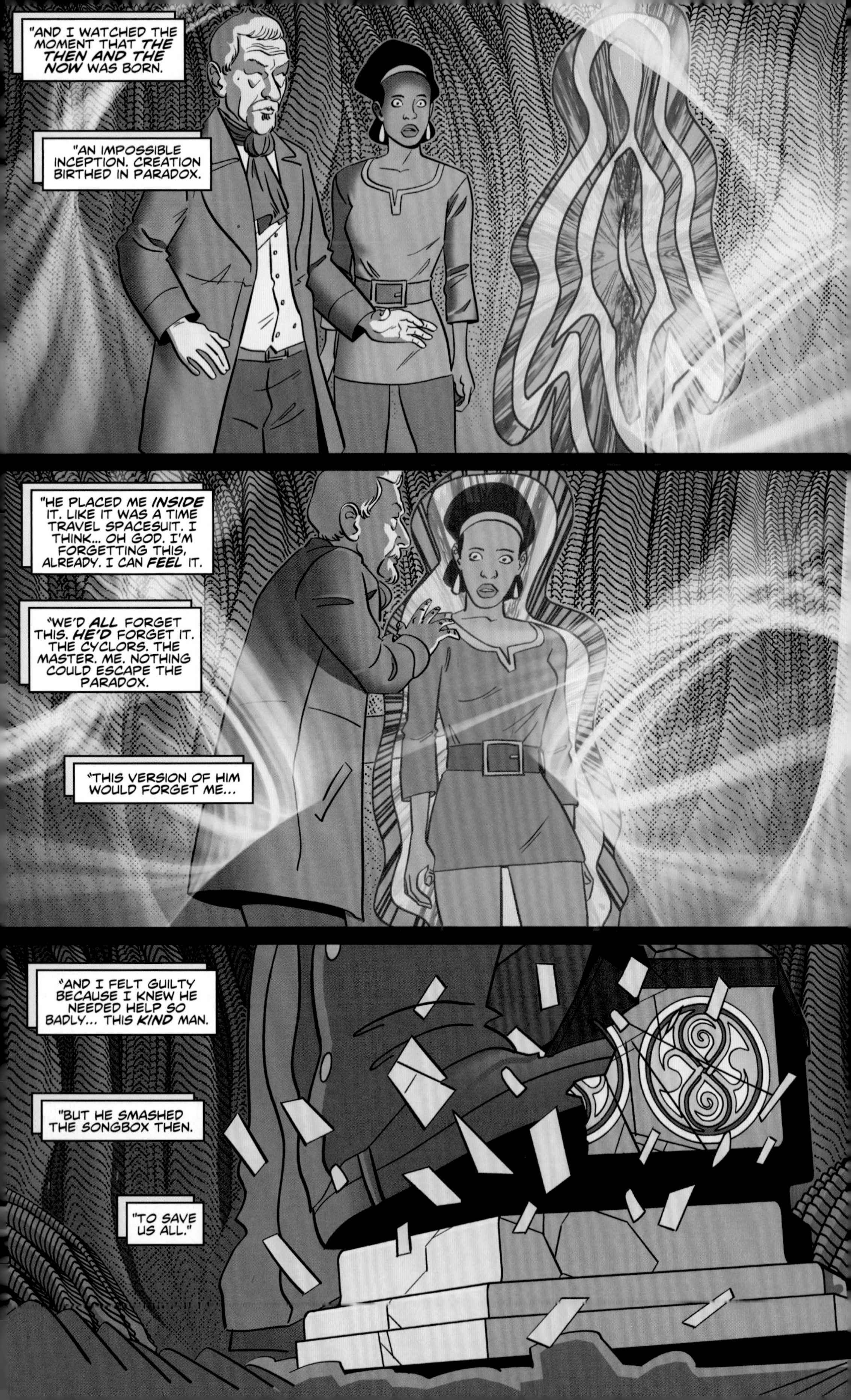
"AND I WATCHED THE MOMENT THAT ***THE THEN AND THE NOW*** WAS BORN.
"AN IMPOSSIBLE INCEPTION. CREATION BIRTHED IN PARADOX.
"HE PLACED ME ***INSIDE*** IT. LIKE IT WAS A TIME TRAVEL SPACESUIT. I THINK... OH GOD. I'M FORGETTING THIS, ALREADY. I CAN ***FEEL*** IT.
"WE'D ***ALL*** FORGET THIS. ***HE'D*** FORGET IT. THE CYCLORS. THE MASTER. ME. NOTHING COULD ESCAPE THE PARADOX.
"THIS VERSION OF HIM WOULD FORGET ME...
"AND I FELT GUILTY BECAUSE I KNEW HE NEEDED HELP SO BADLY... THIS ***KIND*** MAN.
"BUT HE SMASHED THE SONGBOX THEN.
"TO SAVE US ALL."

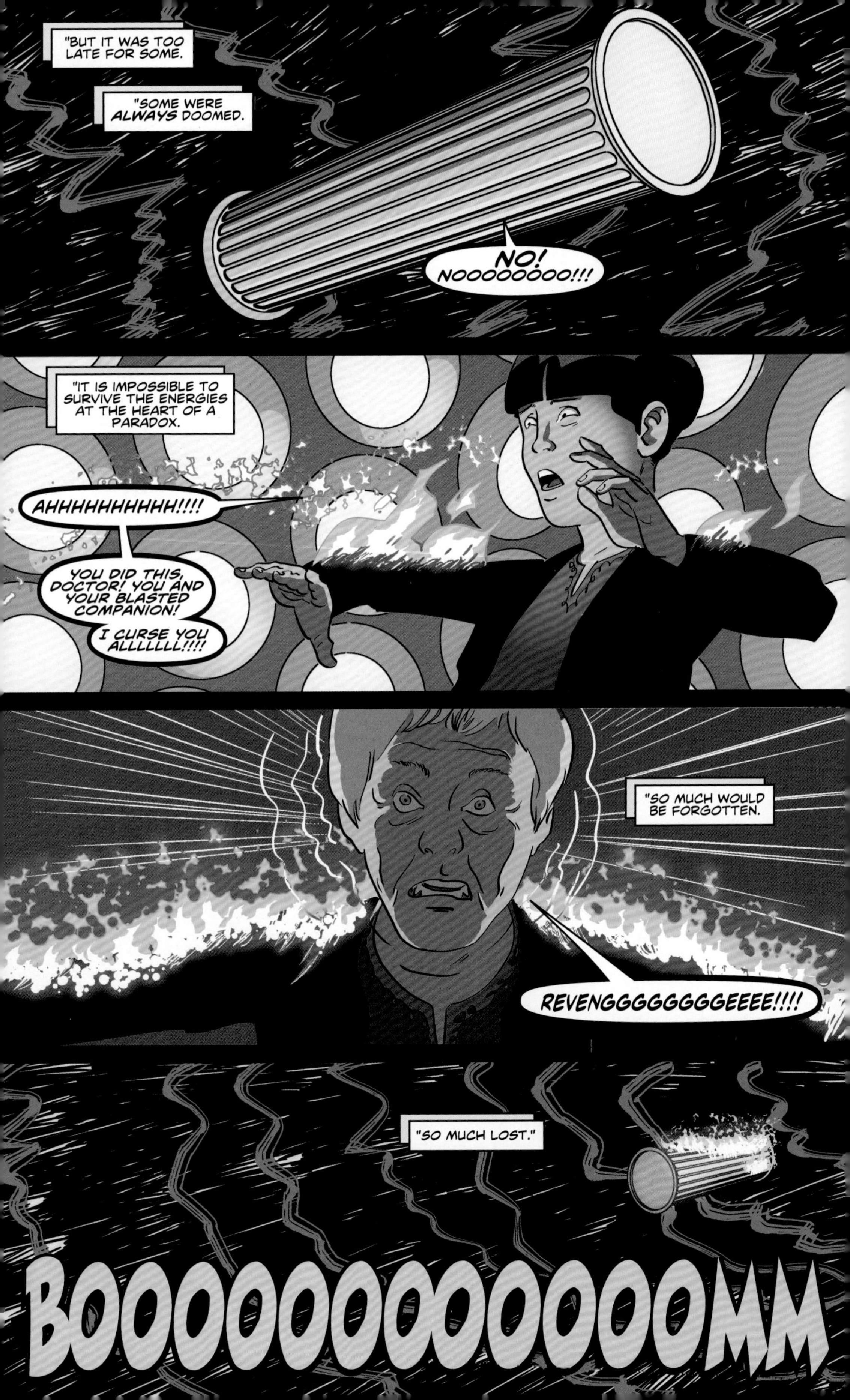
"BUT IT WAS TOO LATE FOR SOME.
"SOME WERE ALWAYS DOOMED.
NO! NOOOOOOOO!!!
"IT IS IMPOSSIBLE TO SURVIVE THE ENERGIES AT THE HEART OF A PARADOX.
AHHHHHHHHHH!!!!
YOU DID THIS, DOCTOR! YOU AND YOUR BLASTED COMPANION!
I CURSE YOU ALLLLLLL!!!!
"SO MUCH WOULD BE FORGOTTEN.
REVENGGGGGGGGEEEE!!!!
"SO MUCH LOST."
BOOOOOOOOOOOOMM

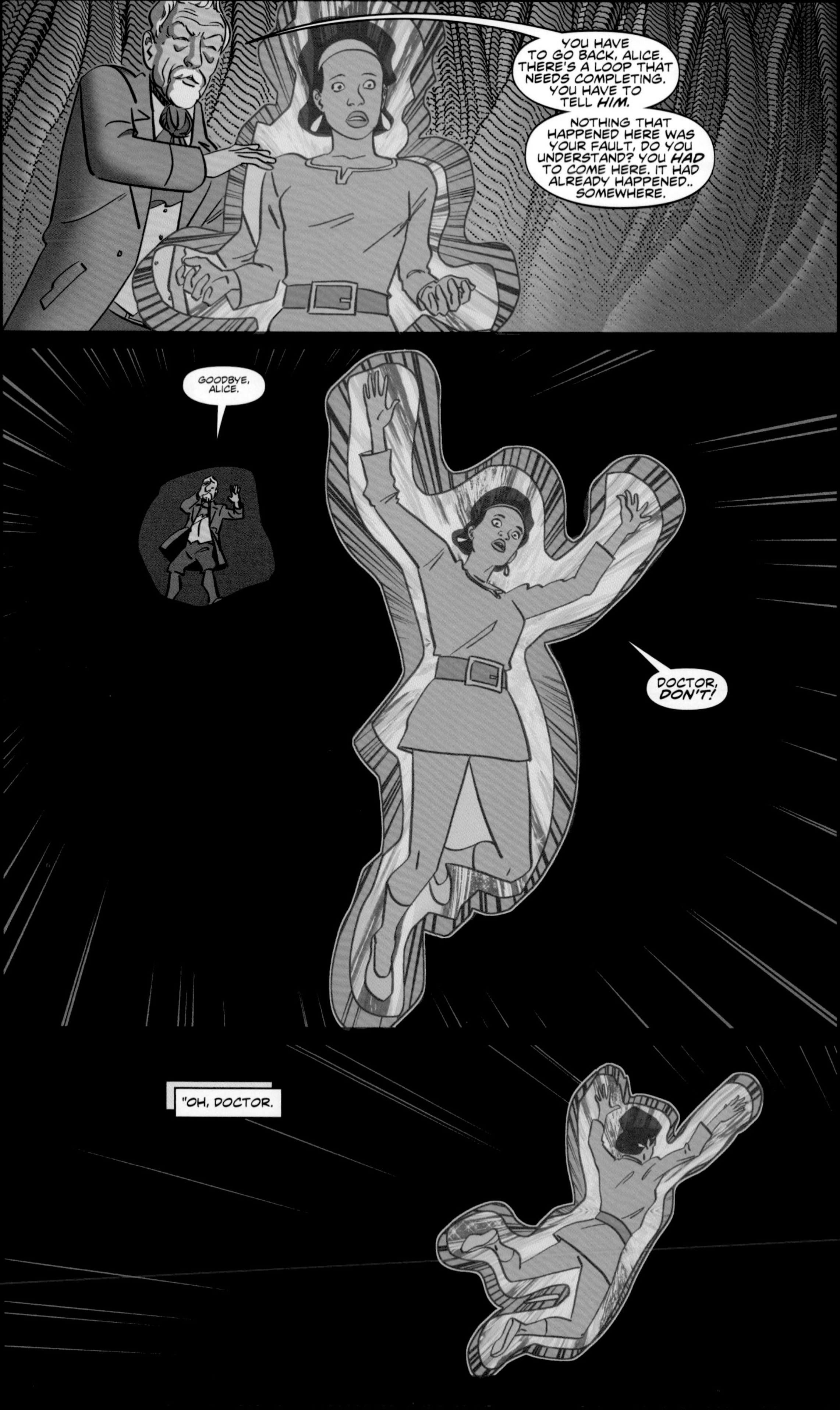
YOU HAVE TO GO BACK, ALICE. THERE'S A LOOP THAT NEEDS COMPLETING. YOU HAVE TO TELL *HIM*.
NOTHING THAT HAPPENED HERE WAS YOUR FAULT, DO YOU UNDERSTAND? YOU *HAD* TO COME HERE. IT HAD ALREADY HAPPENED.. SOMEWHERE.
GOODBYE, ALICE.
DOCTOR, *DON'T!*
"OH, DOCTOR.

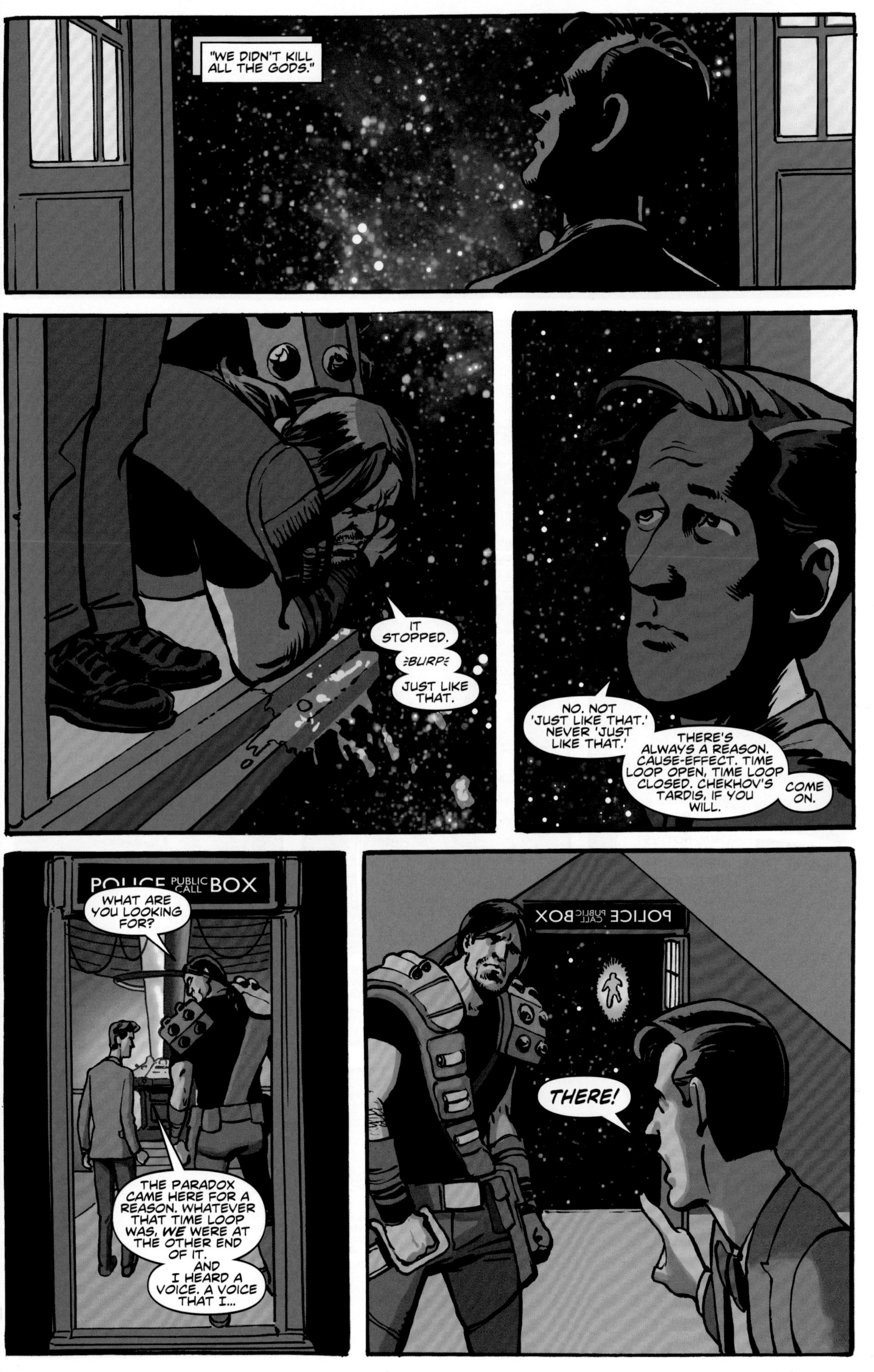

"WE DIDN'T KILL ALL THE GODS."
IT STOPPED.
BURP
JUST LIKE THAT.
NO. NOT 'JUST LIKE THAT.' NEVER 'JUST LIKE THAT.'
THERE'S ALWAYS A REASON. CAUSE-EFFECT. TIME LOOP OPEN, TIME LOOP CLOSED. CHEKHOV'S TARDIS, IF YOU WILL.
COME ON.
POLICE PUBLIC CALL BOX
WHAT ARE YOU LOOKING FOR?
THE PARADOX CAME HERE FOR A REASON. WHATEVER THAT TIME LOOP WAS, WE WERE AT THE OTHER END OF IT.
AND I HEARD A VOICE. A VOICE THAT I...
POLICE PUBLIC CALL BOX
THERE!

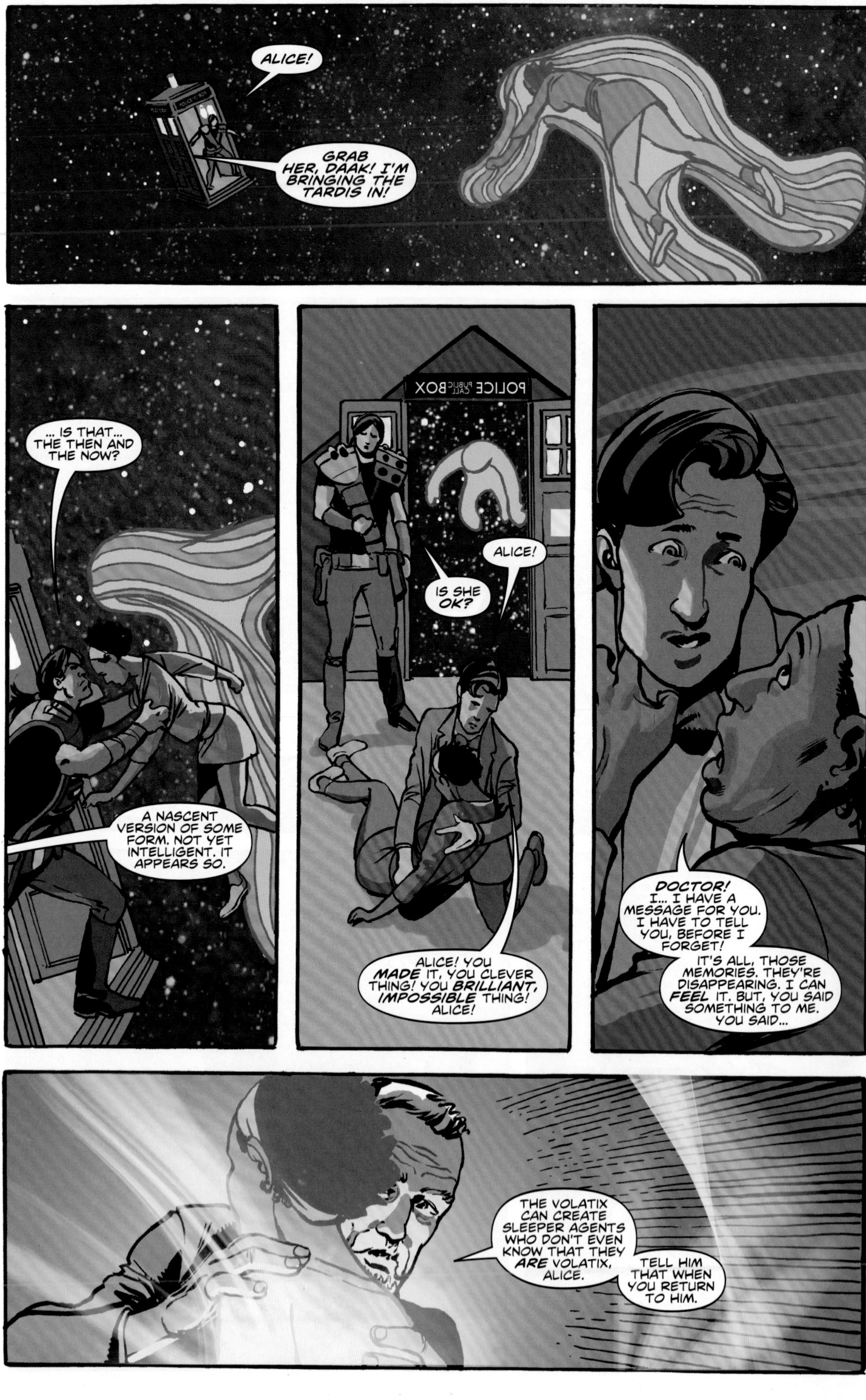
ALICE!
GRAB HER, DAAK! I'M BRINGING THE TARDIS IN!
... IS THAT... THE THEN AND THE NOW?
A NASCENT VERSION OF SOME FORM. NOT YET INTELLIGENT. IT APPEARS SO.
POLICE PUBLIC CALL BOX
IS SHE OK?
ALICE!
ALICE! YOU MADE IT, YOU CLEVER THING! YOU BRILLIANT, IMPOSSIBLE THING! ALICE!
DOCTOR! I... I HAVE A MESSAGE FOR YOU. I HAVE TO TELL YOU, BEFORE I FORGET!
IT'S ALL, THOSE MEMORIES. THEY'RE DISAPPEARING. I CAN FEEL IT. BUT, YOU SAID SOMETHING TO ME. YOU SAID...
THE VOLATIX CAN CREATE SLEEPER AGENTS WHO DON'T EVEN KNOW THAT THEY ARE VOLATIX, ALICE.
TELL HIM THAT WHEN YOU RETURN TO HIM.

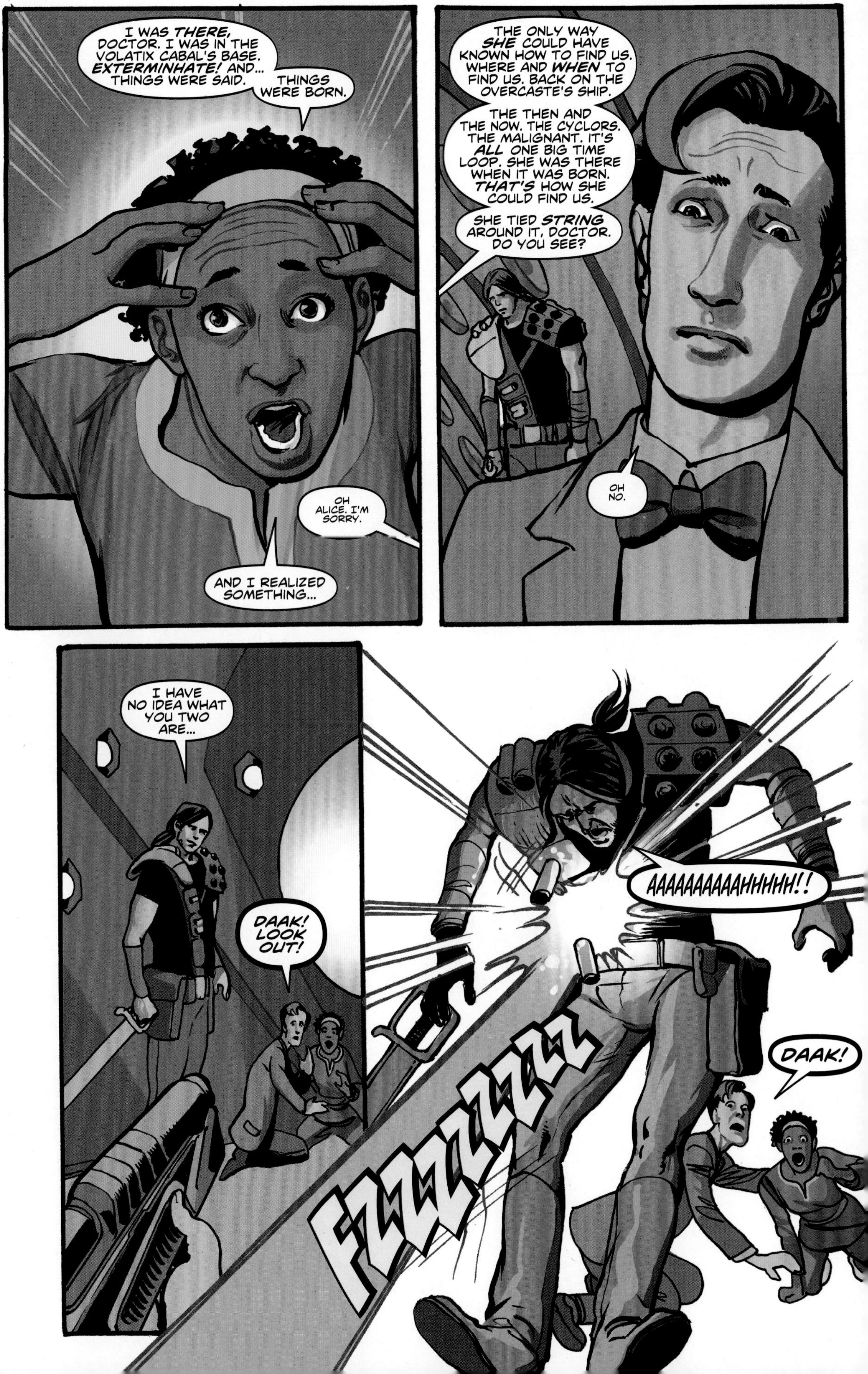
I WAS THERE, DOCTOR. I WAS IN THE VOLATIX CABAL'S BASE. EXTERMINHATE! AND... THINGS WERE SAID.
THINGS WERE BORN.
OH ALICE. I'M SORRY.
AND I REALIZED SOMETHING...
THE ONLY WAY SHE COULD HAVE KNOWN HOW TO FIND US. WHERE AND WHEN TO FIND US. BACK ON THE OVERCASTE'S SHIP.
THE THEN AND THE NOW. THE CYCLORS. THE MALIGNANT. IT'S ALL ONE BIG TIME LOOP. SHE WAS THERE WHEN IT WAS BORN. THAT'S HOW SHE COULD FIND US.
SHE TIED STRING AROUND IT, DOCTOR. DO YOU SEE?
OH NO.
I HAVE NO IDEA WHAT YOU TWO ARE...
DAAK! LOOK OUT!
FZZZZZZZZ
AAAAAAAAAAHHHHH!!
DAAK!

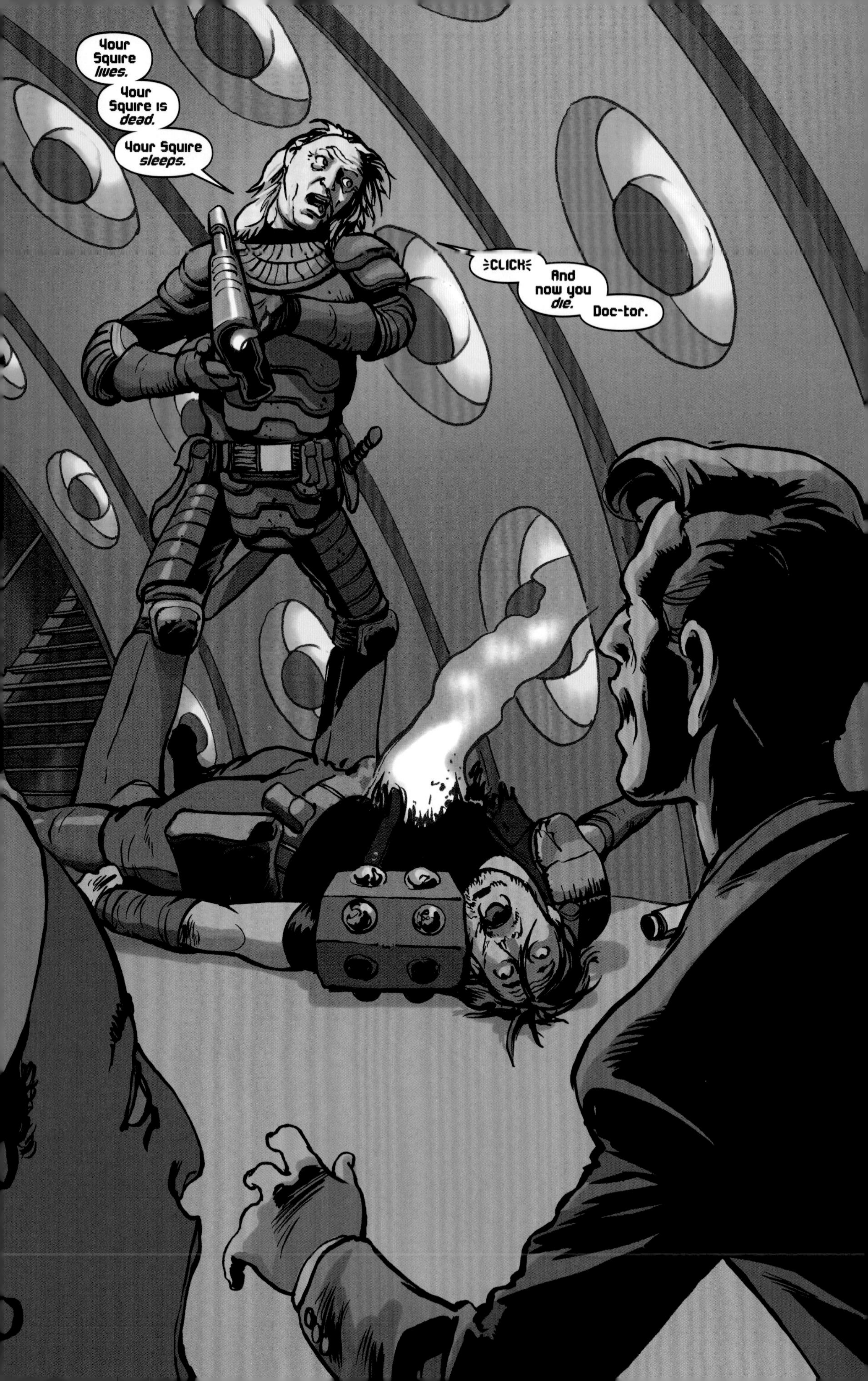
Your Squire lives.
Your Squire is dead.
Your Squire sleeps.
CLICK
And now you die.
Doc-tor.

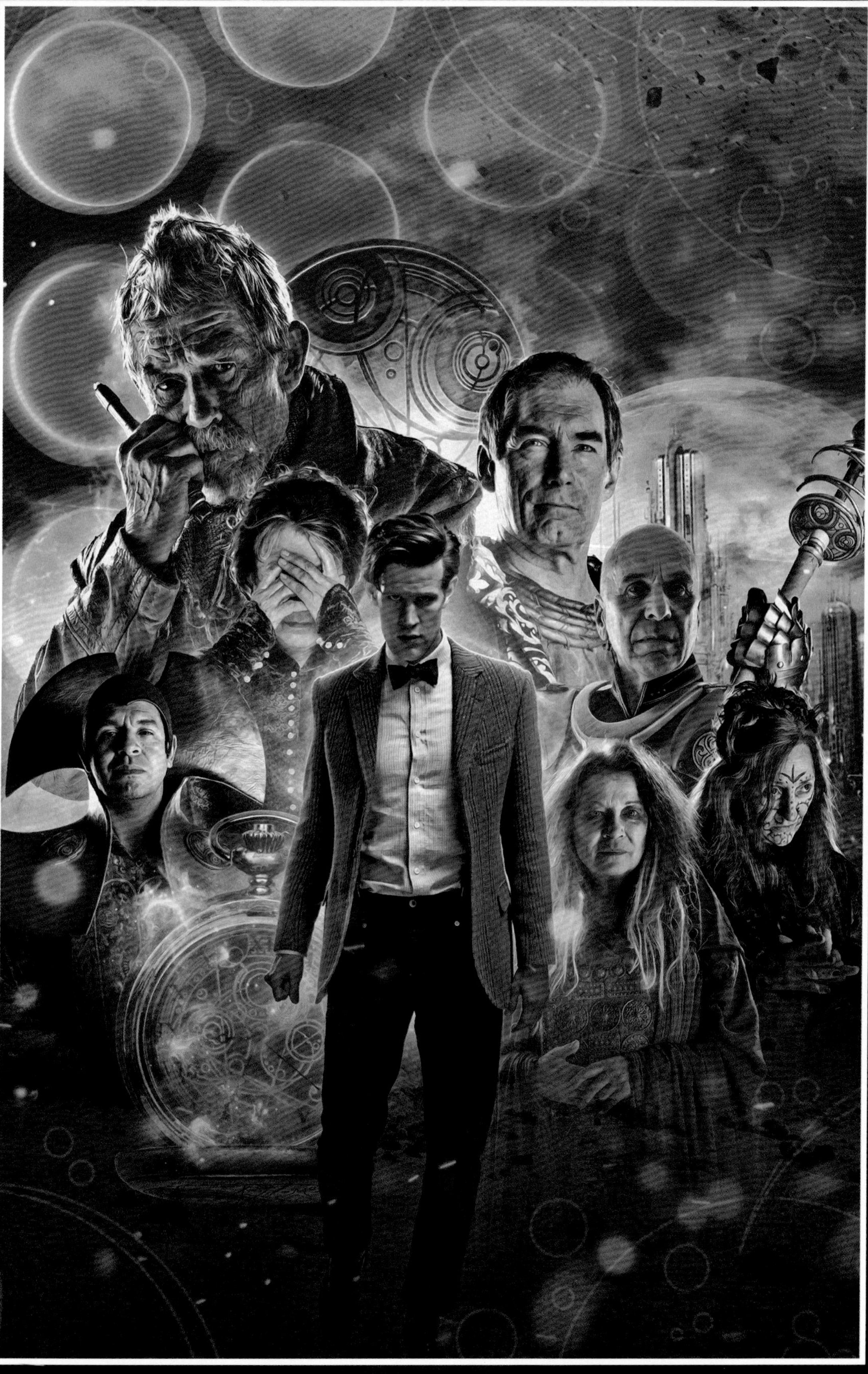

11D #2.13 Cover B: Will Brooks

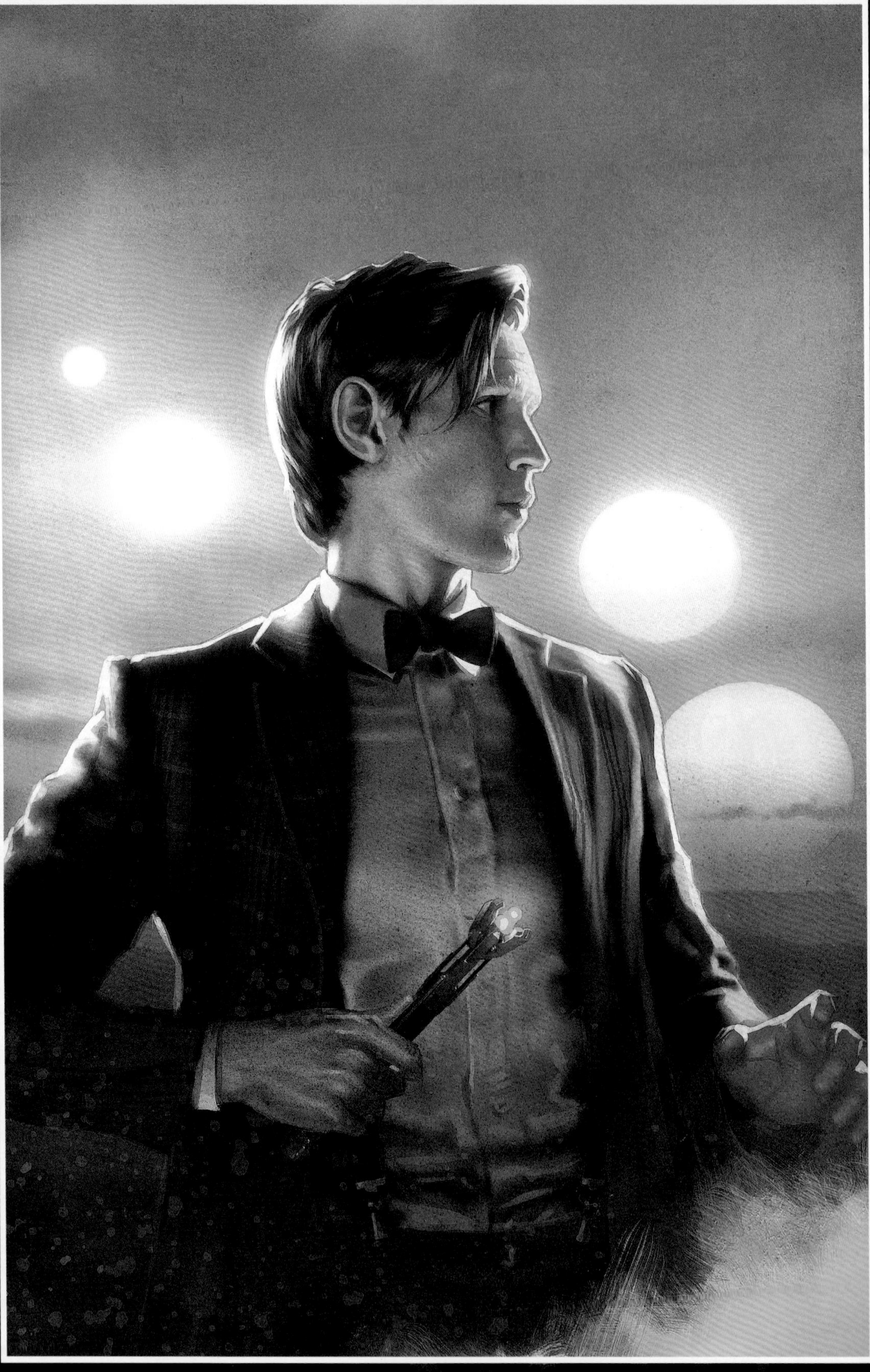

11D #2.14 Cover A: Alex Ronald

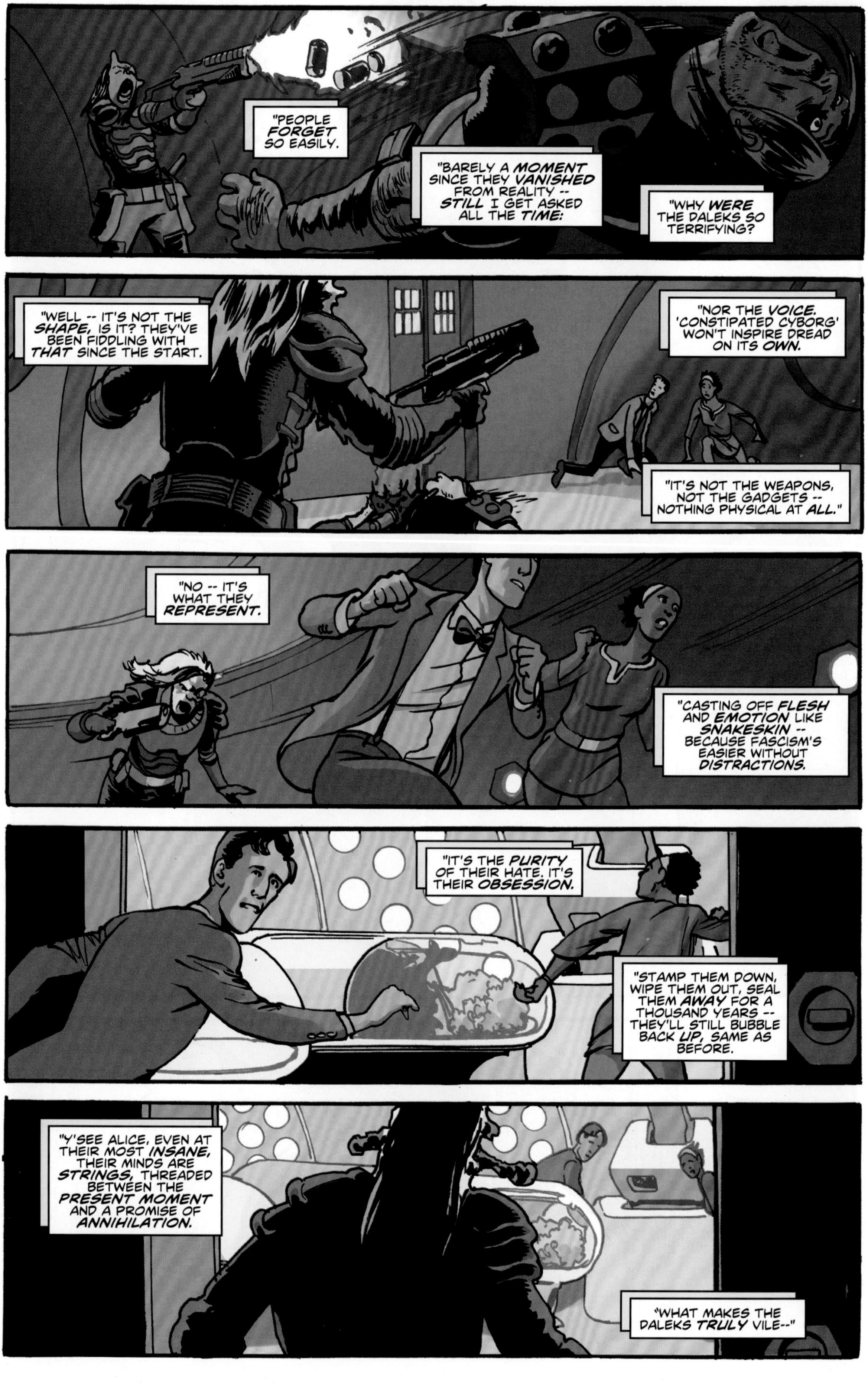
"PEOPLE FORGET SO EASILY.
"BARELY A MOMENT SINCE THEY VANISHED FROM REALITY -- STILL I GET ASKED ALL THE TIME:
"WHY WERE THE DALEKS SO TERRIFYING?
"WELL -- IT'S NOT THE SHAPE, IS IT? THEY'VE BEEN FIDDLING WITH THAT SINCE THE START.
"NOR THE VOICE. 'CONSTIPATED CYBORG' WON'T INSPIRE DREAD ON ITS OWN.
"IT'S NOT THE WEAPONS, NOT THE GADGETS -- NOTHING PHYSICAL AT ALL."
"NO -- IT'S WHAT THEY REPRESENT.
"CASTING OFF FLESH AND EMOTION LIKE SNAKESKIN -- BECAUSE FASCISM'S EASIER WITHOUT DISTRACTIONS.
"IT'S THE PURITY OF THEIR HATE. IT'S THEIR OBSESSION.
"STAMP THEM DOWN, WIPE THEM OUT, SEAL THEM AWAY FOR A THOUSAND YEARS -- THEY'LL STILL BUBBLE BACK UP, SAME AS BEFORE.
"Y'SEE ALICE, EVEN AT THEIR MOST INSANE, THEIR MINDS ARE STRINGS, THREADED BETWEEN THE PRESENT MOMENT AND A PROMISE OF ANNIHILATION.
"WHAT MAKES THE DALEKS TRULY VILE--"

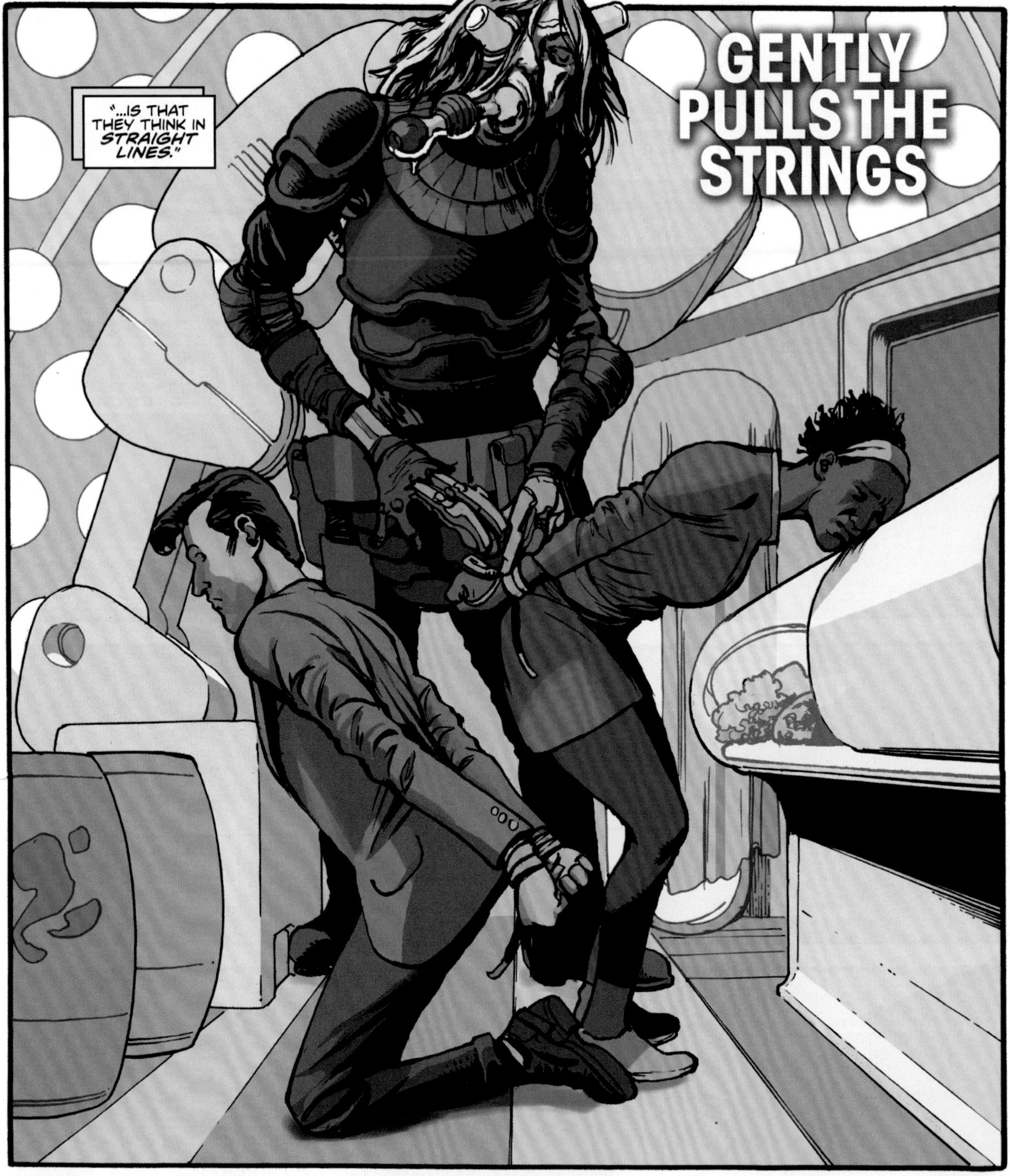
"...IS THAT THEY THINK IN STRAIGHT LINES."
GENTLY PULLS THE STRINGS

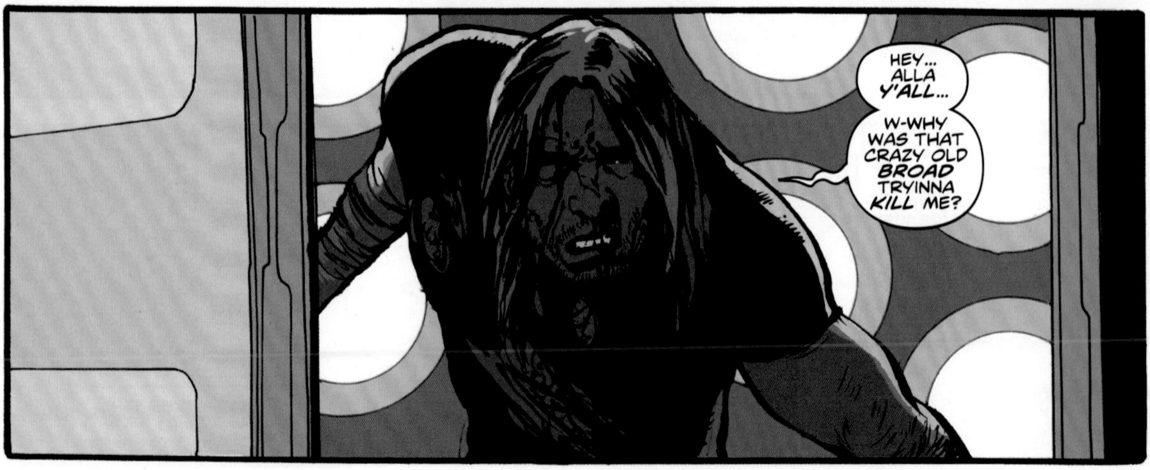
HEY... ALLA Y'ALL...
W-WHY WAS THAT CRAZY OLD BROAD TRYINNA KILL ME?

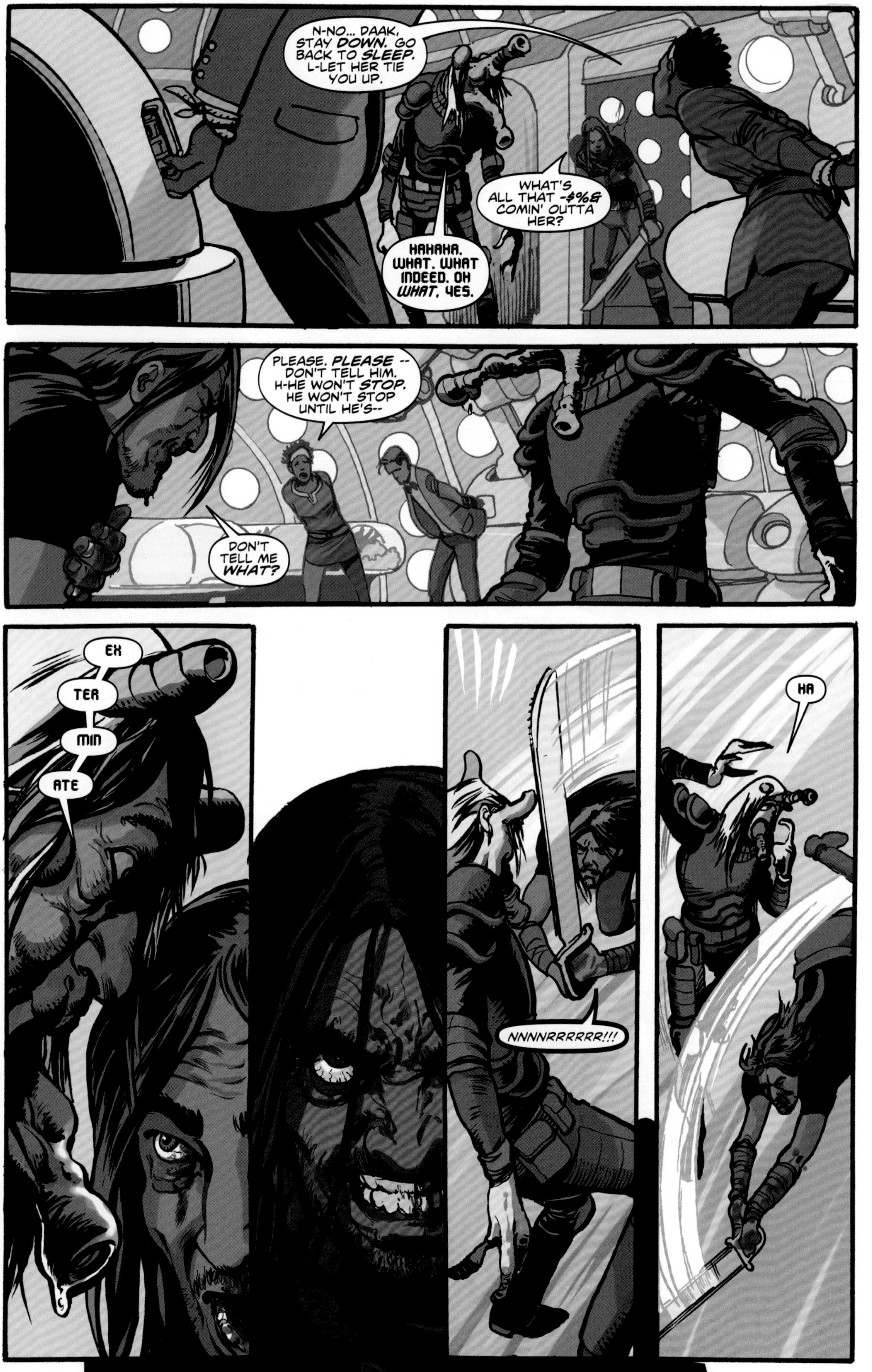
N-NO... DAAK, STAY DOWN. GO BACK TO SLEEP. L-LET HER TIE YOU UP.
HAHAHA. WHAT. WHAT INDEED. OH WHAT, YES.
WHAT'S ALL THAT -$%& COMIN' OUTTA HER?
PLEASE. PLEASE -- DON'T TELL HIM. H-HE WON'T STOP. HE WON'T STOP UNTIL HE'S--
DON'T TELL ME WHAT?
EX
TER
MIN
ATE
NNNNRRRRRR!!!
HA

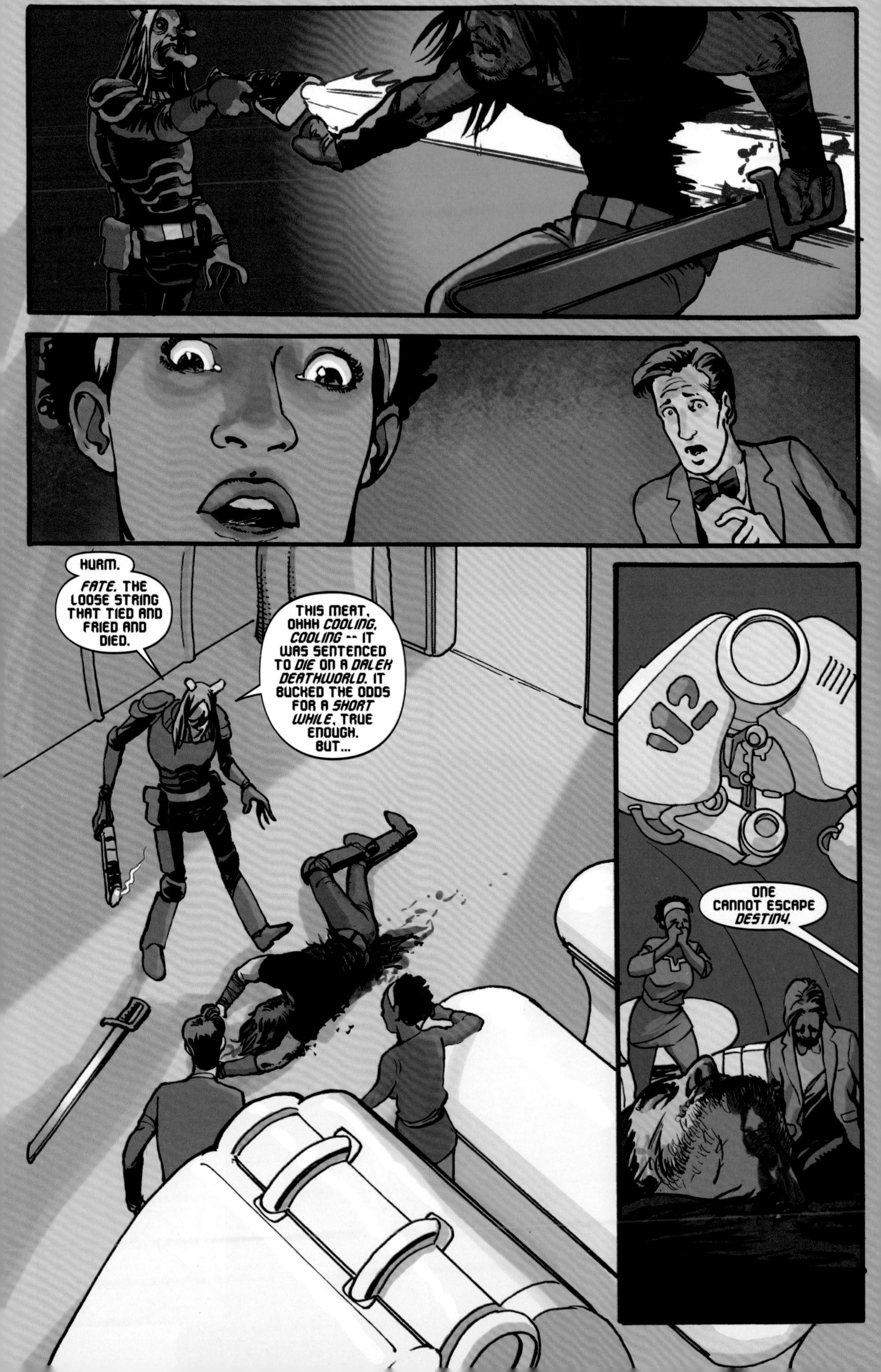
HURM.
FATE. THE LOOSE STRING THAT TIED AND FRIED AND DIED.
THIS MEAT, OHHH COOLING, COOLING -- IT WAS SENTENCED TO DIE ON A DALEK DEATHWORLD. IT BUCKED THE ODDS FOR A SHORT WHILE, TRUE ENOUGH. BUT...
ONE CANNOT ESCAPE DESTINY.

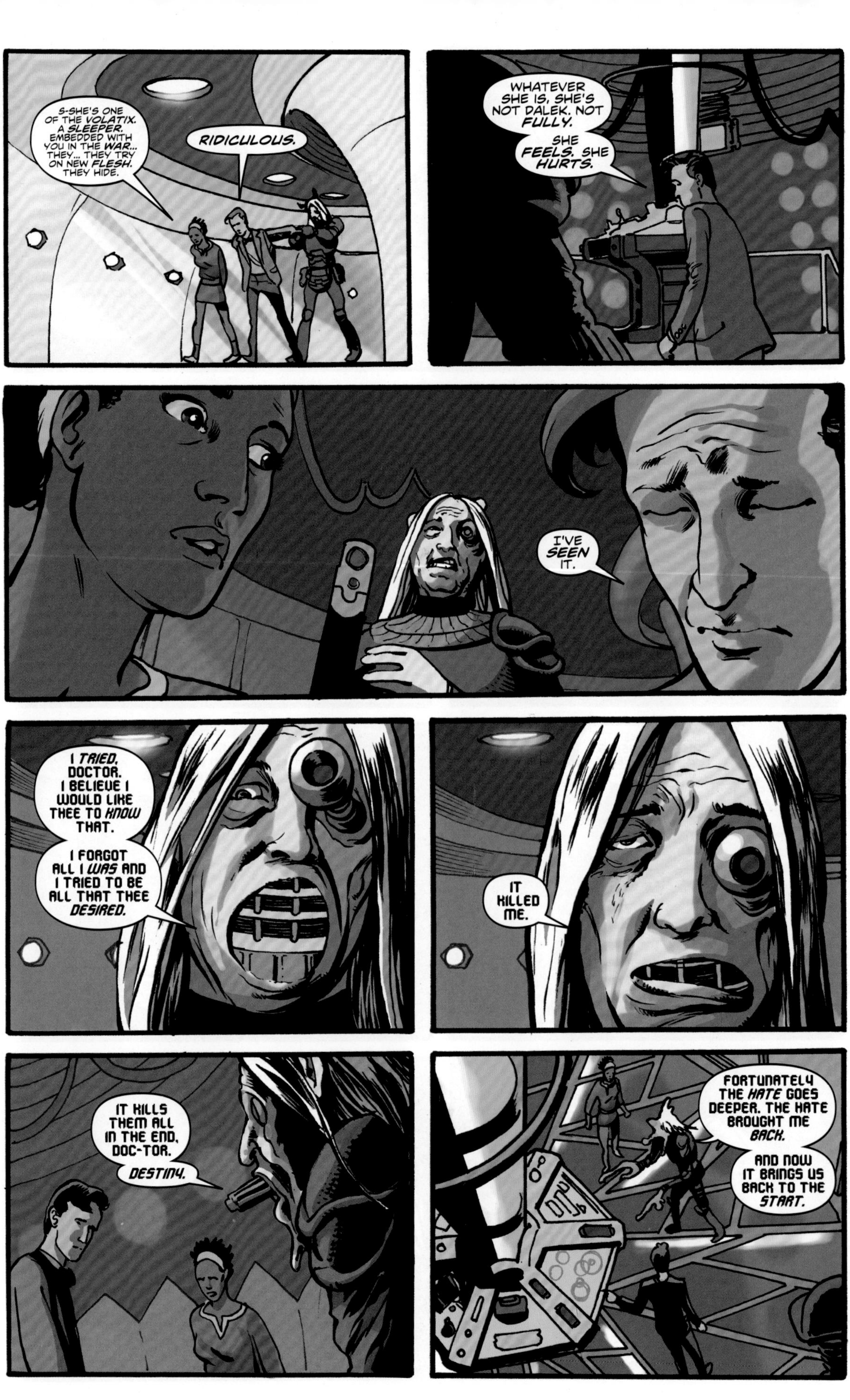
S-SHE'S ONE OF THE VOLATIX. A SLEEPER. EMBEDDED WITH YOU IN THE WAR... THEY... THEY TRY ON NEW FLESH. THEY HIDE.
RIDICULOUS.
WHATEVER SHE IS, SHE'S NOT DALEK. NOT FULLY.
SHE FEELS. SHE HURTS.
I'VE SEEN IT.
I TRIED, DOCTOR. I BELIEVE I WOULD LIKE THEE TO KNOW THAT.
I FORGOT ALL I WAS AND I TRIED TO BE ALL THAT THEE DESIRED.
IT KILLED ME.
IT KILLS THEM ALL IN THE END, DOC-TOR. DESTINY.
FORTUNATELY THE HATE GOES DEEPER. THE HATE BROUGHT ME BACK.
AND NOW IT BRINGS US BACK TO THE START.

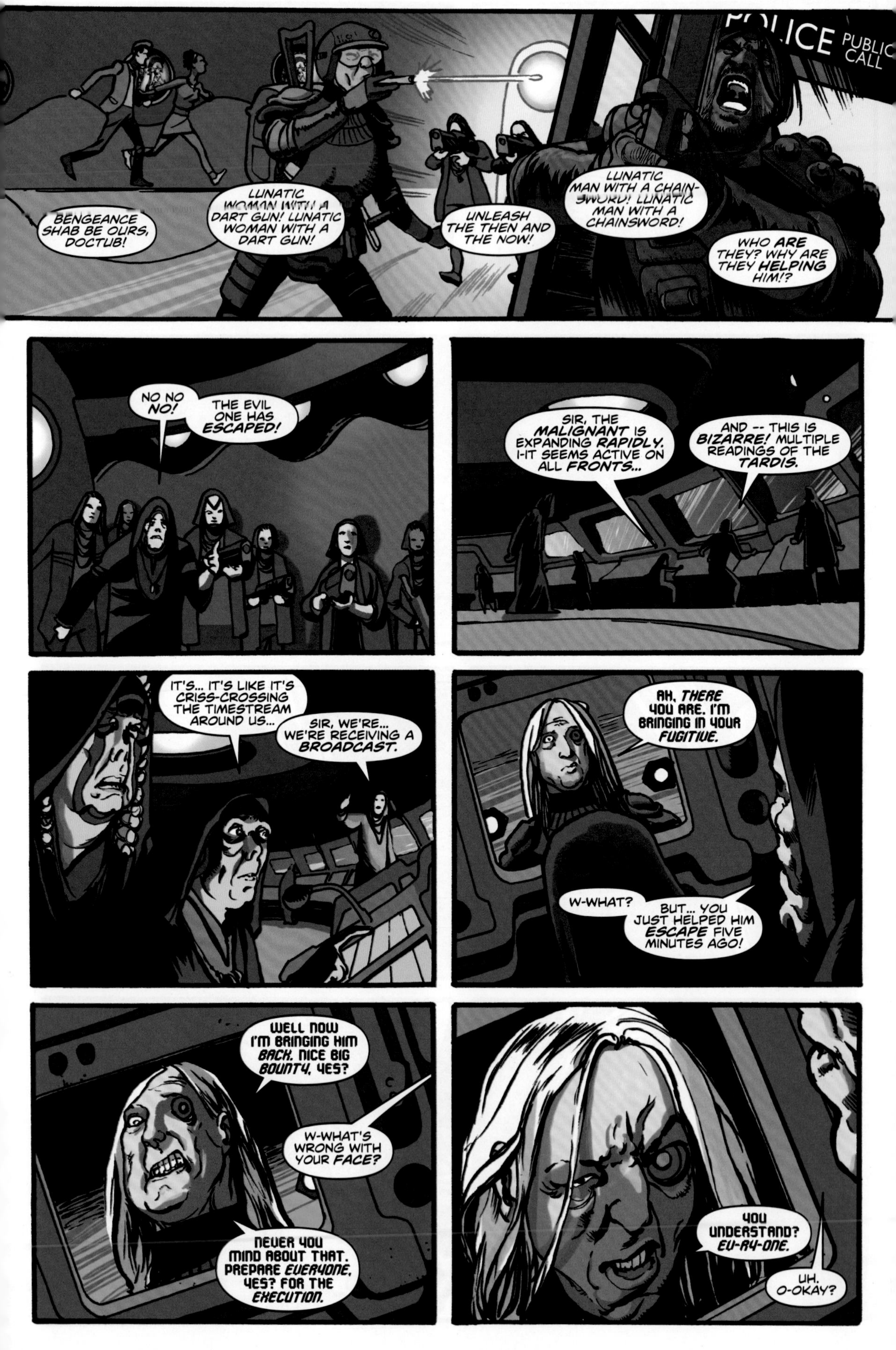
BENGEANCE SHAB BE OURS, DOCTUB!
LUNATIC WOMAN WITH A DART GUN! LUNATIC WOMAN WITH A DART GUN!
UNLEASH THE THEN AND THE NOW!
LUNATIC MAN WITH A CHAIN-SWORD! LUNATIC MAN WITH A CHAINSWORD!
WHO ARE THEY? WHY ARE THEY HELPING HIM!?
POLICE PUBLIC CALL
NO NO NO!
THE EVIL ONE HAS ESCAPED!
SIR, THE MALIGNANT IS EXPANDING RAPIDLY. I-IT SEEMS ACTIVE ON ALL FRONTS...
AND -- THIS IS BIZARRE! MULTIPLE READINGS OF THE TARDIS.
IT'S... IT'S LIKE IT'S CRISS-CROSSING THE TIMESTREAM AROUND US...
SIR, WE'RE... WE'RE RECEIVING A BROADCAST.
AH, THERE YOU ARE. I'M BRINGING IN YOUR FUGITIVE.
W-WHAT?
BUT... YOU JUST HELPED HIM ESCAPE FIVE MINUTES AGO!
WELL NOW I'M BRINGING HIM BACK. NICE BIG BOUNTY, YES?
W-WHAT'S WRONG WITH YOUR FACE?
NEVER YOU MIND ABOUT THAT. PREPARE EVERYONE, YES? FOR THE EXECUTION.
YOU UNDERSTAND? EV-RY-ONE.
UH, O-OKAY?

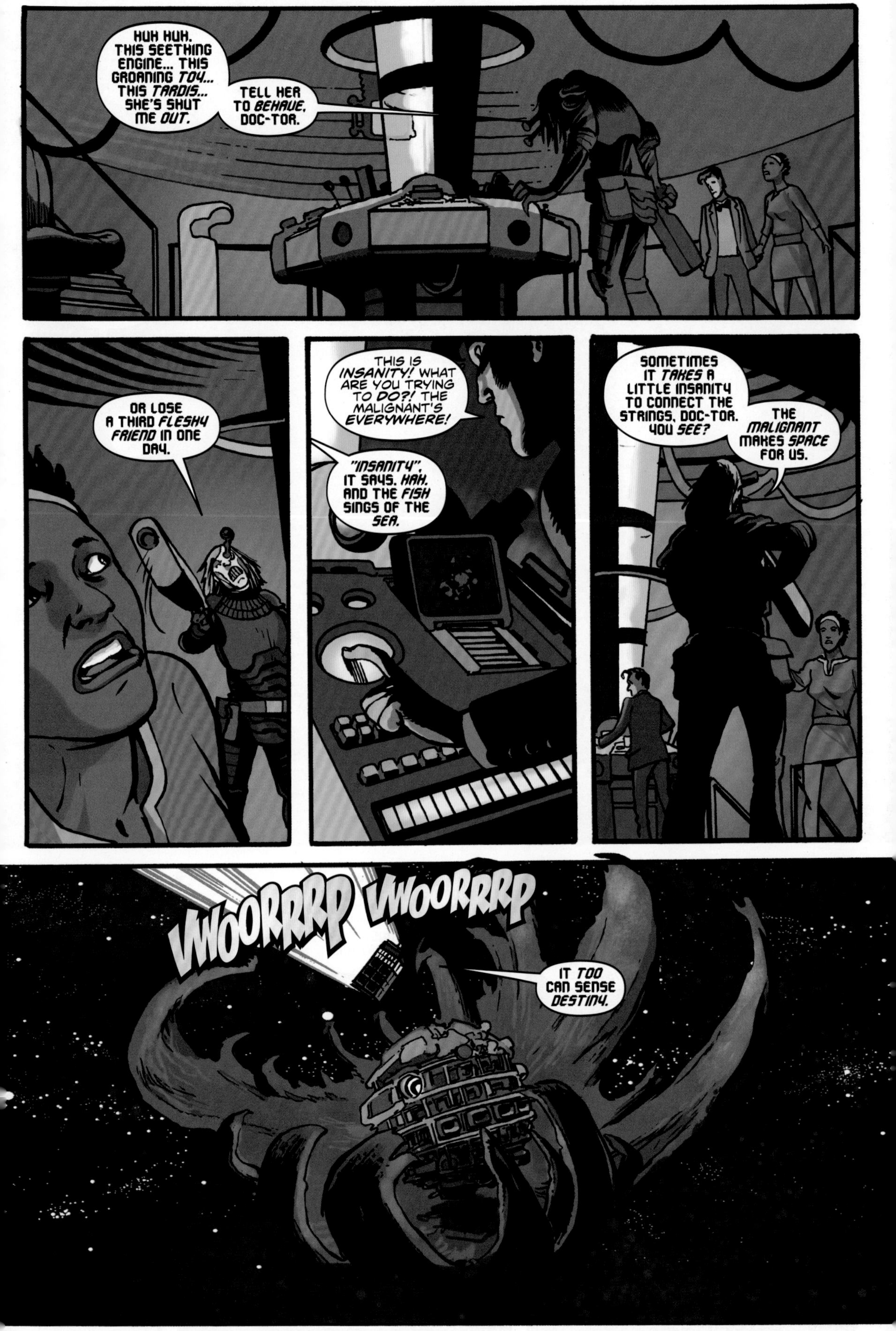
HUH HUH. THIS SEETHING ENGINE... THIS GROANING TOY... THIS TARDIS... SHE'S SHUT ME OUT.
TELL HER TO BEHAVE, DOC-TOR.
OR LOSE A THIRD FLESHY FRIEND IN ONE DAY.
THIS IS INSANITY! WHAT ARE YOU TRYING TO DO?! THE MALIGNANT'S EVERYWHERE!
"INSANITY", IT SAYS. HAH. AND THE FISH SINGS OF THE SEA.
SOMETIMES IT TAKES A LITTLE INSANITY TO CONNECT THE STRINGS, DOC-TOR. YOU SEE?
THE MALIGNANT MAKES SPACE FOR US.
VWOORRRP VWOORRRP
IT TOO CAN SENSE DESTINY.

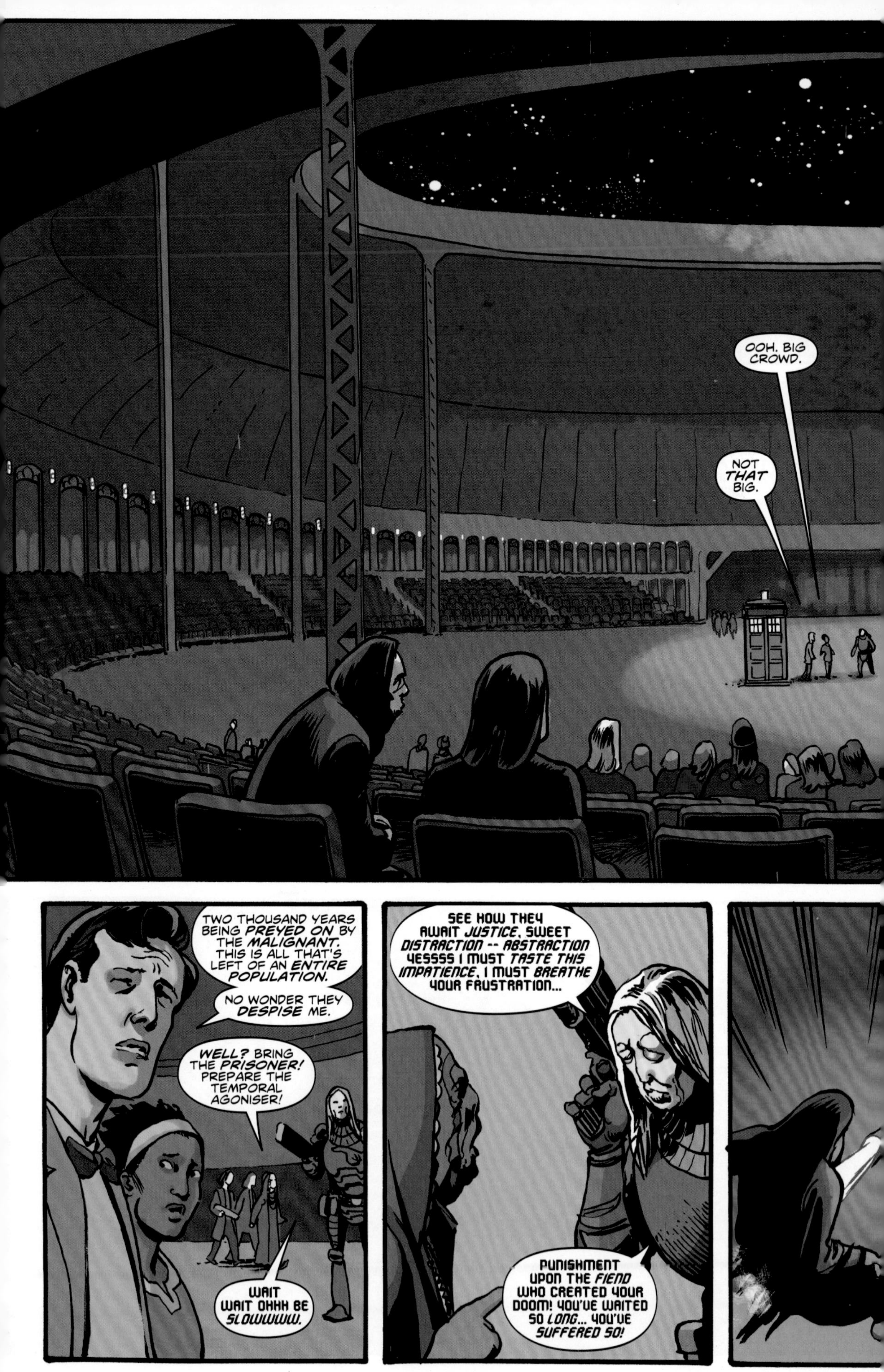
OOH. BIG CROWD.
NOT THAT BIG.
TWO THOUSAND YEARS BEING PREYED ON BY THE MALIGNANT. THIS IS ALL THAT'S LEFT OF AN ENTIRE POPULATION.
NO WONDER THEY DESPISE ME.
WELL? BRING THE PRISONER! PREPARE THE TEMPORAL AGONISER!
WAIT WAIT OHHH BE SLOWWWW.
SEE HOW THEY AWAIT JUSTICE, SWEET DISTRACTION -- ABSTRACTION YESSSS I MUST TASTE THIS IMPATIENCE, I MUST BREATHE YOUR FRUSTRATION...
PUNISHMENT UPON THE FIEND WHO CREATED YOUR DOOM! YOU'VE WAITED SO LONG... YOU'VE SUFFERED SO!

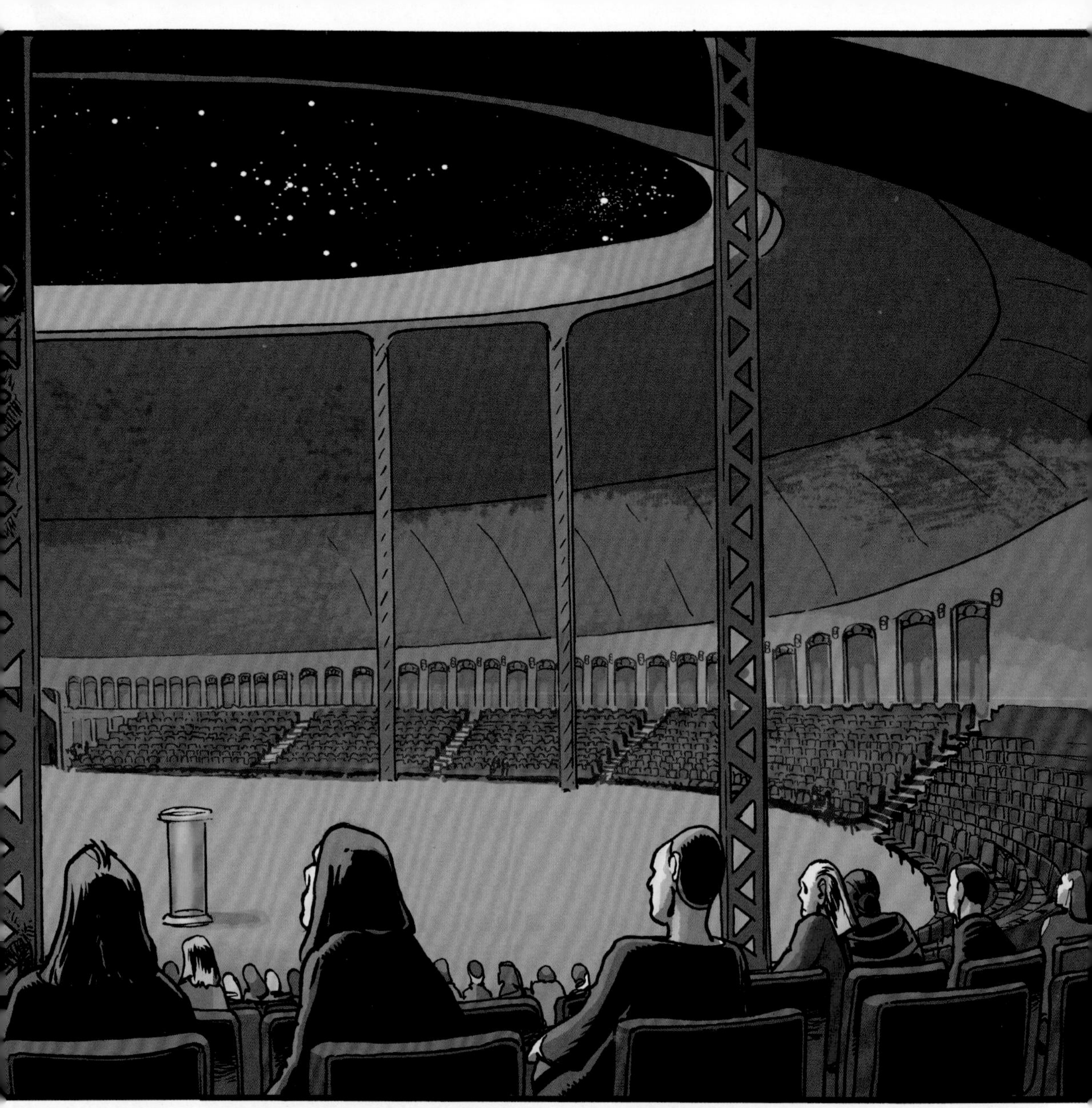
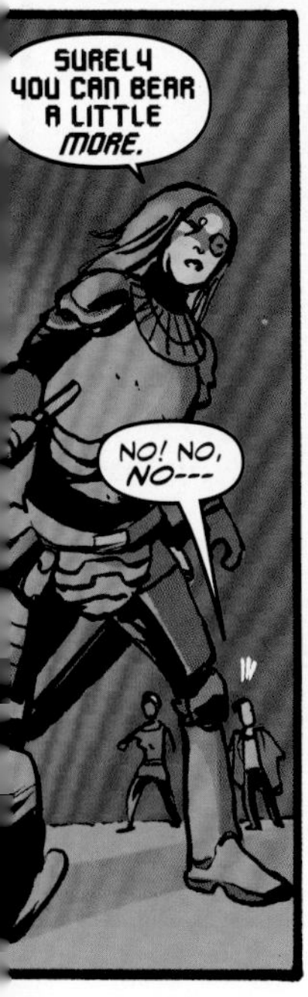
SURELY YOU CAN BEAR A LITTLE MORE.
NO! NO, NO---
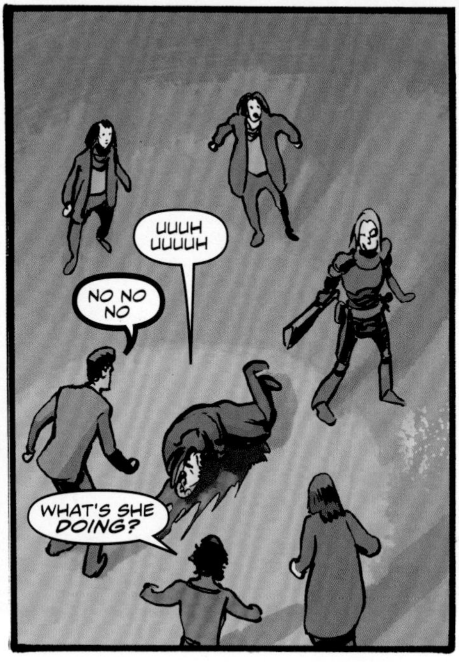
UUUH UUUUH
NO NO NO
WHAT'S SHE DOING?
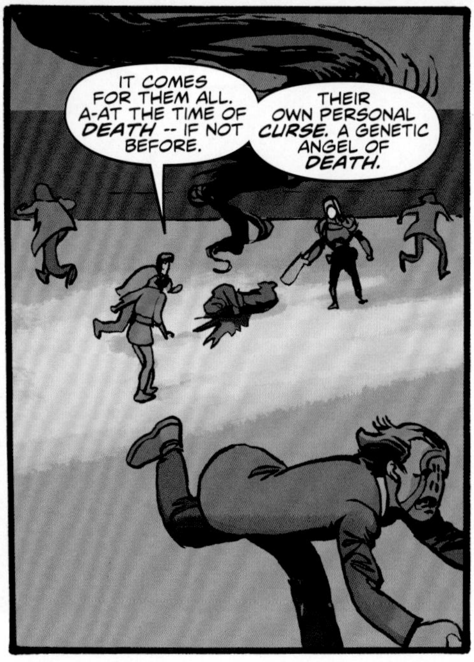
IT COMES FOR THEM ALL. A-AT THE TIME OF DEATH -- IF NOT BEFORE.
THEIR OWN PERSONAL CURSE. A GENETIC ANGEL OF DEATH.

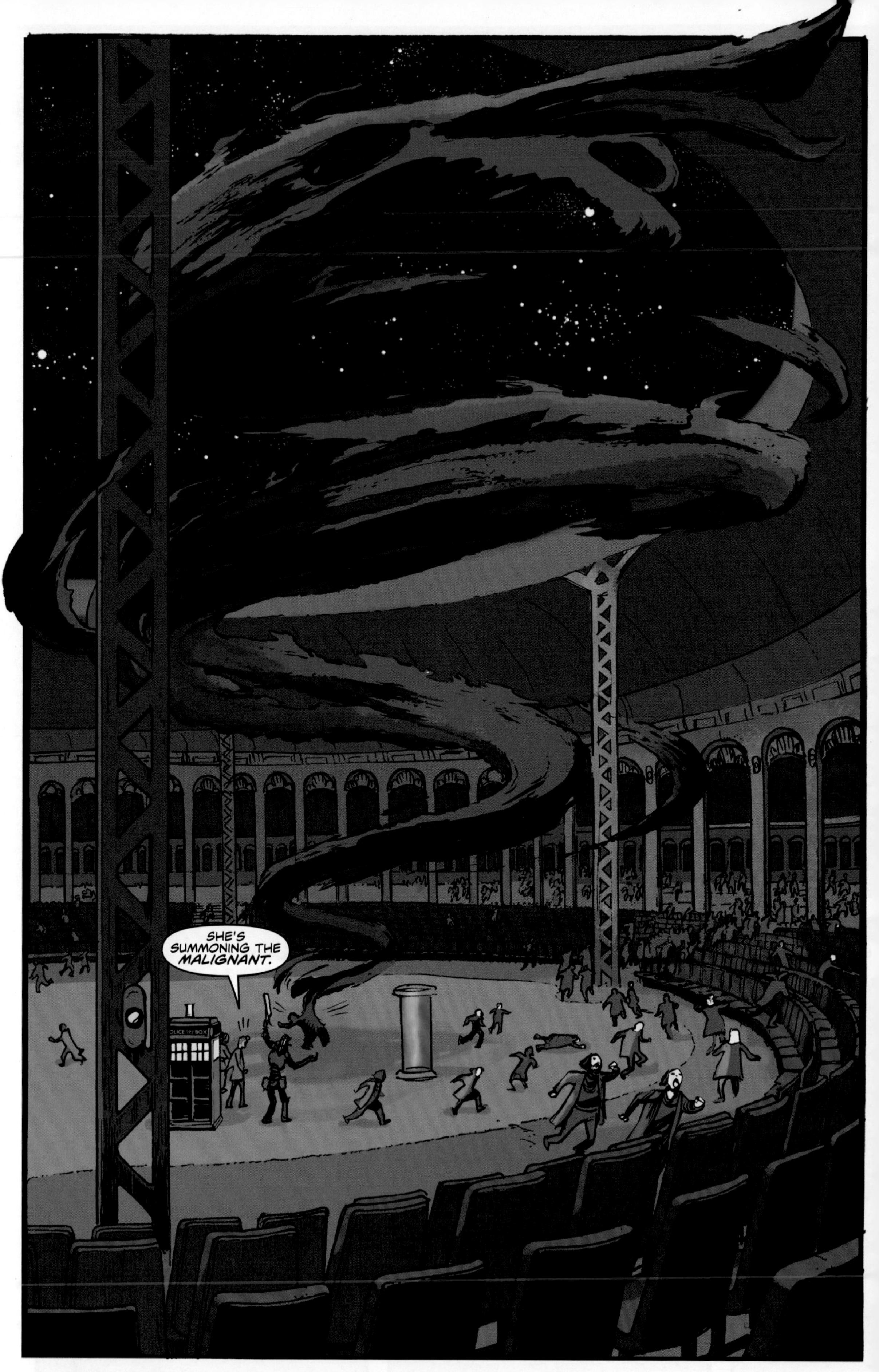
SHE'S SUMMONING THE *MALIGNANT.*

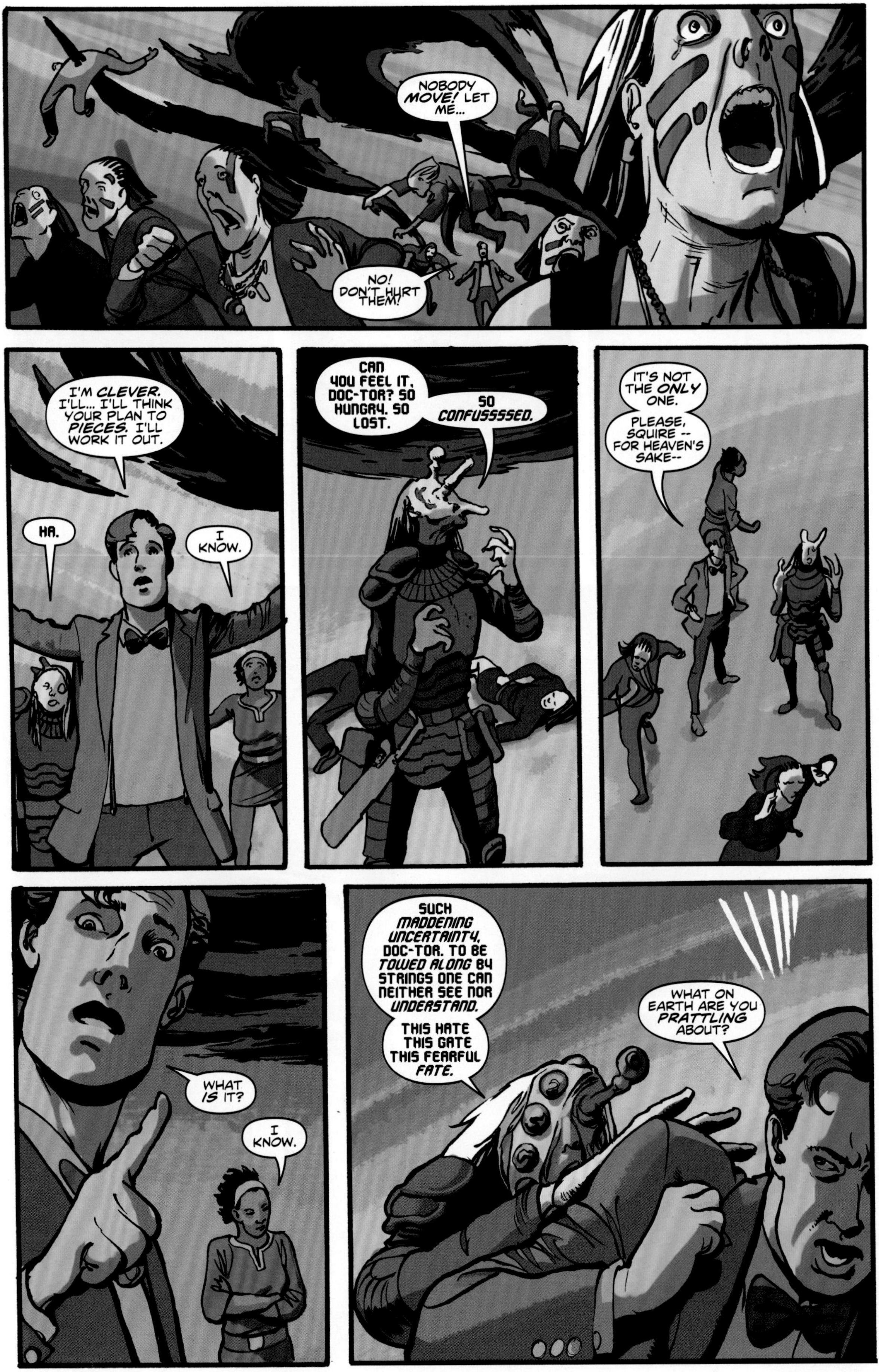
NOBODY MOVE! LET ME...
NO! DON'T HURT THEM!
I'M CLEVER. I'LL... I'LL THINK YOUR PLAN TO PIECES. I'LL WORK IT OUT.
HA.
I KNOW.
CAN YOU FEEL IT, DOC-TOR? SO HUNGRY. SO LOST.
SO CONFUSSSSED.
IT'S NOT THE ONLY ONE.
PLEASE, SQUIRE -- FOR HEAVEN'S SAKE--
WHAT IS IT?
I KNOW.
SUCH MADDENING UNCERTAINTY, DOC-TOR. TO BE TOWED ALONG BY STRINGS ONE CAN NEITHER SEE NOR UNDERSTAND.
THIS HATE THIS GATE THIS FEARFUL FATE.
WHAT ON EARTH ARE YOU PRATTLING ABOUT?

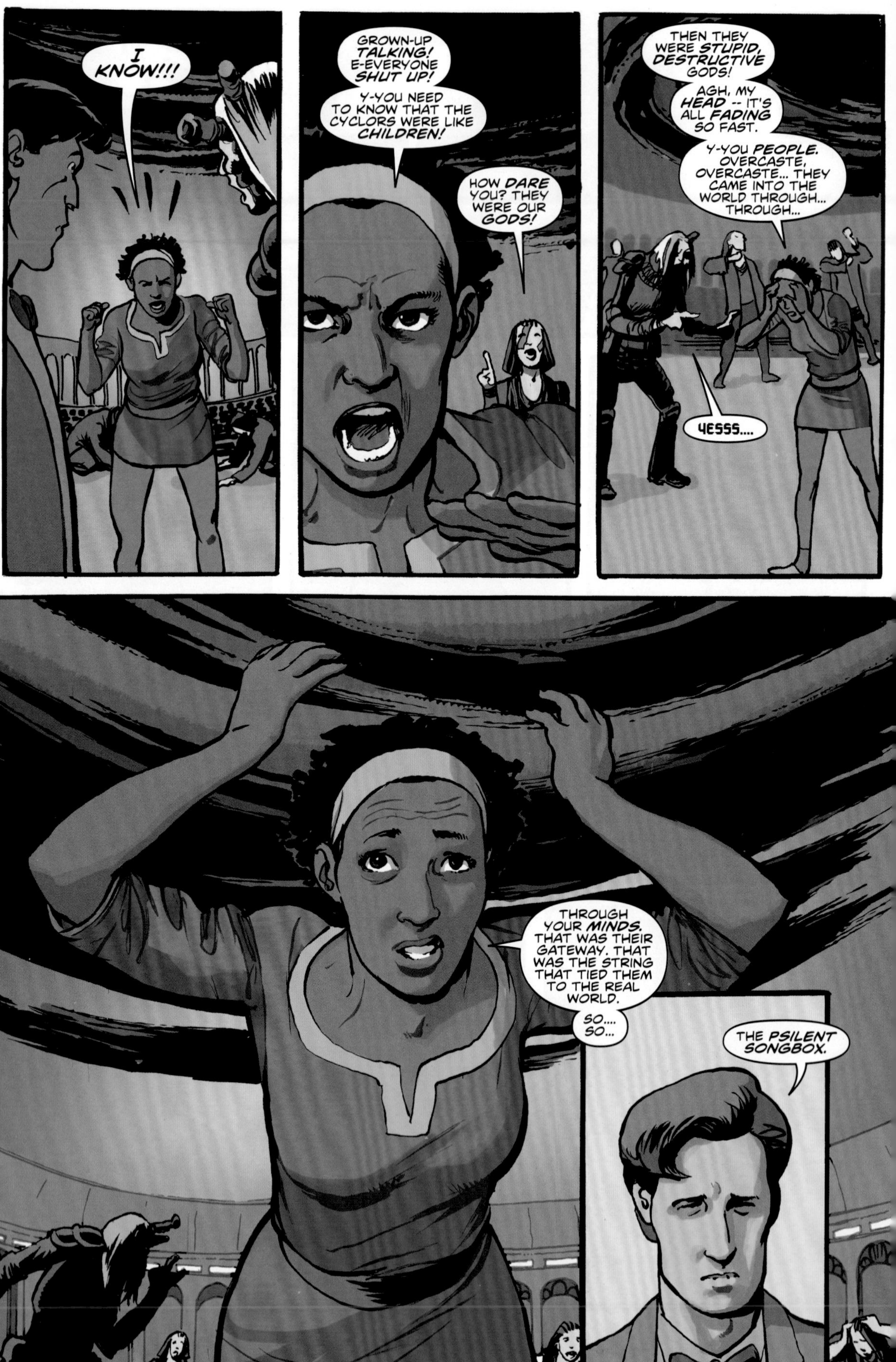
I KNOW!!!
GROWN-UP TALKING! E-EVERYONE SHUT UP!
Y-YOU NEED TO KNOW THAT THE CYCLORS WERE LIKE CHILDREN!
HOW DARE YOU? THEY WERE OUR GODS!
THEN THEY WERE STUPID, DESTRUCTIVE GODS!
AGH, MY HEAD -- IT'S ALL FADING SO FAST.
Y-YOU PEOPLE. OVERCASTE, OVERCASTE... THEY CAME INTO THE WORLD THROUGH... THROUGH...
YESSS....
THROUGH YOUR MINDS. THAT WAS THEIR GATEWAY. THAT WAS THE STRING THAT TIED THEM TO THE REAL WORLD.
SO.... SO...
THE PSILENT SONGBOX.

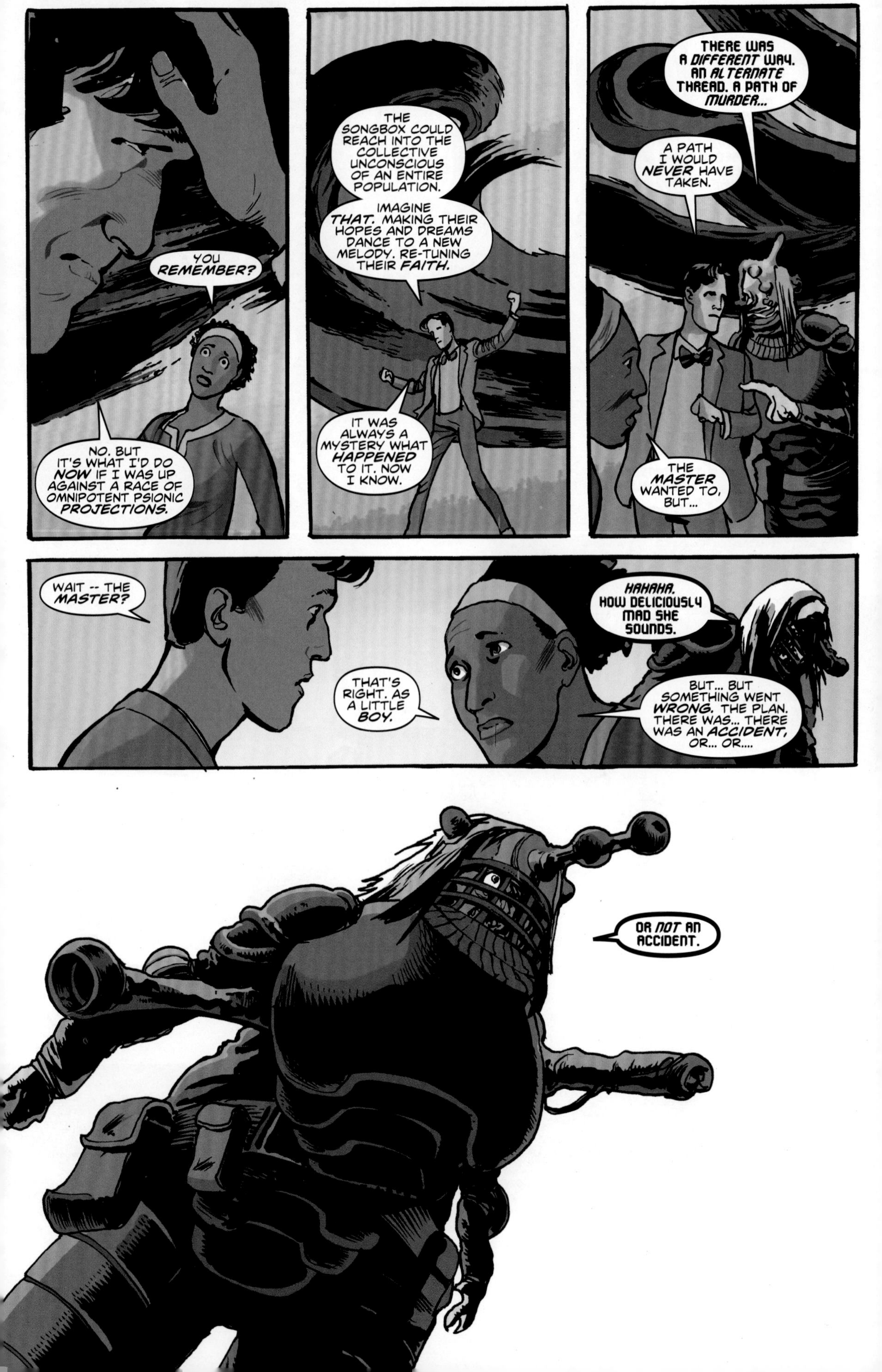
YOU REMEMBER?
NO. BUT IT'S WHAT I'D DO NOW IF I WAS UP AGAINST A RACE OF OMNIPOTENT PSIONIC PROJECTIONS.
THE SONGBOX COULD REACH INTO THE COLLECTIVE UNCONSCIOUS OF AN ENTIRE POPULATION.
IMAGINE THAT. MAKING THEIR HOPES AND DREAMS DANCE TO A NEW MELODY. RE-TUNING THEIR FAITH.
IT WAS ALWAYS A MYSTERY WHAT HAPPENED TO IT. NOW I KNOW.
THERE WAS A DIFFERENT WAY. AN ALTERNATE THREAD. A PATH OF MURDER...
A PATH I WOULD NEVER HAVE TAKEN.
THE MASTER WANTED TO, BUT...
WAIT -- THE MASTER?
THAT'S RIGHT. AS A LITTLE BOY.
HAHAHA. HOW DELICIOUSLY MAD SHE SOUNDS.
BUT... BUT SOMETHING WENT WRONG. THE PLAN. THERE WAS... THERE WAS AN ACCIDENT, OR... OR....
OR NOT AN ACCIDENT.

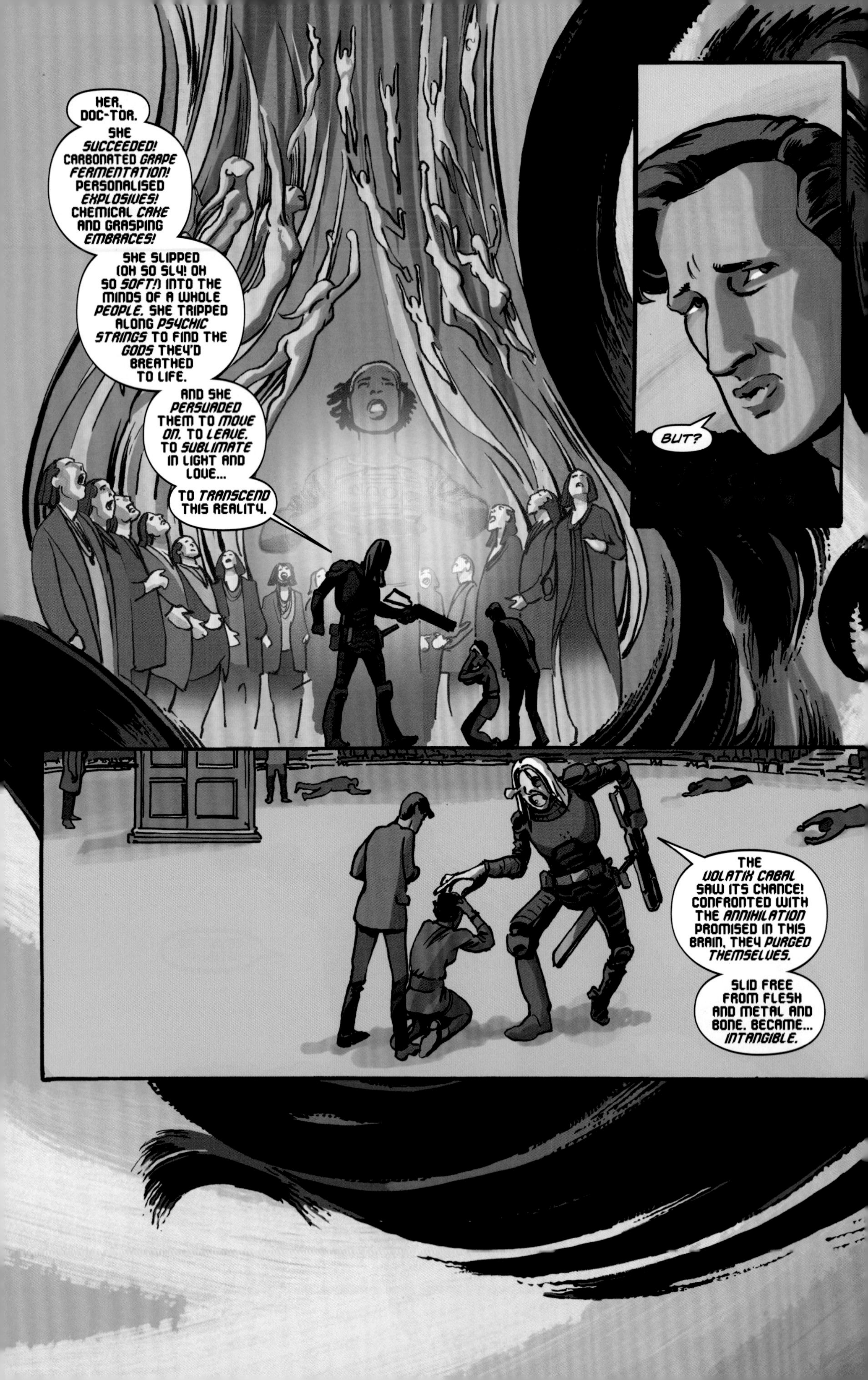
HER, DOC-TOR.
SHE *SUCCEEDED!* CARBONATED *GRAPE FERMENTATION!* PERSONALISED *EXPLOSIVES!* CHEMICAL *CAKE* AND GRASPING *EMBRACES!*
SHE SLIPPED (OH SO SLY! OH SO *SOFT!*) INTO THE MINDS OF A WHOLE *PEOPLE*. SHE TRIPPED ALONG *PSYCHIC STRINGS* TO FIND THE *GODS* THEY'D BREATHED TO LIFE.
AND SHE *PERSUADED* THEM TO *MOVE ON*. TO *LEAVE*. TO *SUBLIMATE* IN LIGHT AND LOVE...
TO *TRANSCEND* THIS REALITY.
BUT?
THE *VOLATIX CABAL* SAW ITS CHANCE! CONFRONTED WITH THE *ANNIHILATION* PROMISED IN THIS BRAIN, THEY *PURGED THEMSELVES*.
SLID FREE FROM FLESH AND METAL AND BONE. BECAME... *INTANGIBLE*.

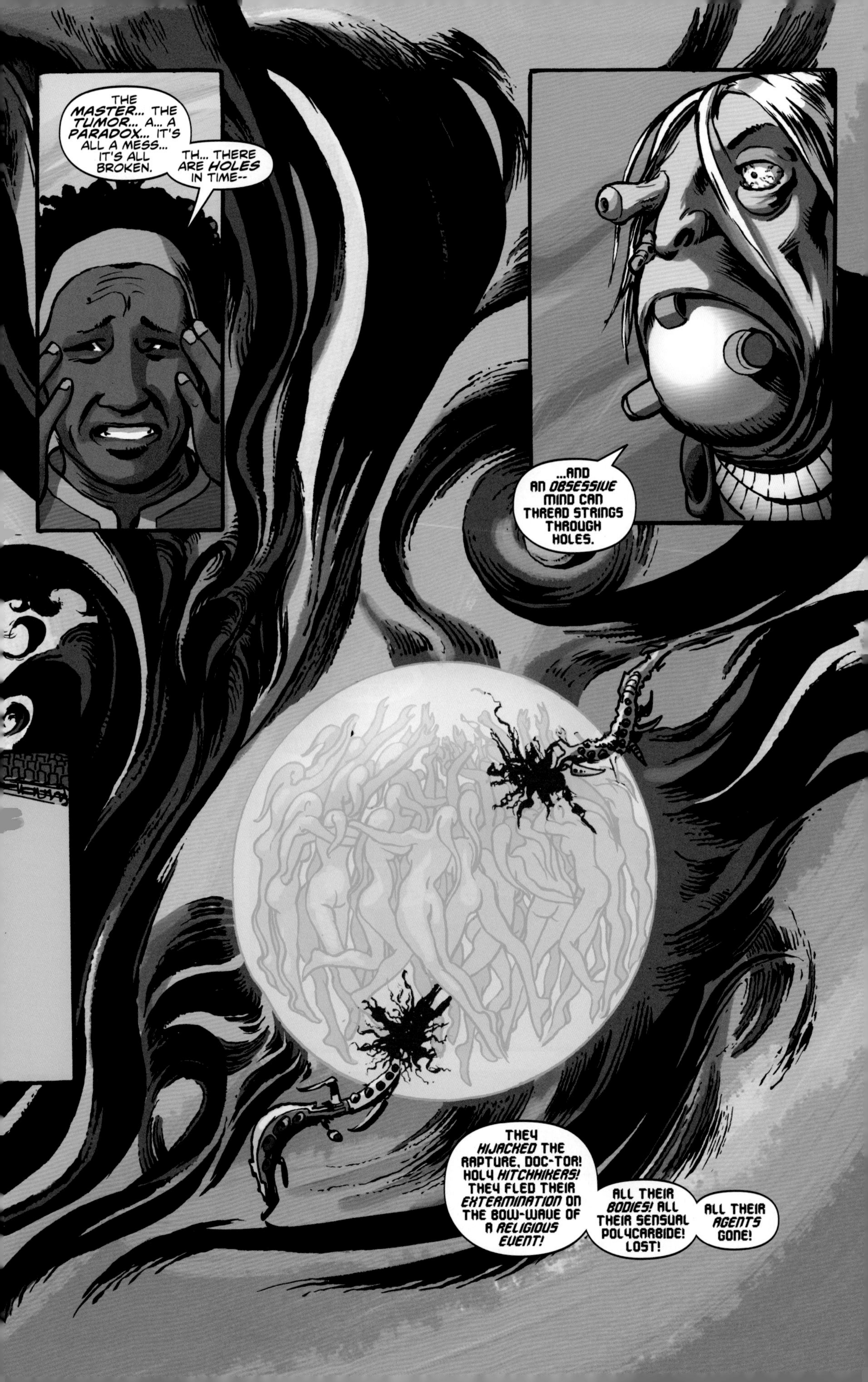
THE MASTER... THE TUMOR... A... A PARADOX... IT'S ALL A MESS... IT'S ALL BROKEN.
TH... THERE ARE HOLES IN TIME--
...AND AN OBSESSIVE MIND CAN THREAD STRINGS THROUGH HOLES.
THEY HIJACKED THE RAPTURE, DOC-TOR! HOLY HITCHHIKERS! THEY FLED THEIR EXTERMINATION ON THE BOW-WAVE OF A RELIGIOUS EVENT!
ALL THEIR BODIES! ALL THEIR SENSUAL POLYCARBIDE! LOST!
ALL THEIR AGENTS GONE!

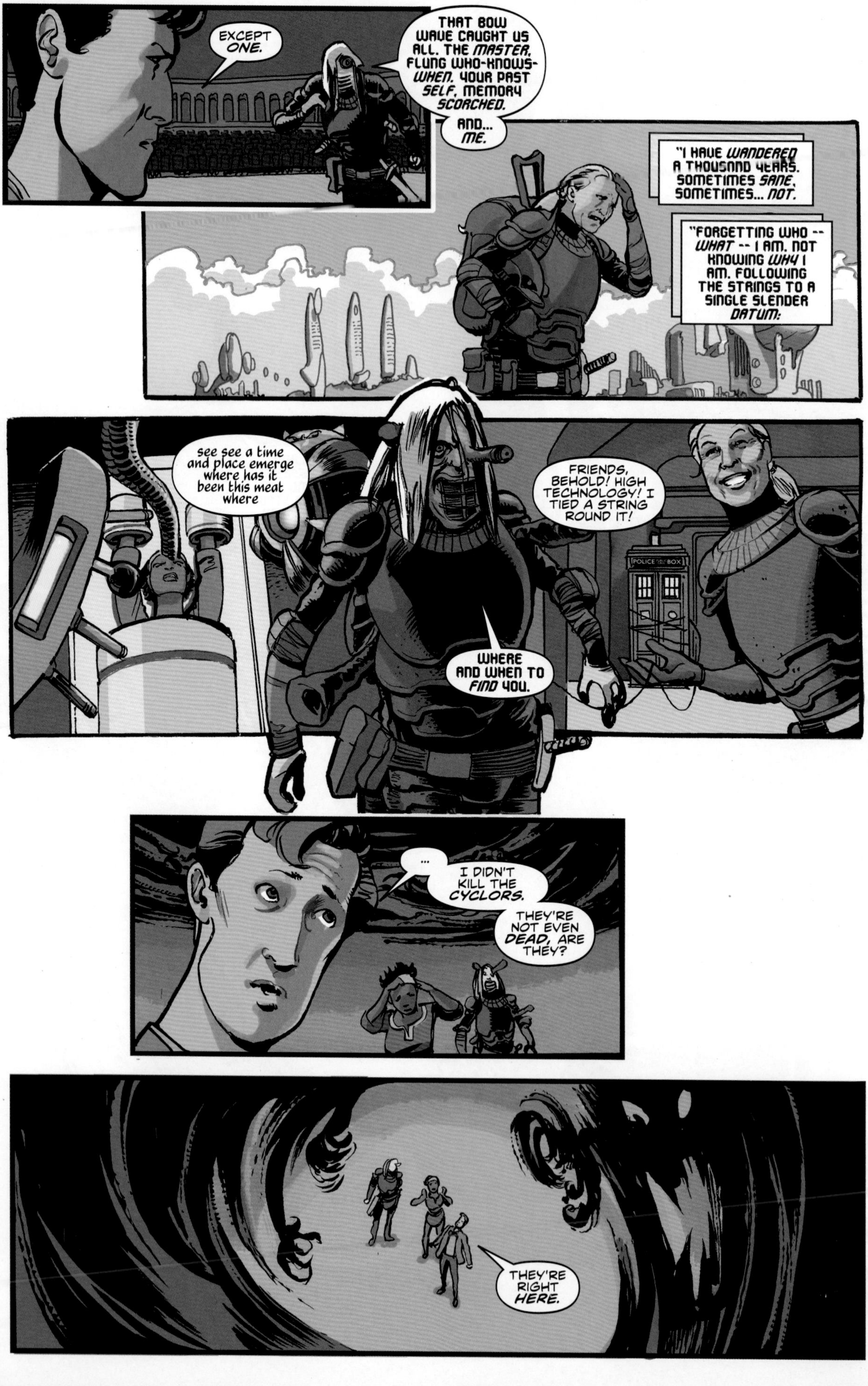
EXCEPT ONE.
THAT BOW WAVE CAUGHT US ALL. THE MASTER, FLUNG WHO-KNOWS-WHEN. YOUR PAST SELF, MEMORY SCORCHED.
AND... ME.
"I HAVE WANDERED A THOUSAND YEARS. SOMETIMES SANE, SOMETIMES... NOT.
"FORGETTING WHO -- WHAT -- I AM. NOT KNOWING WHY I AM. FOLLOWING THE STRINGS TO A SINGLE SLENDER DATUM:
see see a time and place emerge where has it been this meat where
FRIENDS, BEHOLD! HIGH TECHNOLOGY! I TIED A STRING ROUND IT!
POLICE BOX
WHERE AND WHEN TO FIND YOU.
... I DIDN'T KILL THE CYCLORS.
THEY'RE NOT EVEN DEAD, ARE THEY?
THEY'RE RIGHT HERE.

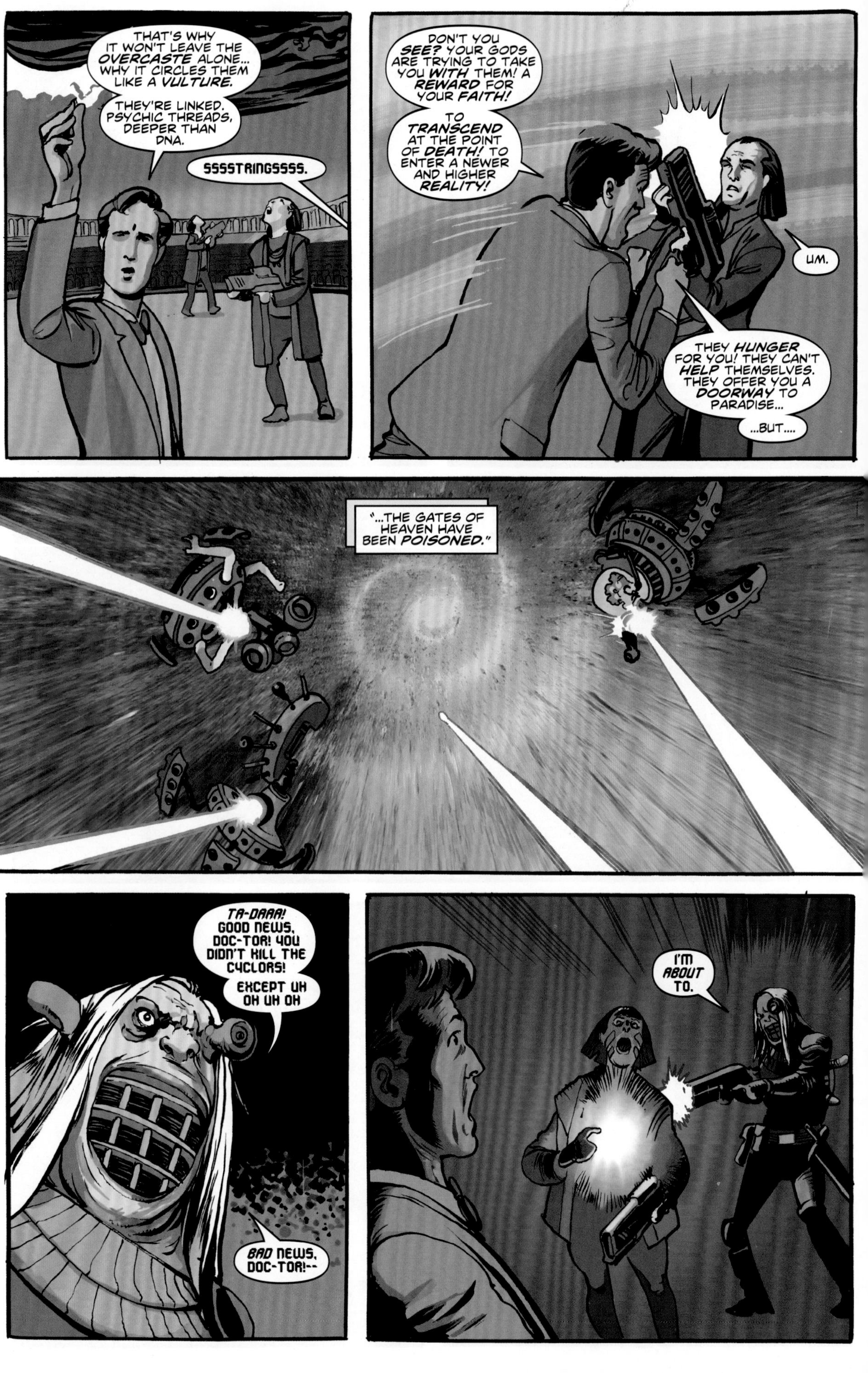
THAT'S WHY IT WON'T LEAVE THE OVERCASTE ALONE... WHY IT CIRCLES THEM LIKE A VULTURE.
THEY'RE LINKED. PSYCHIC THREADS, DEEPER THAN DNA.
SSSSTRINGSSSS.
DON'T YOU SEE? YOUR GODS ARE TRYING TO TAKE YOU WITH THEM! A REWARD FOR YOUR FAITH!
TO TRANSCEND AT THE POINT OF DEATH! TO ENTER A NEWER AND HIGHER REALITY!
UM.
THEY HUNGER FOR YOU! THEY CAN'T HELP THEMSELVES. THEY OFFER YOU A DOORWAY TO PARADISE...
...BUT....
"...THE GATES OF HEAVEN HAVE BEEN POISONED."
TA-DAAA! GOOD NEWS, DOC-TOR! YOU DIDN'T KILL THE CYCLORS!
EXCEPT UH OH UH OH
BAD NEWS, DOC-TOR!--
I'M ABOUT TO.

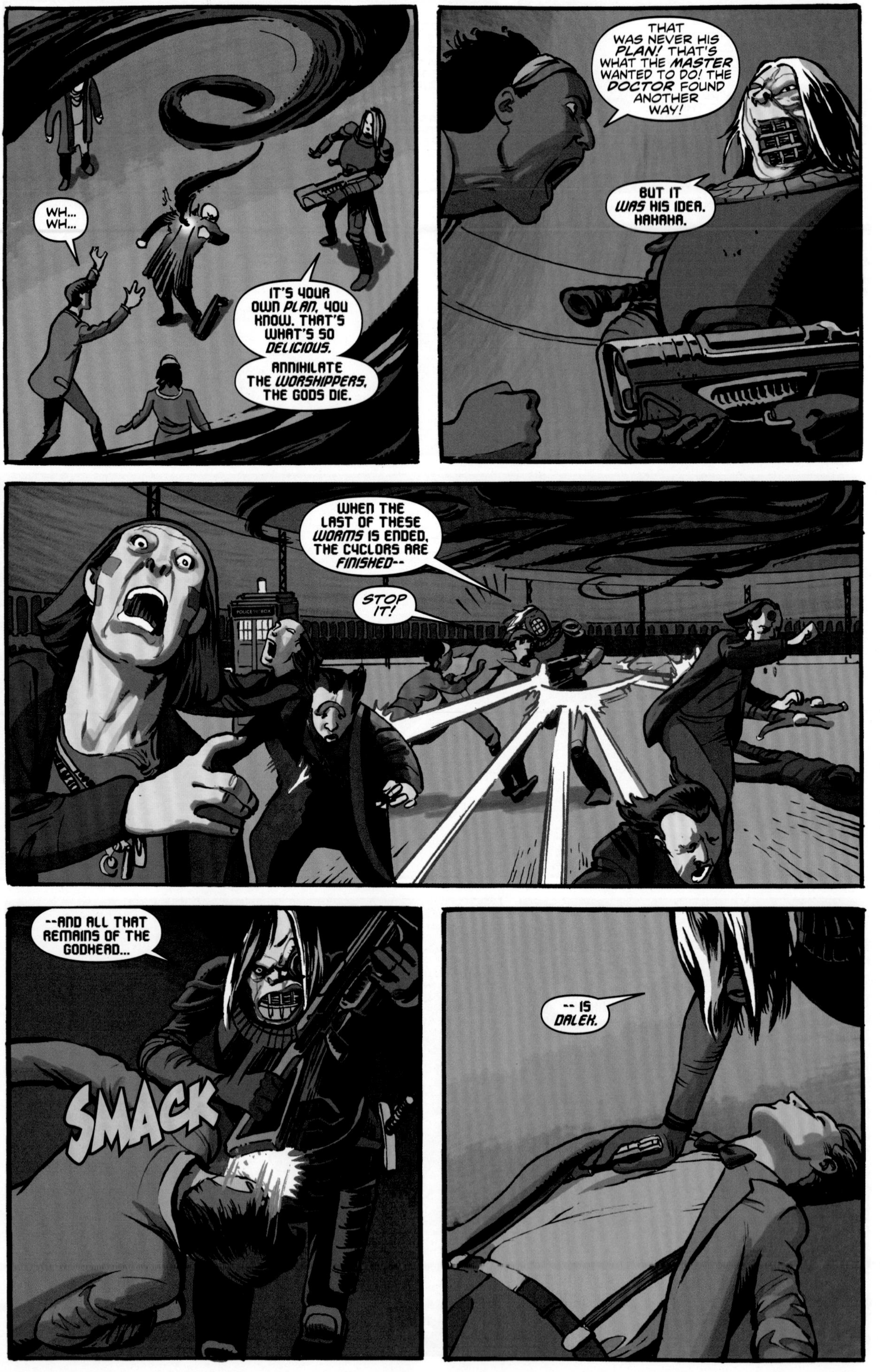
WH... WH...
IT'S YOUR OWN PLAN, YOU KNOW. THAT'S WHAT'S SO DELICIOUS.
ANNIHILATE THE WORSHIPPERS, THE GODS DIE.
THAT WAS NEVER HIS PLAN! THAT'S WHAT THE MASTER WANTED TO DO! THE DOCTOR FOUND ANOTHER WAY!
BUT IT WAS HIS IDEA. HAHAHA.
WHEN THE LAST OF THESE WORMS IS ENDED, THE CYCLORS ARE FINISHED--
STOP IT!
POLICE BOX
--AND ALL THAT REMAINS OF THE GODHEAD...
SMACK
-- IS DALEK.

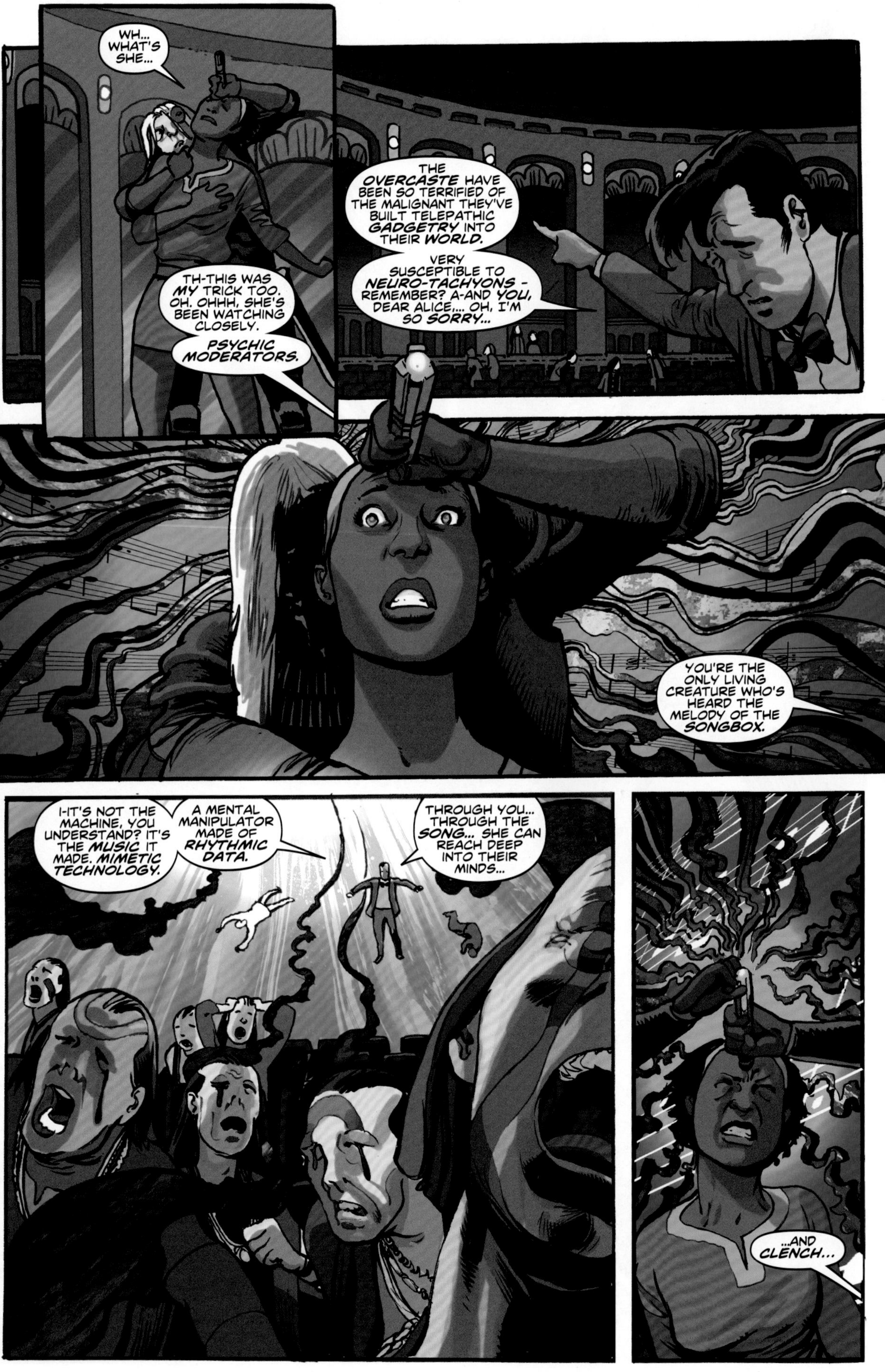
WH... WHAT'S SHE...
THE OVERCASTE HAVE BEEN SO TERRIFIED OF THE MALIGNANT THEY'VE BUILT TELEPATHIC GADGETRY INTO THEIR WORLD.
VERY SUSCEPTIBLE TO NEURO-TACHYONS - REMEMBER? A-AND YOU, DEAR ALICE.... OH, I'M SO SORRY...
TH-THIS WAS MY TRICK TOO. OH. OHHH, SHE'S BEEN WATCHING CLOSELY.
PSYCHIC MODERATORS.
YOU'RE THE ONLY LIVING CREATURE WHO'S HEARD THE MELODY OF THE SONGBOX.
I-IT'S NOT THE MACHINE, YOU UNDERSTAND? IT'S THE MUSIC IT MADE. MIMETIC TECHNOLOGY.
A MENTAL MANIPULATOR MADE OF RHYTHMIC DATA.
THROUGH YOU... THROUGH THE SONG... SHE CAN REACH DEEP INTO THEIR MINDS...
...AND CLENCH...

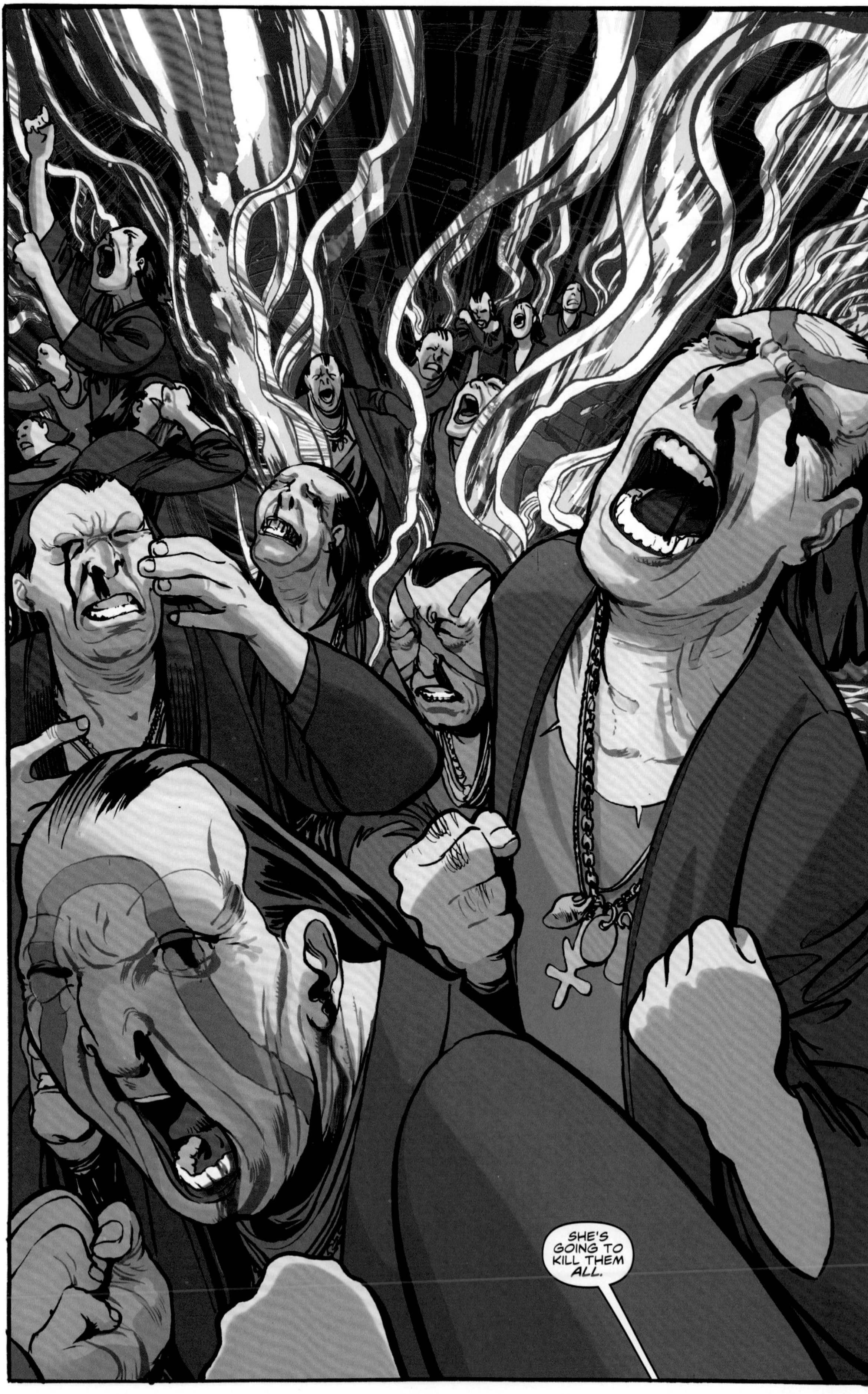
SHE'S GOING TO KILL THEM ALL.

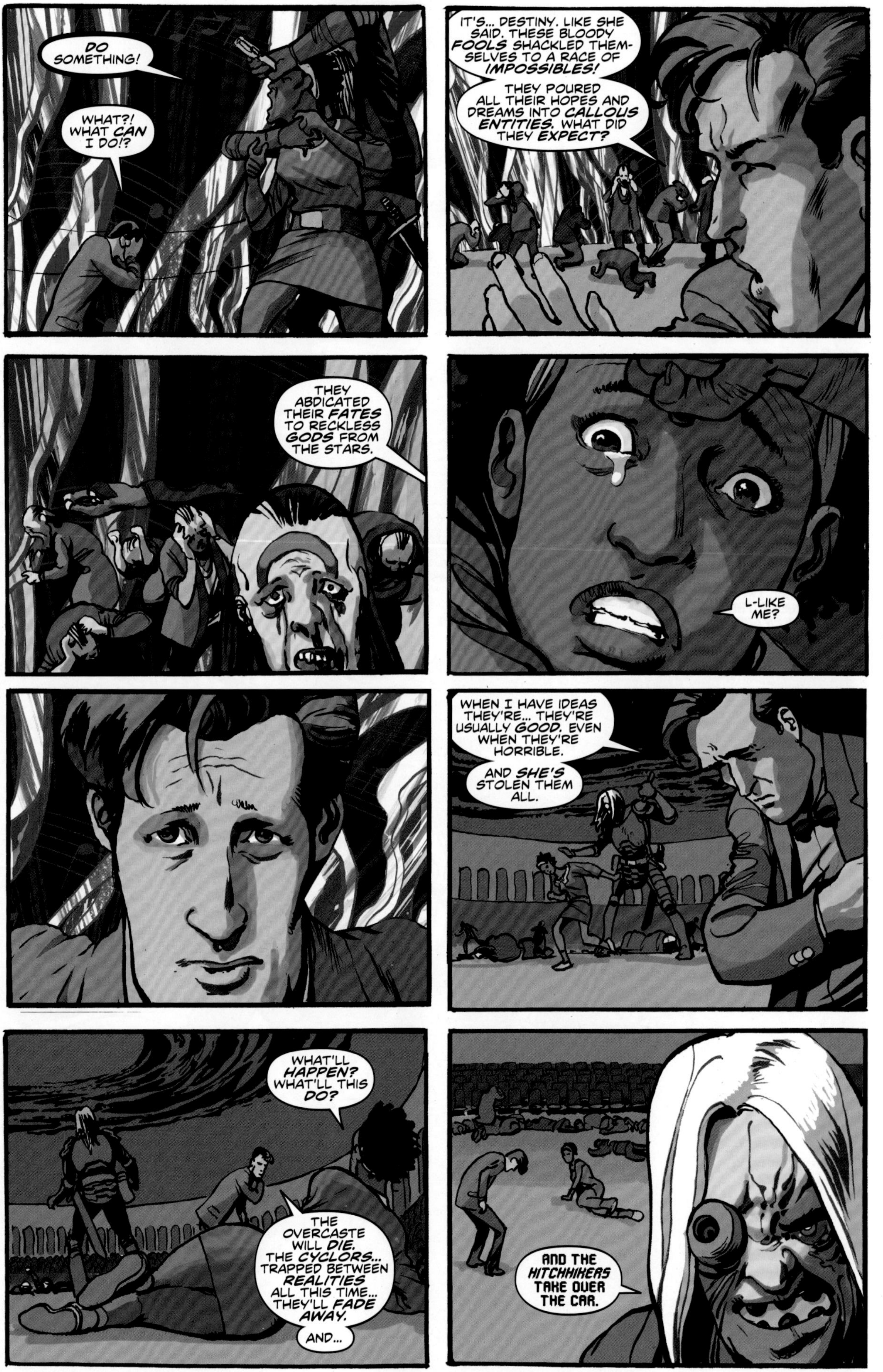

DO SOMETHING!
WHAT?! WHAT CAN I DO!?
IT'S... DESTINY. LIKE SHE SAID. THESE BLOODY FOOLS SHACKLED THEMSELVES TO A RACE OF IMPOSSIBLES!
THEY POURED ALL THEIR HOPES AND DREAMS INTO CALLOUS ENTITIES. WHAT DID THEY EXPECT?
THEY ABDICATED THEIR FATES TO RECKLESS GODS FROM THE STARS.
L-LIKE ME?
WHEN I HAVE IDEAS THEY'RE... THEY'RE USUALLY GOOD. EVEN WHEN THEY'RE HORRIBLE.
AND SHE'S STOLEN THEM ALL.
WHAT'LL HAPPEN? WHAT'LL THIS DO?
THE OVERCASTE WILL DIE. THE CYCLORS... TRAPPED BETWEEN REALITIES ALL THIS TIME... THEY'LL FADE AWAY.
AND...
AND THE HITCHHIKERS TAKE OVER THE CAR.

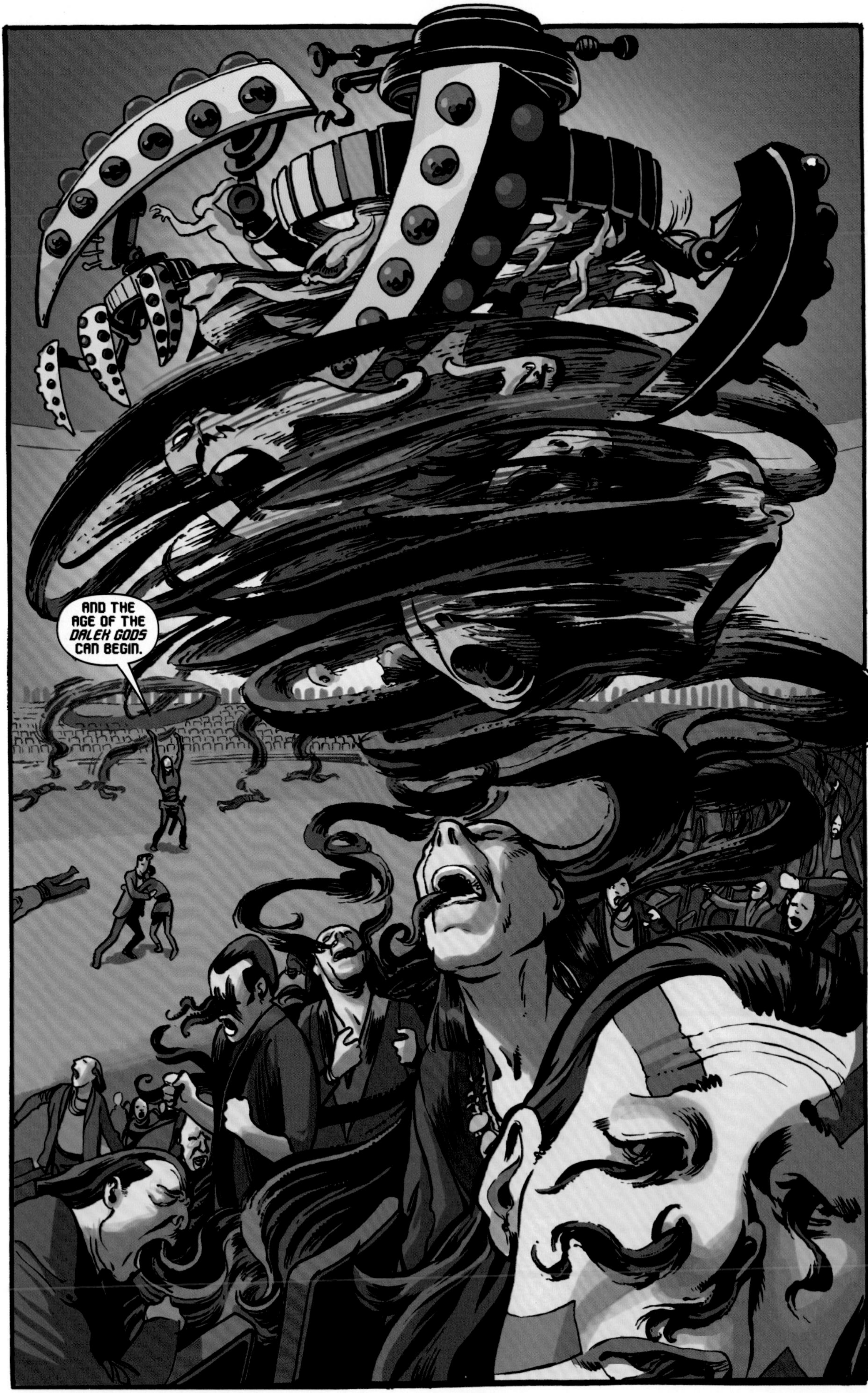
AND THE AGE OF THE *DALEK GODS* CAN BEGIN.

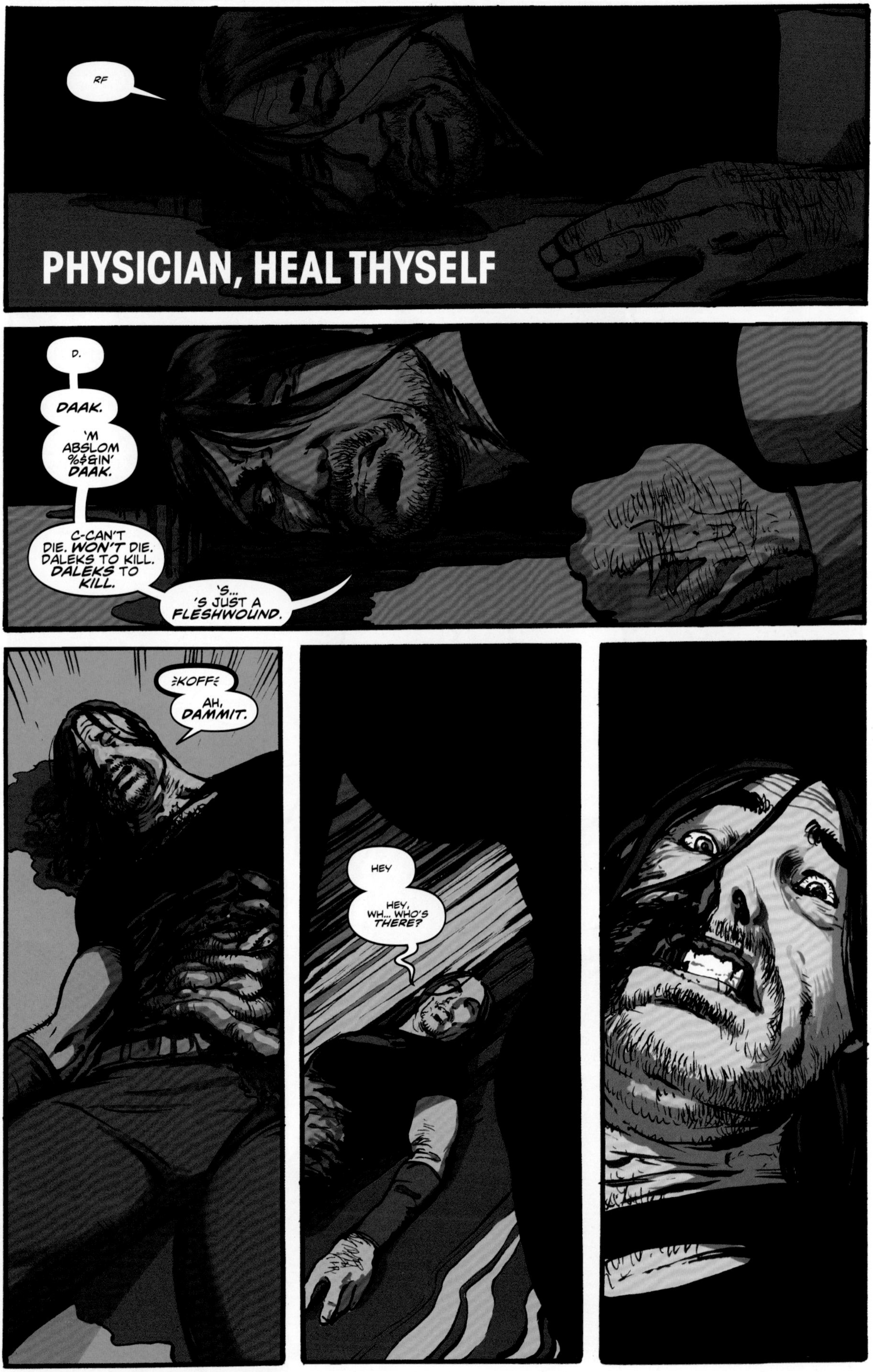
RF
PHYSICIAN, HEAL THYSELF
D.
DAAK.
'M ABSLOM %$&IN' DAAK.
C-CAN'T DIE. WON'T DIE. DALEKS TO KILL. DALEKS TO KILL.
'S... 'S JUST A FLESHWOUND.
KOFF
AH, DAMMIT.
HEY
HEY, WH... WHO'S THERE?

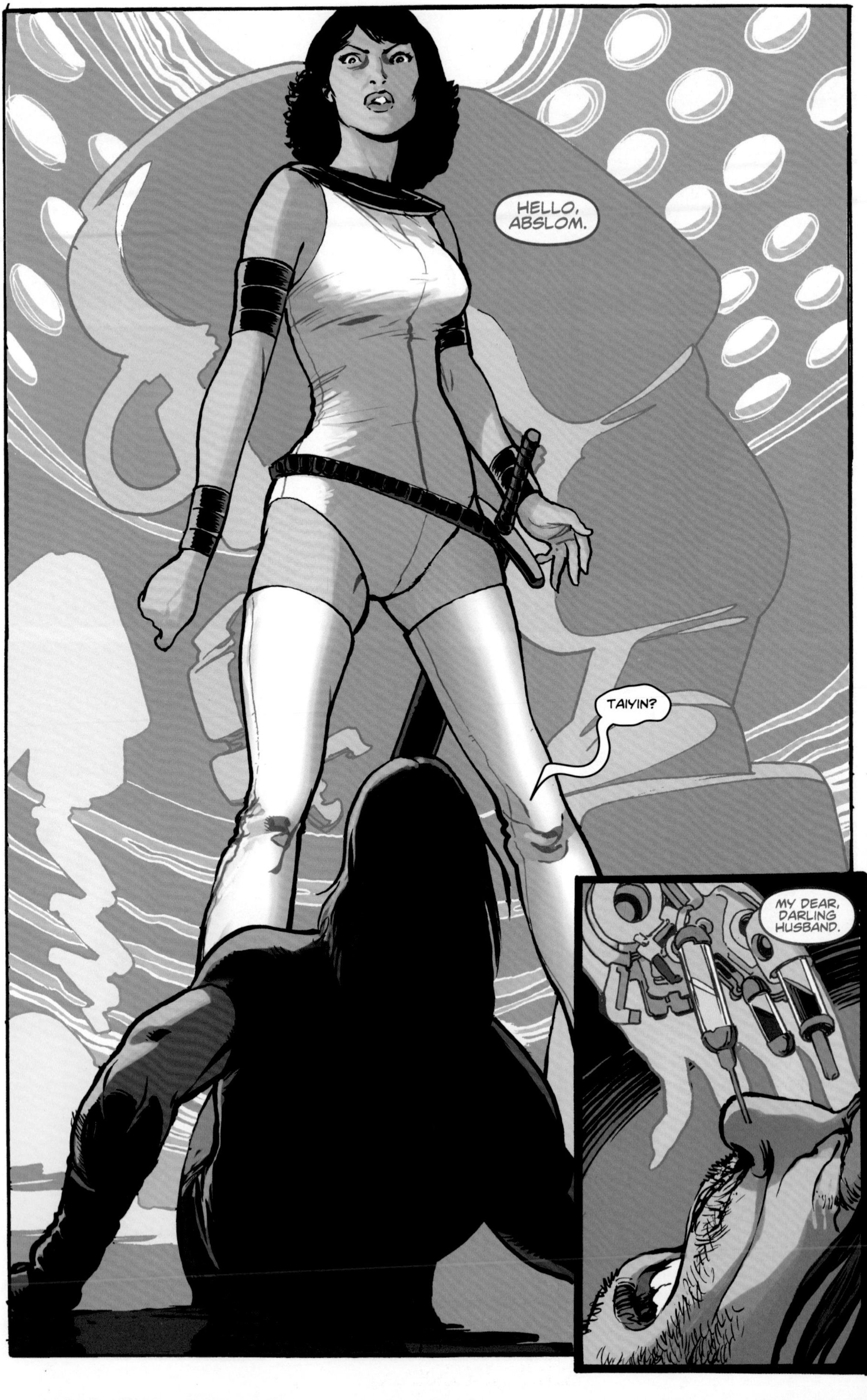
HELLO, ABSLOM.
TAIYIN?
MY DEAR, DARLING HUSBAND.

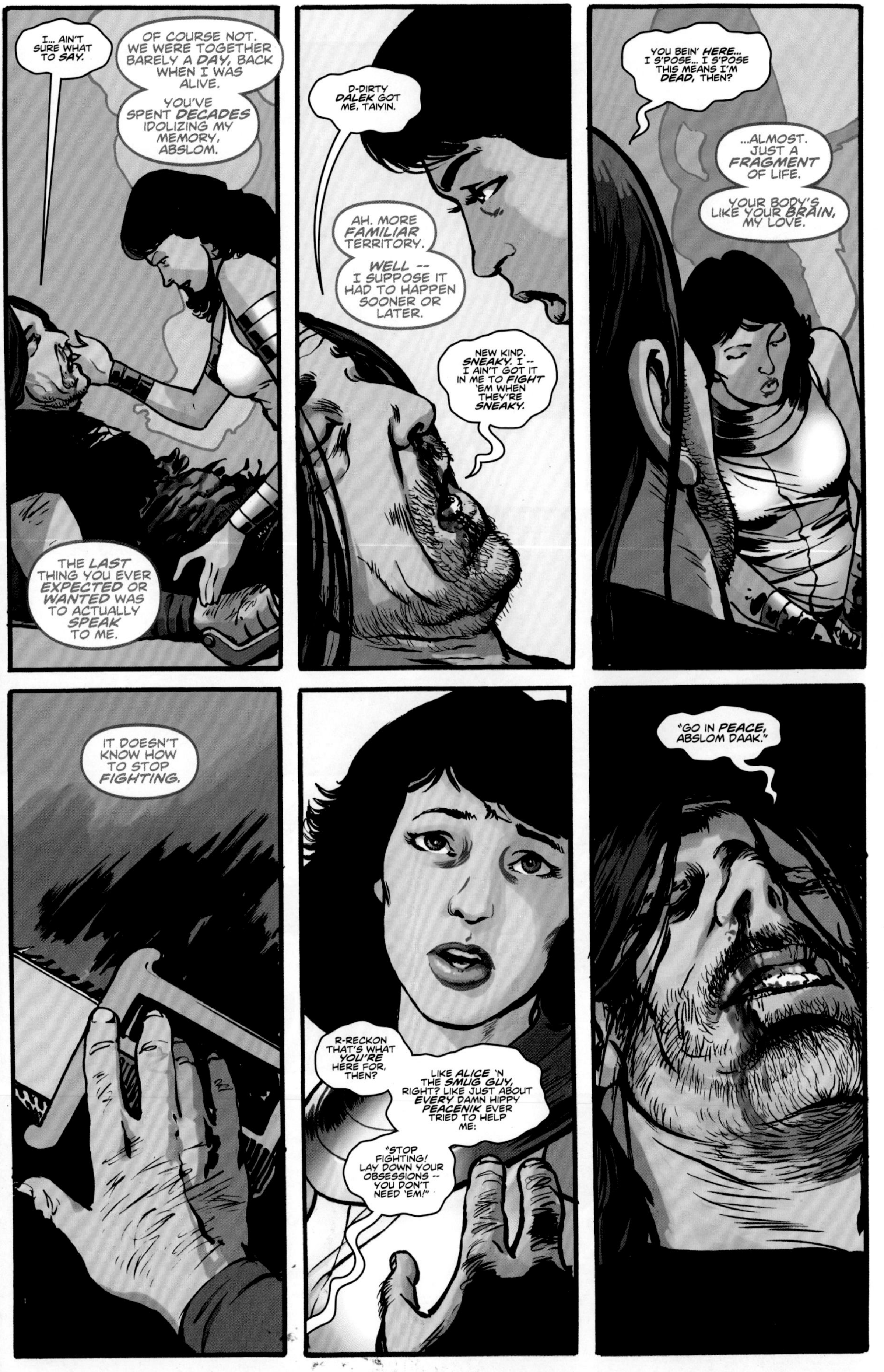
I... AIN'T SURE WHAT TO SAY.
OF COURSE NOT. WE WERE TOGETHER BARELY A DAY, BACK WHEN I WAS ALIVE.
YOU'VE SPENT DECADES IDOLIZING MY MEMORY, ABSLOM.
THE LAST THING YOU EVER EXPECTED OR WANTED WAS TO ACTUALLY SPEAK TO ME.
D-DIRTY DALEK GOT ME, TAIYIN.
AH. MORE FAMILIAR TERRITORY.
WELL -- I SUPPOSE IT HAD TO HAPPEN SOONER OR LATER.
NEW KIND. SNEAKY. I -- I AIN'T GOT IT IN ME TO FIGHT 'EM WHEN THEY'RE SNEAKY.
YOU BEIN' HERE... I S'POSE... I S'POSE THIS MEANS I'M DEAD, THEN?
...ALMOST. JUST A FRAGMENT OF LIFE.
YOUR BODY'S LIKE YOUR BRAIN, MY LOVE.
IT DOESN'T KNOW HOW TO STOP FIGHTING.
R-RECKON THAT'S WHAT YOU'RE HERE FOR, THEN?
LIKE ALICE 'N THE SMUG GUY, RIGHT? LIKE JUST ABOUT EVERY DAMN HIPPY PEACENIK EVER TRIED TO HELP ME:
"STOP FIGHTING! LAY DOWN YOUR OBSESSIONS -- YOU DON'T NEED 'EM!"
"GO IN PEACE, ABSLOM DAAK."

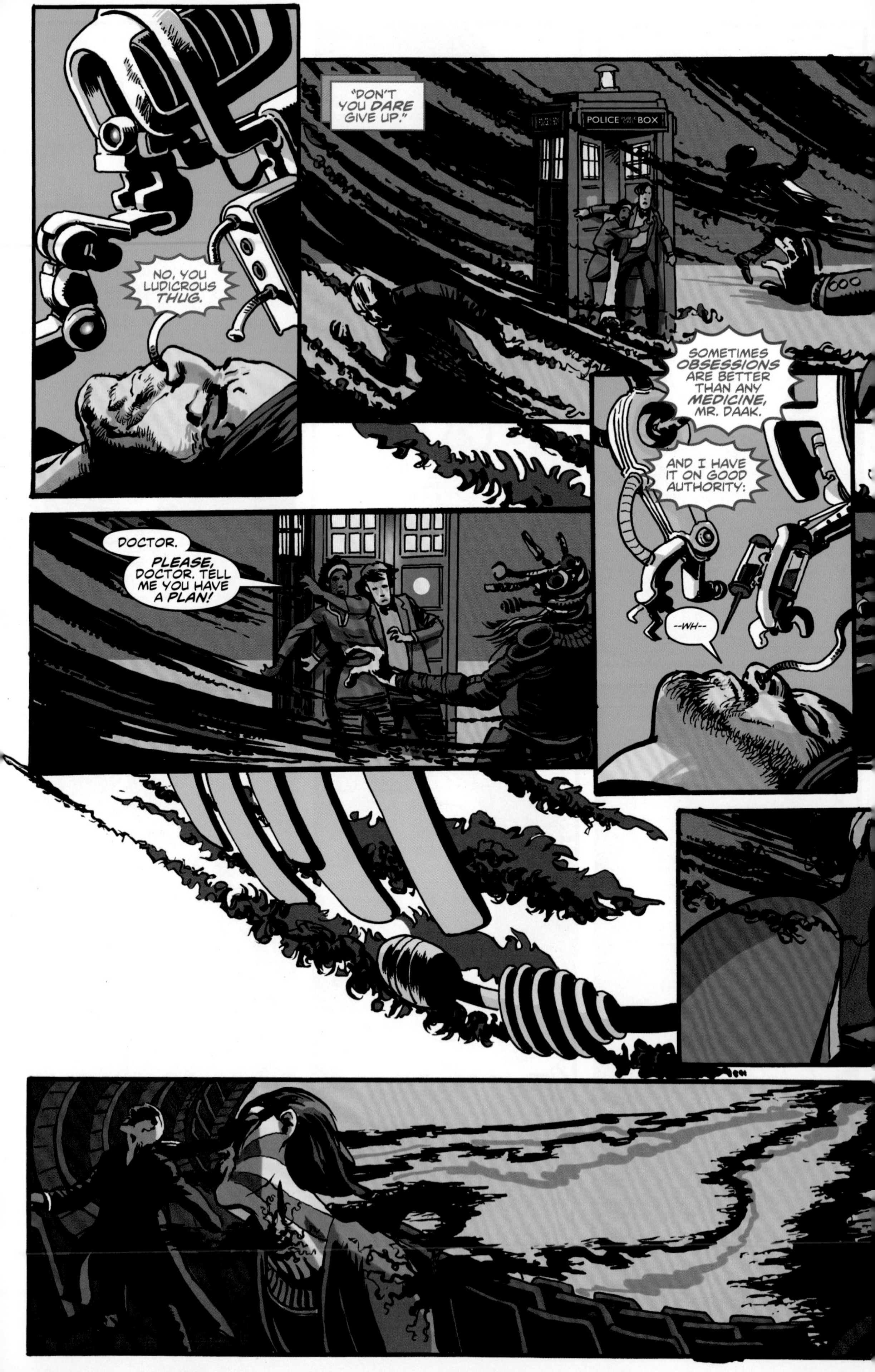
NO, YOU LUDICROUS THUG.
"DON'T YOU DARE GIVE UP."
POLICE PUBLIC CALL BOX
SOMETIMES OBSESSIONS ARE BETTER THAN ANY MEDICINE, MR. DAAK.
AND I HAVE IT ON GOOD AUTHORITY:
--WH--
DOCTOR.
PLEASE, DOCTOR. TELL ME YOU HAVE A PLAN!

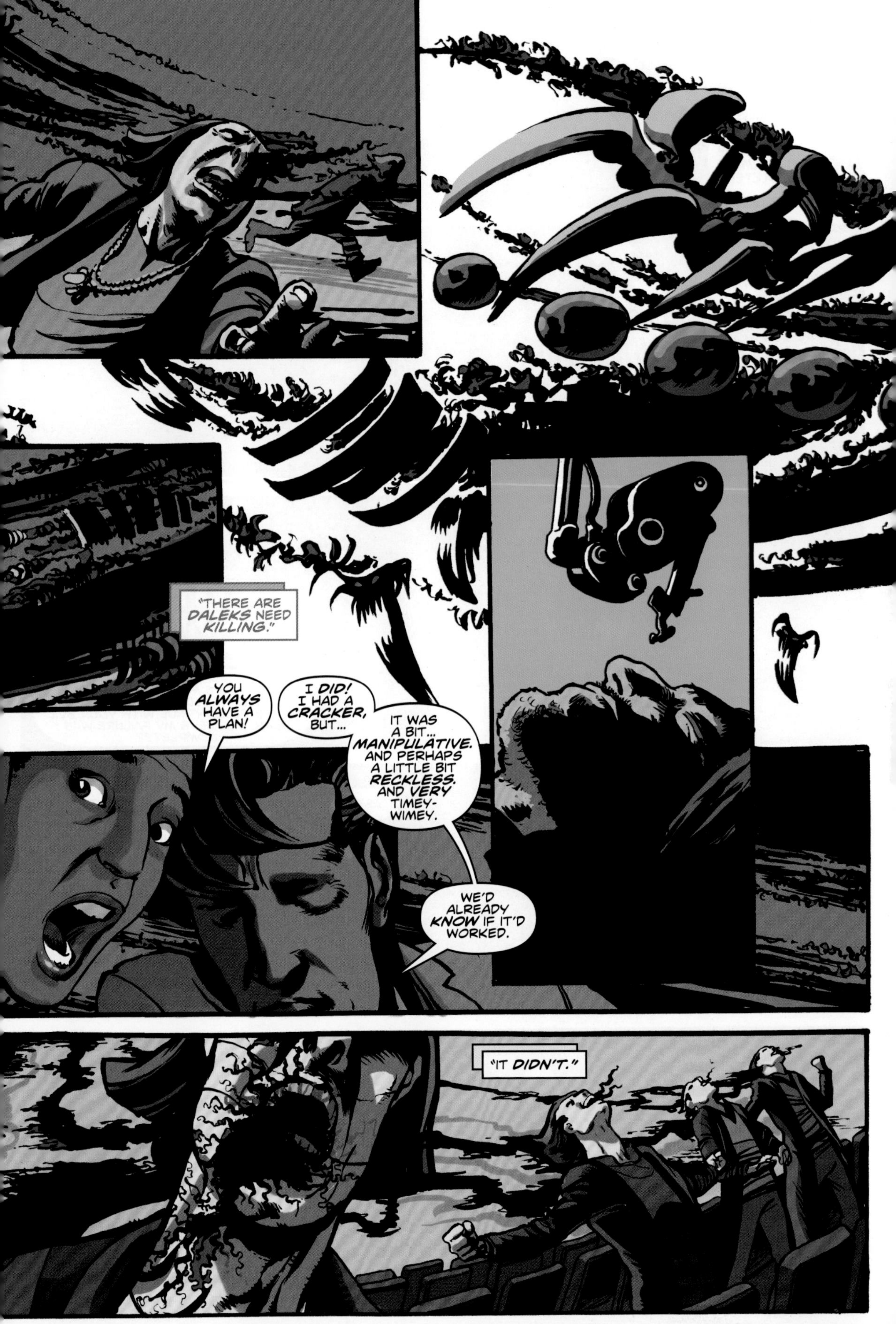
"THERE ARE DALEKS NEED KILLING."
YOU ALWAYS HAVE A PLAN!
I DID! I HAD A CRACKER, BUT...
IT WAS A BIT... MANIPULATIVE. AND PERHAPS A LITTLE BIT RECKLESS. AND VERY TIMEY-WIMEY.
WE'D ALREADY KNOW IF IT'D WORKED.
"IT DIDN'T."

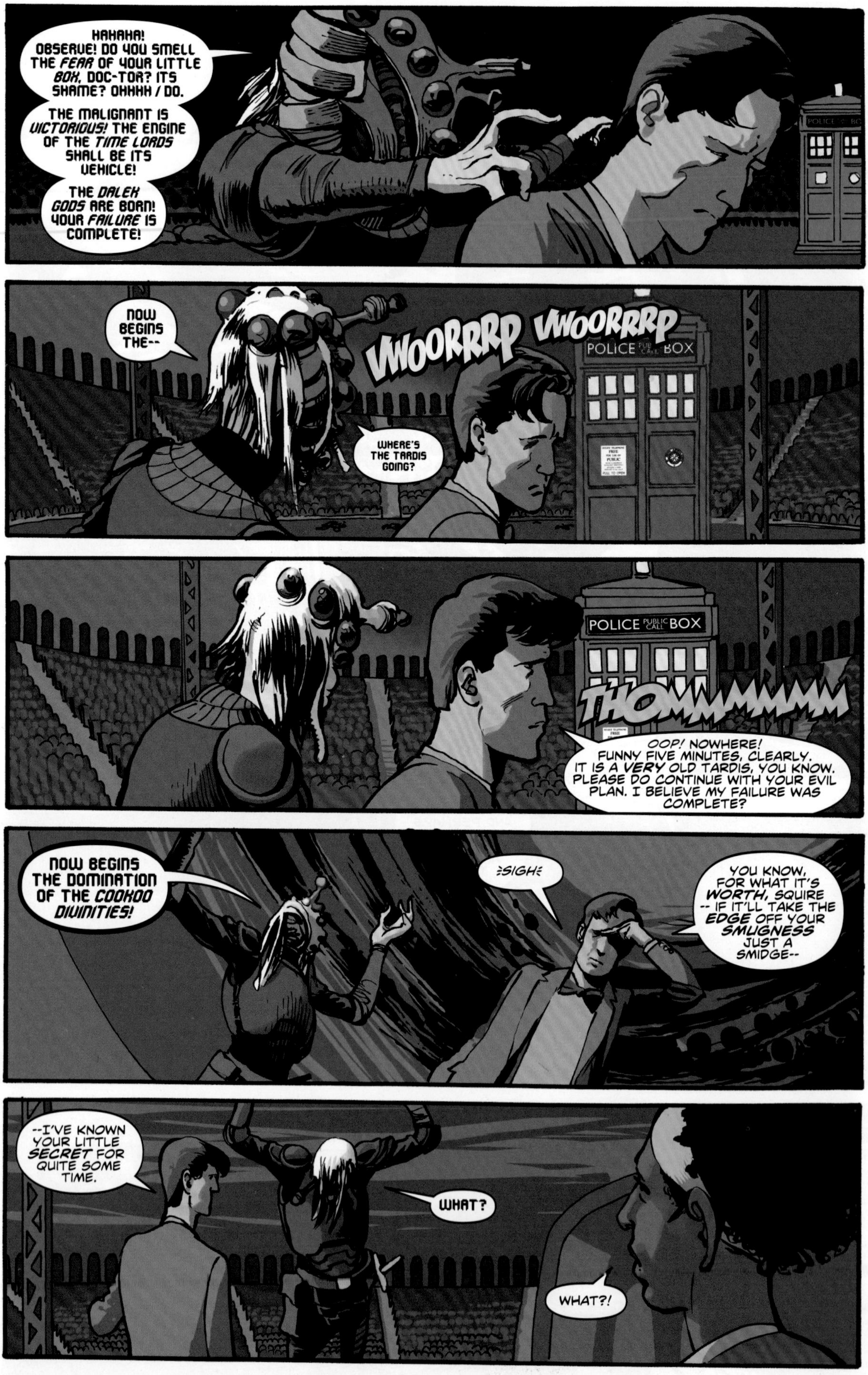
HAHAHA! OBSERVE! DO YOU SMELL THE FEAR OF YOUR LITTLE BOX, DOC-TOR? ITS SHAME? OHHHH I DO.
THE MALIGNANT IS VICTORIOUS! THE ENGINE OF THE TIME LORDS SHALL BE ITS VEHICLE!
THE DALEK GODS ARE BORN! YOUR FAILURE IS COMPLETE!
NOW BEGINS THE--
VWOORRRP VWOORRRP
POLICE PUBLIC CALL BOX
WHERE'S THE TARDIS GOING?
POLICE PUBLIC CALL BOX
THOMMMMMM
OOP! NOWHERE! FUNNY FIVE MINUTES, CLEARLY. IT IS A VERY OLD TARDIS, YOU KNOW. PLEASE DO CONTINUE WITH YOUR EVIL PLAN. I BELIEVE MY FAILURE WAS COMPLETE?
NOW BEGINS THE DOMINATION OF THE COOKOO DIVINITIES!
SIGH
YOU KNOW, FOR WHAT IT'S WORTH, SQUIRE -- IF IT'LL TAKE THE EDGE OFF YOUR SMUGNESS JUST A SMIDGE--
--I'VE KNOWN YOUR LITTLE SECRET FOR QUITE SOME TIME.
WHAT?
WHAT?!

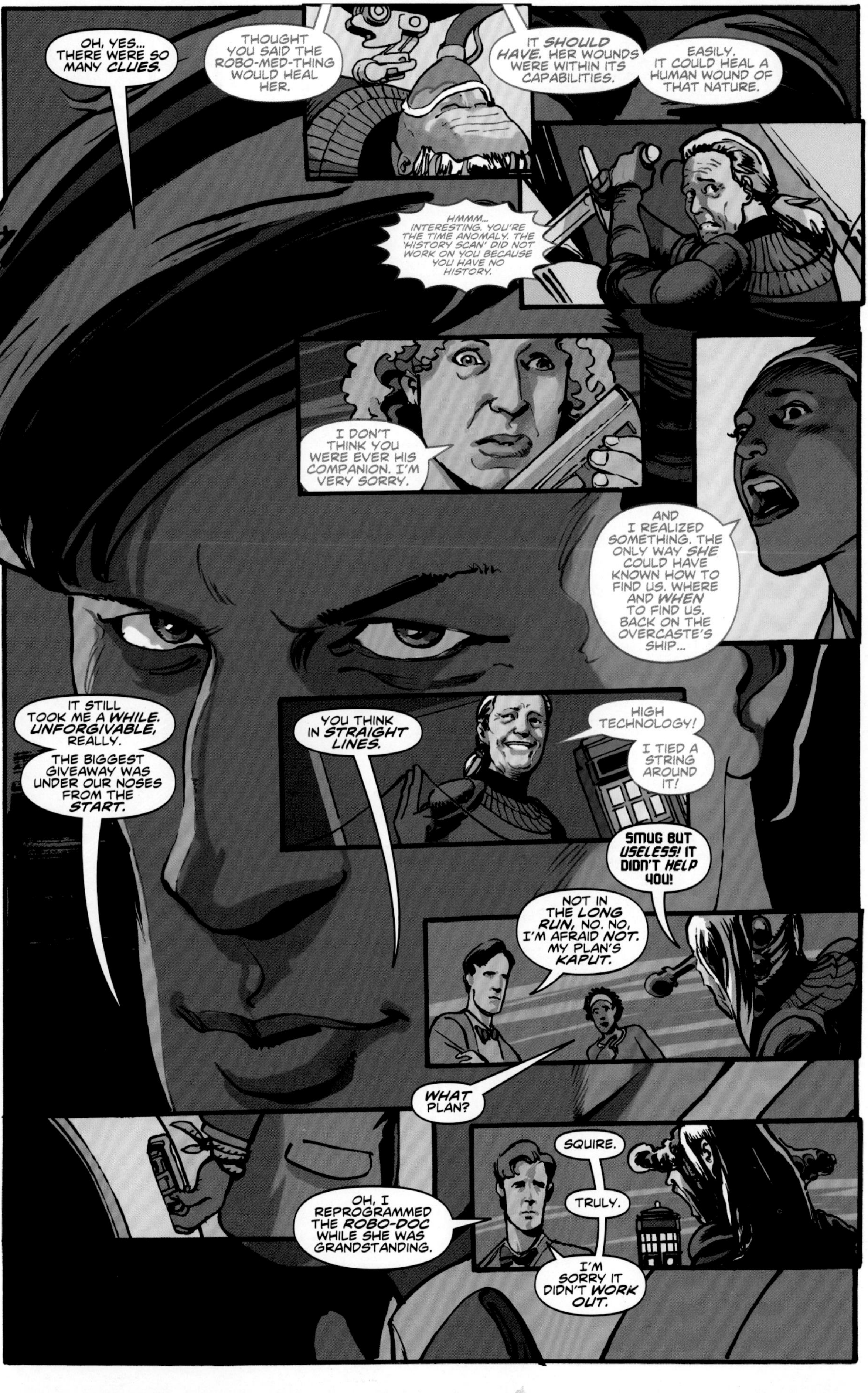
OH, YES... THERE WERE SO MANY CLUES.
THOUGHT YOU SAID THE ROBO-MED-THING WOULD HEAL HER.
IT SHOULD HAVE. HER WOUNDS WERE WITHIN ITS CAPABILITIES.
EASILY. IT COULD HEAL A HUMAN WOUND OF THAT NATURE.
HMMM... INTERESTING. YOU'RE THE TIME ANOMALY. THE 'HISTORY SCAN' DID NOT WORK ON YOU BECAUSE YOU HAVE NO HISTORY.
I DON'T THINK YOU WERE EVER HIS COMPANION. I'M VERY SORRY.
AND I REALIZED SOMETHING. THE ONLY WAY SHE COULD HAVE KNOWN HOW TO FIND US. WHERE AND WHEN TO FIND US. BACK ON THE OVERCASTE'S SHIP...
IT STILL TOOK ME A WHILE. UNFORGIVABLE, REALLY.
THE BIGGEST GIVEAWAY WAS UNDER OUR NOSES FROM THE START.
YOU THINK IN STRAIGHT LINES.
HIGH TECHNOLOGY!
I TIED A STRING AROUND IT!
SMUG BUT USELESS! IT DIDN'T HELP YOU!
NOT IN THE LONG RUN, NO. NO, I'M AFRAID NOT. MY PLAN'S KAPUT.
WHAT PLAN?
OH, I REPROGRAMMED THE ROBO-DOC WHILE SHE WAS GRANDSTANDING.
SQUIRE.
TRULY.
I'M SORRY IT DIDN'T WORK OUT.

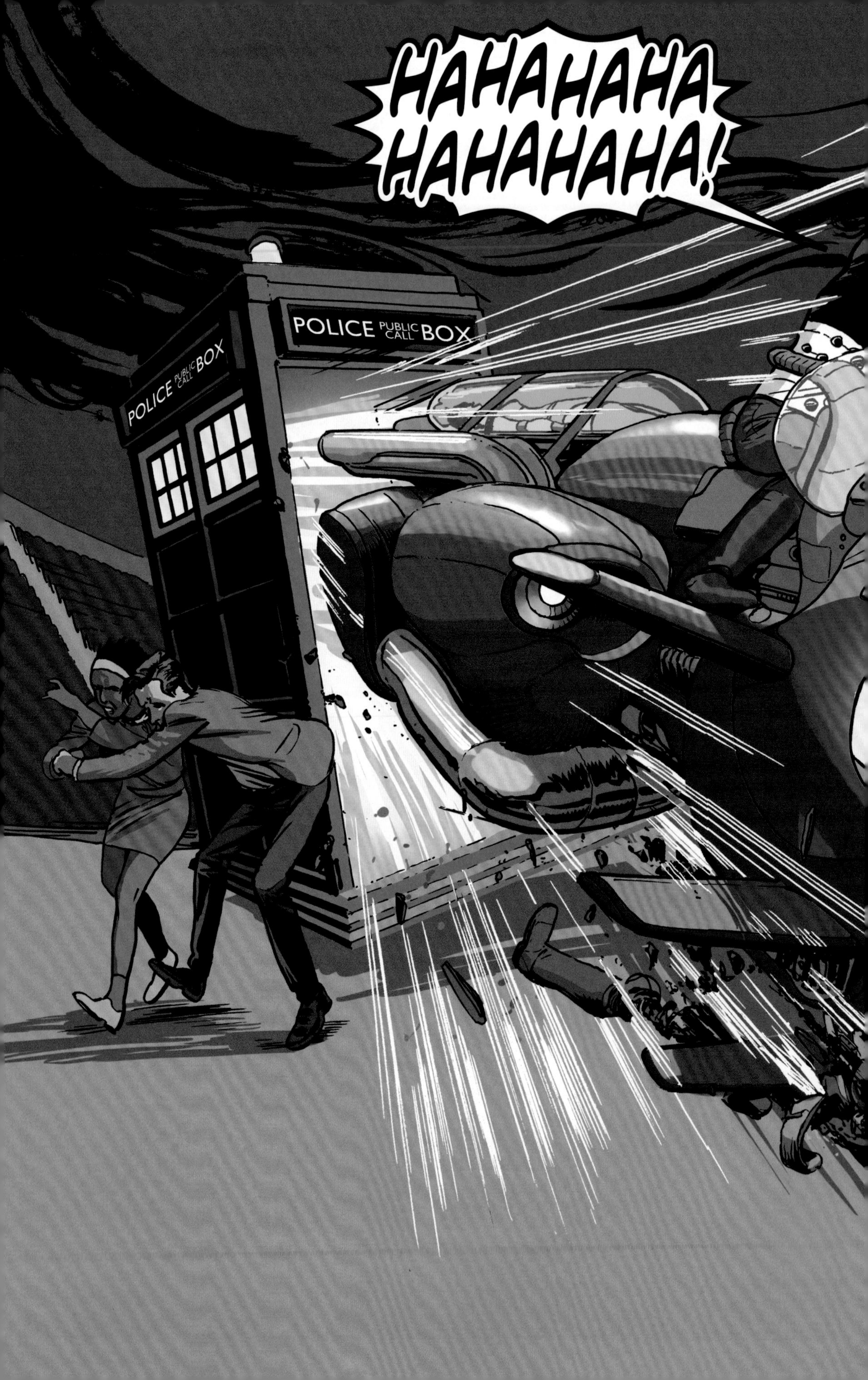
HAHAHAHA
HAHAHAHA!
POLICE PUBLIC CALL BOX
POLICE PUBLIC CALL BOX

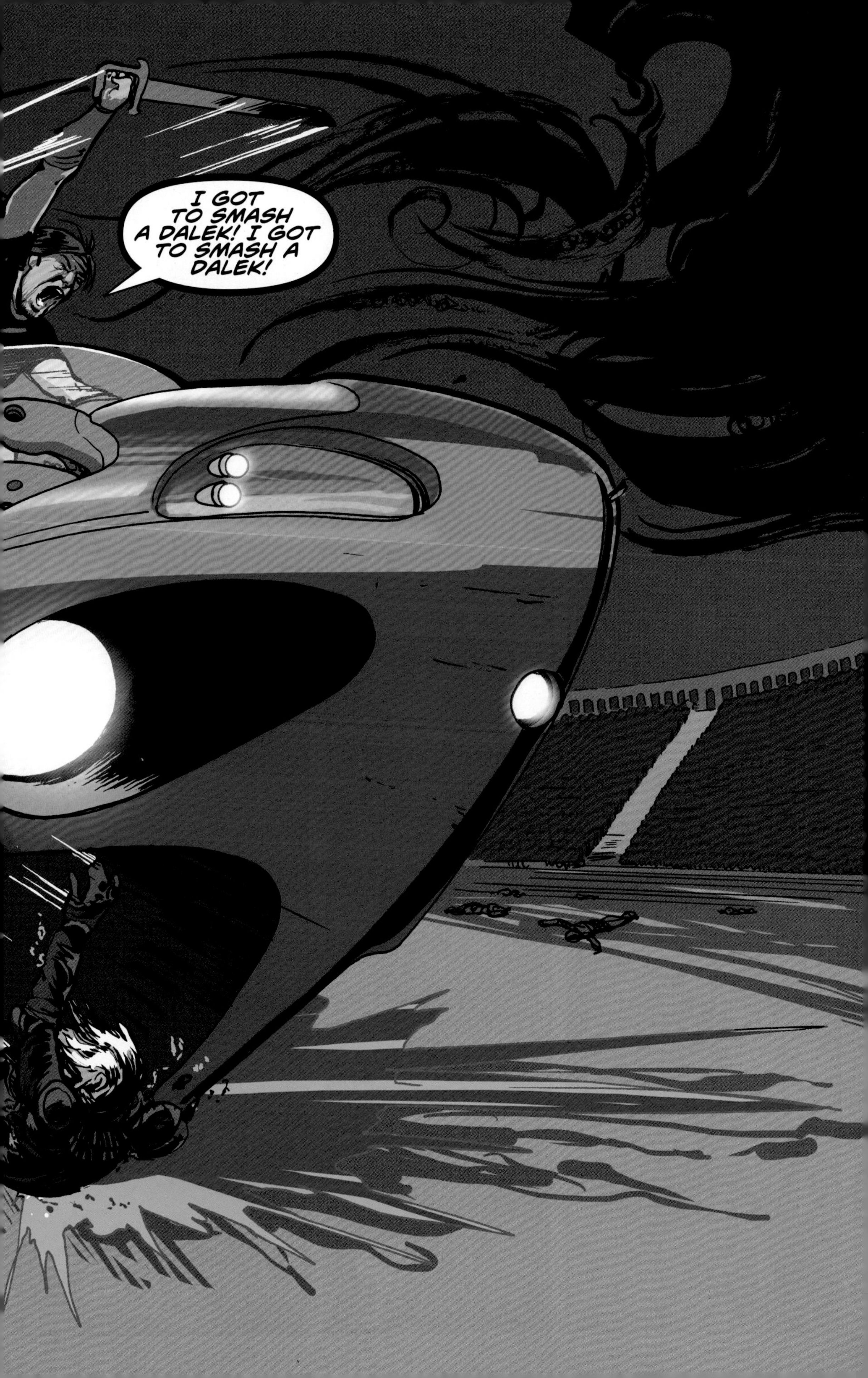
I GOT TO SMASH A DALEK! I GOT TO SMASH A DALEK!

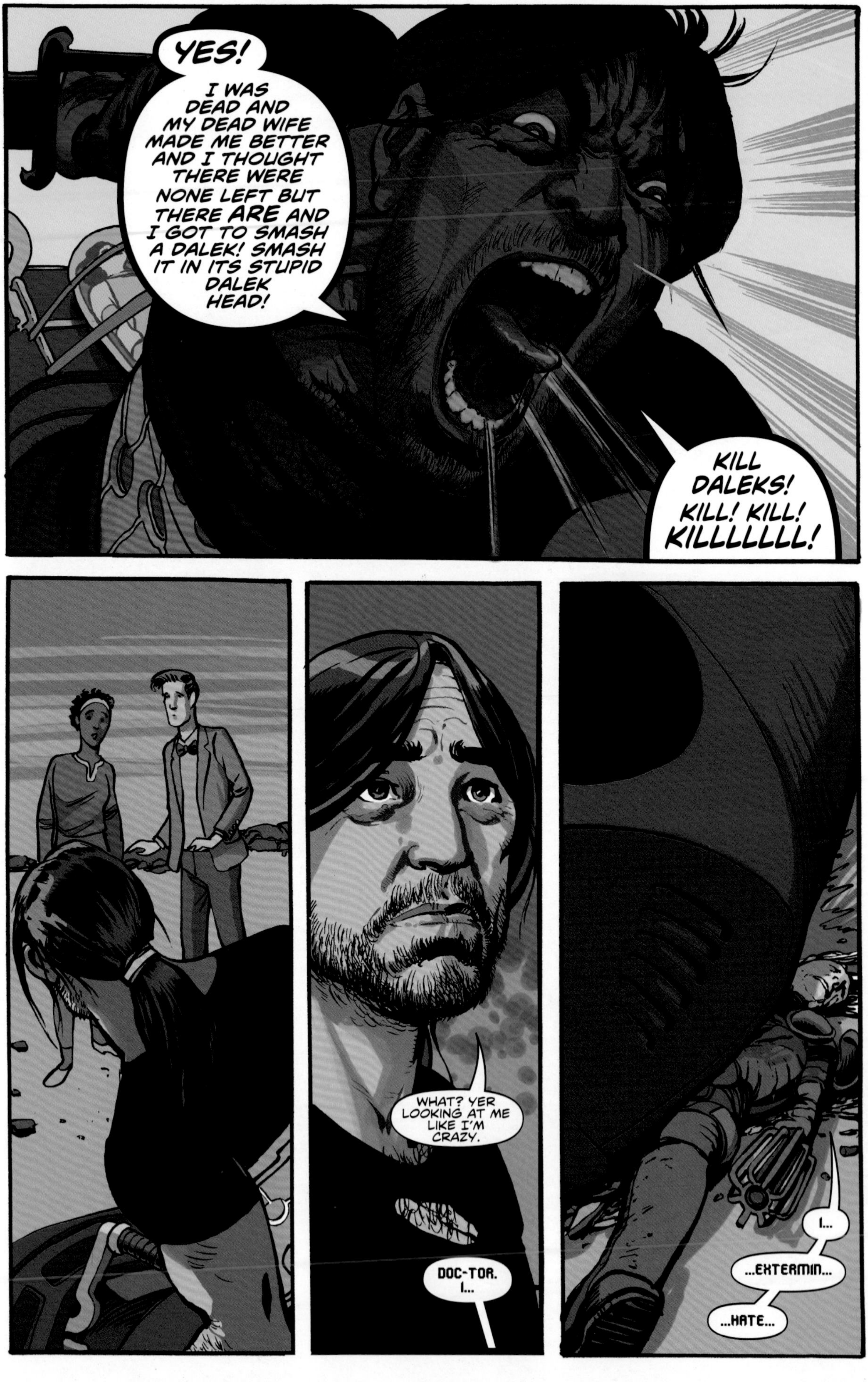
YES!
I WAS DEAD AND MY DEAD WIFE MADE ME BETTER AND I THOUGHT THERE WERE NONE LEFT BUT THERE ARE AND I GOT TO SMASH A DALEK! SMASH IT IN ITS STUPID DALEK HEAD!
KILL DALEKS! KILL! KILL! KILLLLLLL!
WHAT? YER LOOKING AT ME LIKE I'M CRAZY.
DOC-TOR. I...
I...
...EXTERMIN...
...HATE...

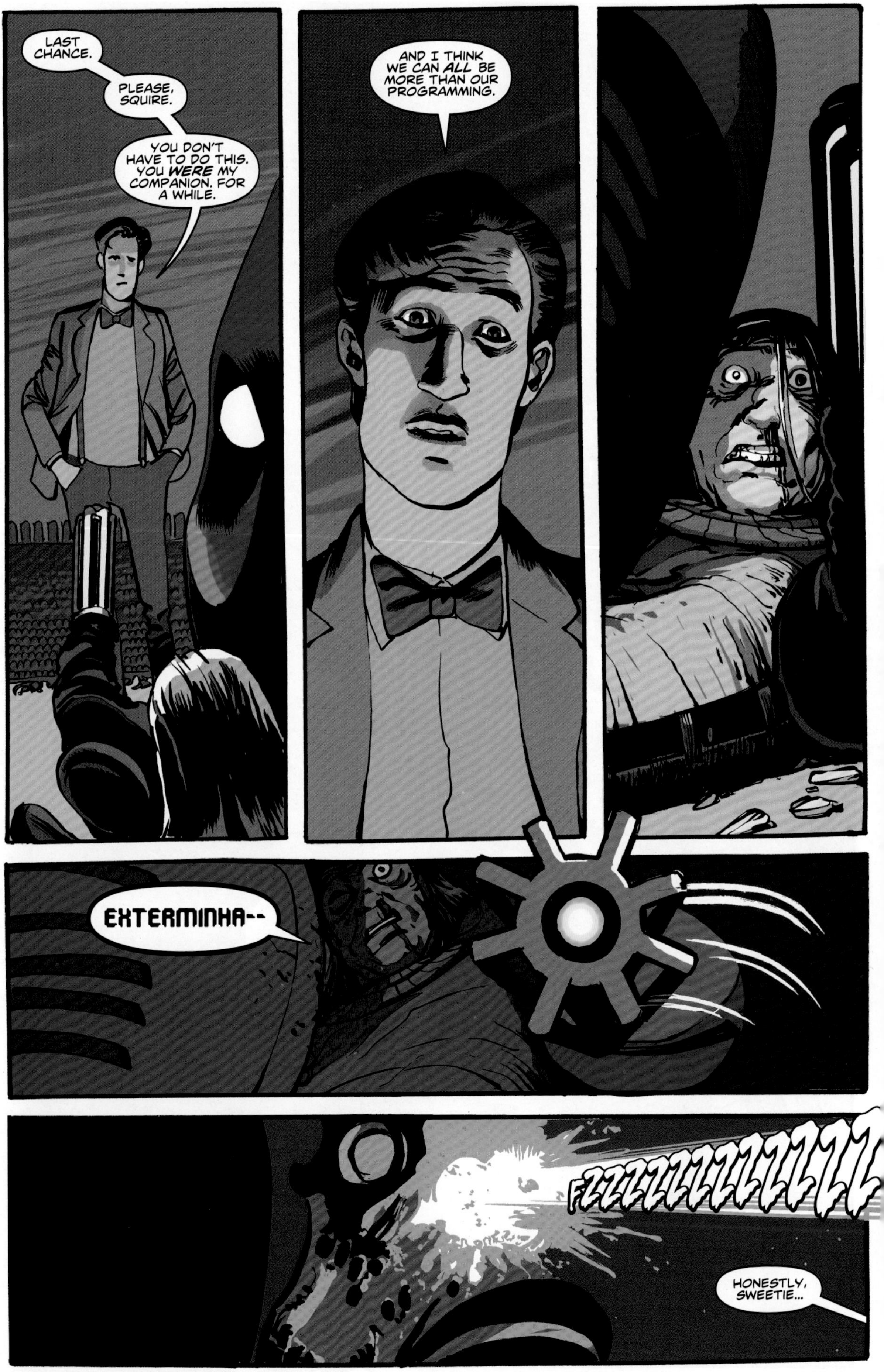
LAST CHANCE.
PLEASE, SQUIRE.
YOU DON'T HAVE TO DO THIS. YOU WERE MY COMPANION. FOR A WHILE.
AND I THINK WE CAN ALL BE MORE THAN OUR PROGRAMMING.
EXTERMINHA--
FZZZZZZZZZZZZZZZZ
HONESTLY, SWEETIE...

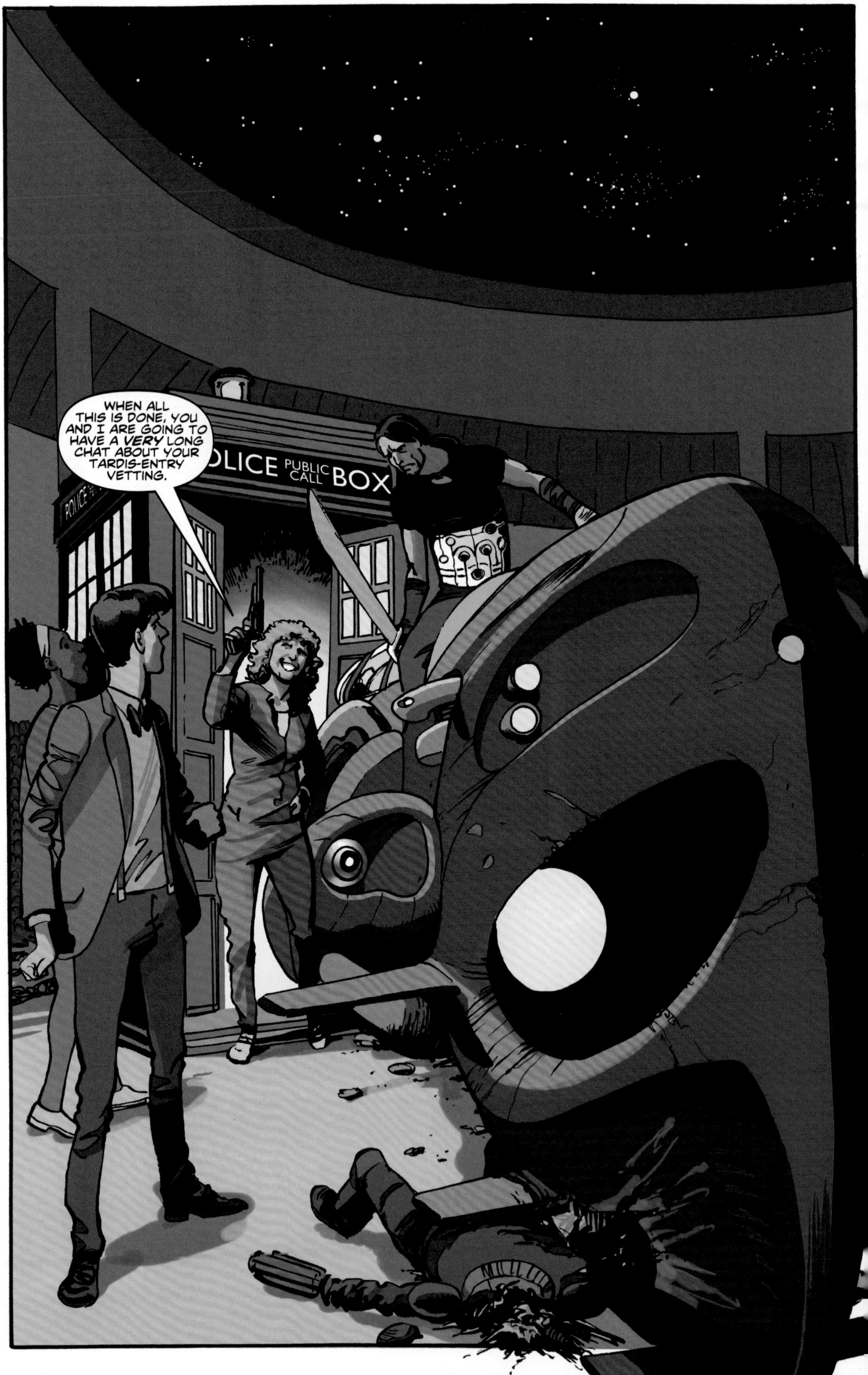
WHEN ALL THIS IS DONE, YOU AND I ARE GOING TO HAVE A *VERY* LONG CHAT ABOUT YOUR TARDIS-ENTRY VETTING.
POLICE PUBLIC CALL BOX

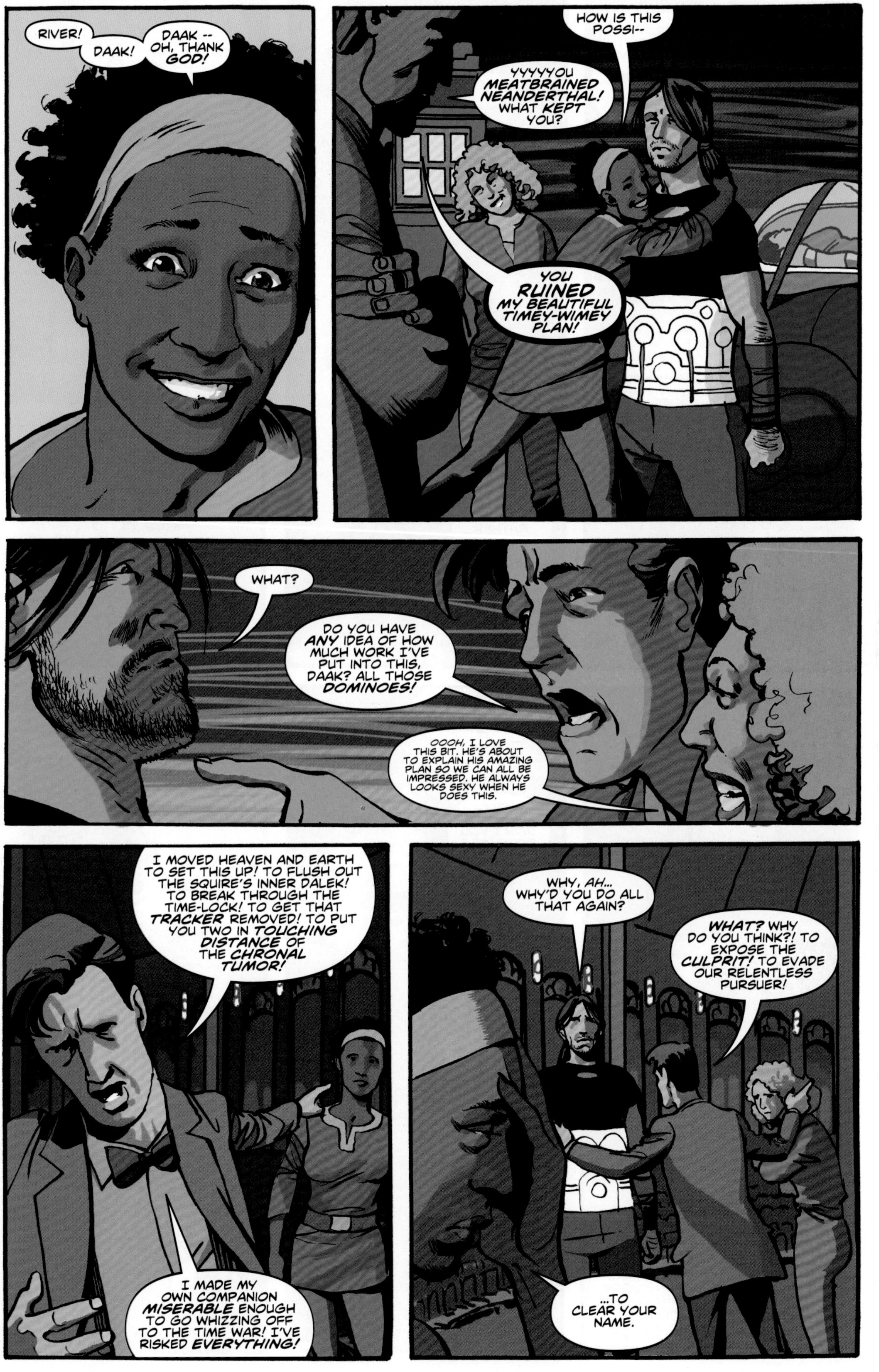
RIVER!
DAAK!
DAAK -- OH, THANK GOD!
HOW IS THIS POSSI--
YYYYYOU MEATBRAINED NEANDERTHAL! WHAT KEPT YOU?
YOU RUINED MY BEAUTIFUL TIMEY-WIMEY PLAN!
WHAT?
DO YOU HAVE ANY IDEA OF HOW MUCH WORK I'VE PUT INTO THIS, DAAK? ALL THOSE DOMINOES!
OOOH, I LOVE THIS BIT. HE'S ABOUT TO EXPLAIN HIS AMAZING PLAN SO WE CAN ALL BE IMPRESSED. HE ALWAYS LOOKS SEXY WHEN HE DOES THIS.
I MOVED HEAVEN AND EARTH TO SET THIS UP! TO FLUSH OUT THE SQUIRE'S INNER DALEK! TO BREAK THROUGH THE TIME-LOCK! TO GET THAT TRACKER REMOVED! TO PUT YOU TWO IN TOUCHING DISTANCE OF THE CHRONAL TUMOR!
I MADE MY OWN COMPANION MISERABLE ENOUGH TO GO WHIZZING OFF TO THE TIME WAR! I'VE RISKED EVERYTHING!
WHY, AH... WHY'D YOU DO ALL THAT AGAIN?
WHAT? WHY DO YOU THINK?! TO EXPOSE THE CULPRIT! TO EVADE OUR RELENTLESS PURSUER!
...TO CLEAR YOUR NAME.

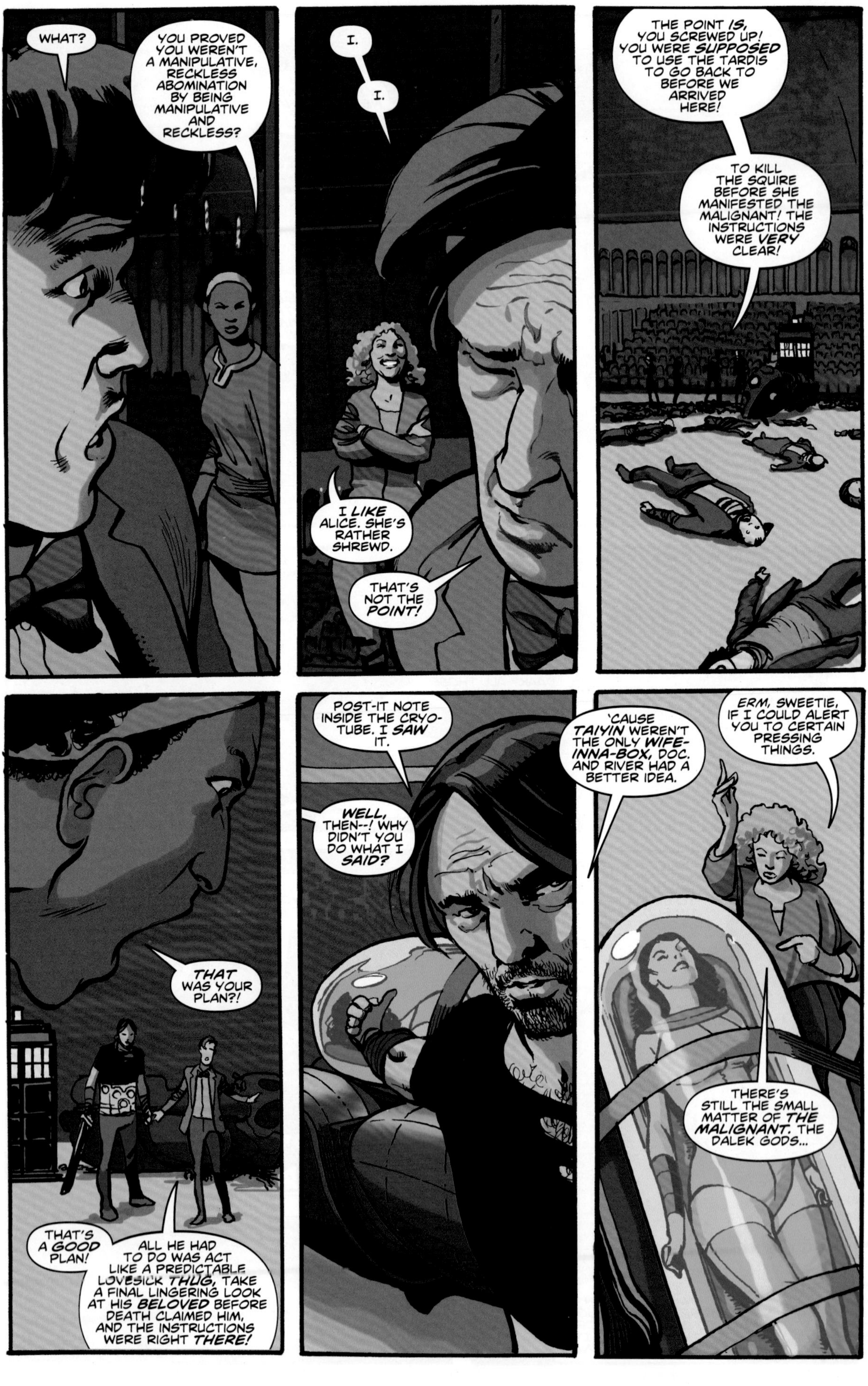
WHAT?
YOU PROVED YOU WEREN'T A MANIPULATIVE, RECKLESS ABOMINATION BY BEING MANIPULATIVE AND RECKLESS?
I.
I.
I LIKE ALICE. SHE'S RATHER SHREWD.
THAT'S NOT THE POINT!
THE POINT IS, YOU SCREWED UP! YOU WERE SUPPOSED TO USE THE TARDIS TO GO BACK TO BEFORE WE ARRIVED HERE!
TO KILL THE SQUIRE BEFORE SHE MANIFESTED THE MALIGNANT! THE INSTRUCTIONS WERE VERY CLEAR!
THAT WAS YOUR PLAN?!
THAT'S A GOOD PLAN!
ALL HE HAD TO DO WAS ACT LIKE A PREDICTABLE LOVESICK THUG, TAKE A FINAL LINGERING LOOK AT HIS BELOVED BEFORE DEATH CLAIMED HIM, AND THE INSTRUCTIONS WERE RIGHT THERE!
POST-IT NOTE INSIDE THE CRYO-TUBE. I SAW IT.
WELL, THEN--! WHY DIDN'T YOU DO WHAT I SAID?
'CAUSE TAIYIN WEREN'T THE ONLY WIFE-INNA-BOX, DOC. AND RIVER HAD A BETTER IDEA.
ERM, SWEETIE, IF I COULD ALERT YOU TO CERTAIN PRESSING THINGS.
THERE'S STILL THE SMALL MATTER OF THE MALIGNANT. THE DALEK GODS...

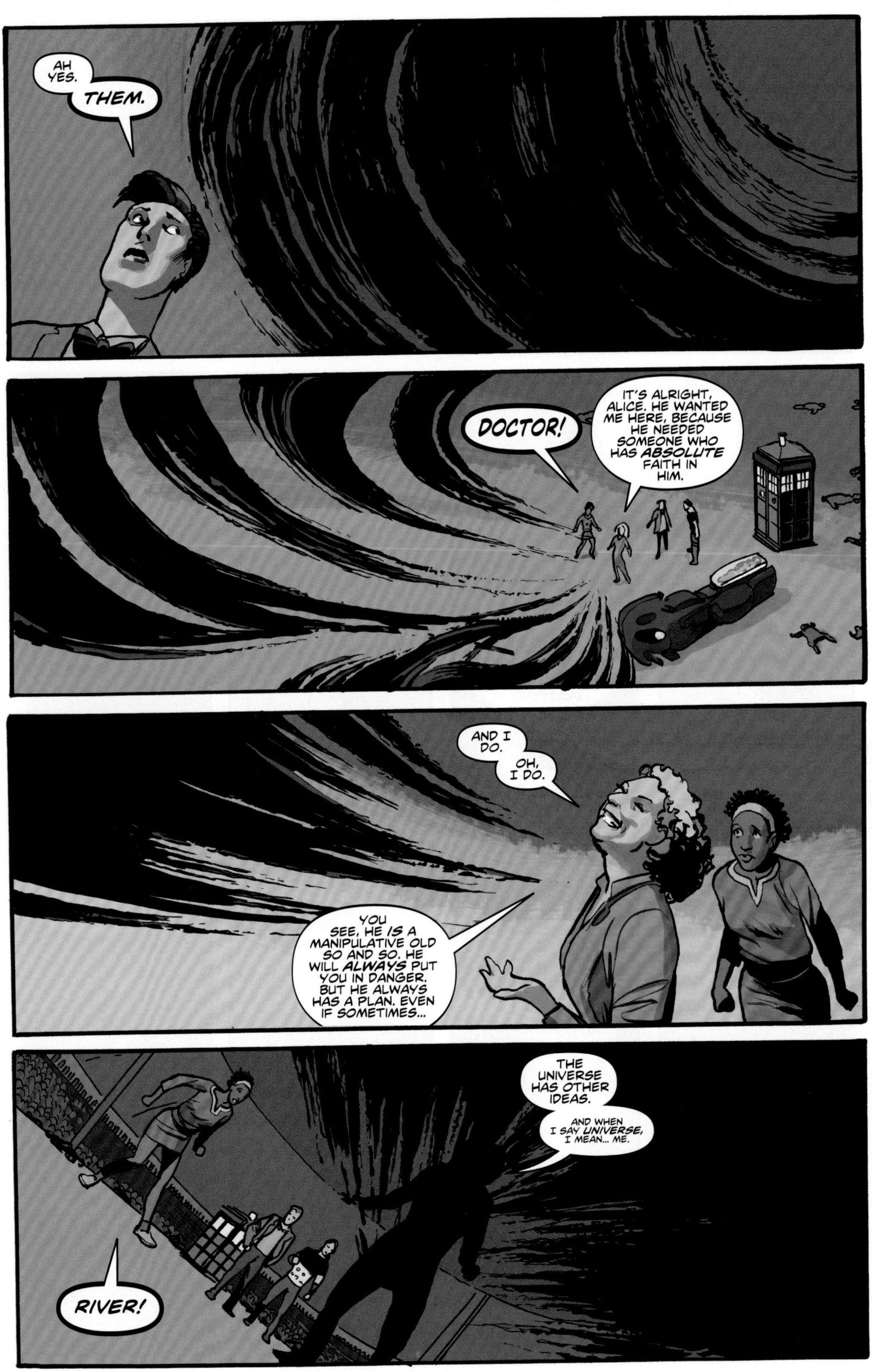
AH YES.
THEM.
DOCTOR!
IT'S ALRIGHT, ALICE. HE WANTED ME HERE, BECAUSE HE NEEDED SOMEONE WHO HAS ABSOLUTE FAITH IN HIM.
AND I DO.
OH, I DO.
YOU SEE, HE IS A MANIPULATIVE OLD SO AND SO. HE WILL ALWAYS PUT YOU IN DANGER. BUT HE ALWAYS HAS A PLAN. EVEN IF SOMETIMES...
THE UNIVERSE HAS OTHER IDEAS.
AND WHEN I SAY UNIVERSE, I MEAN... ME.
RIVER!

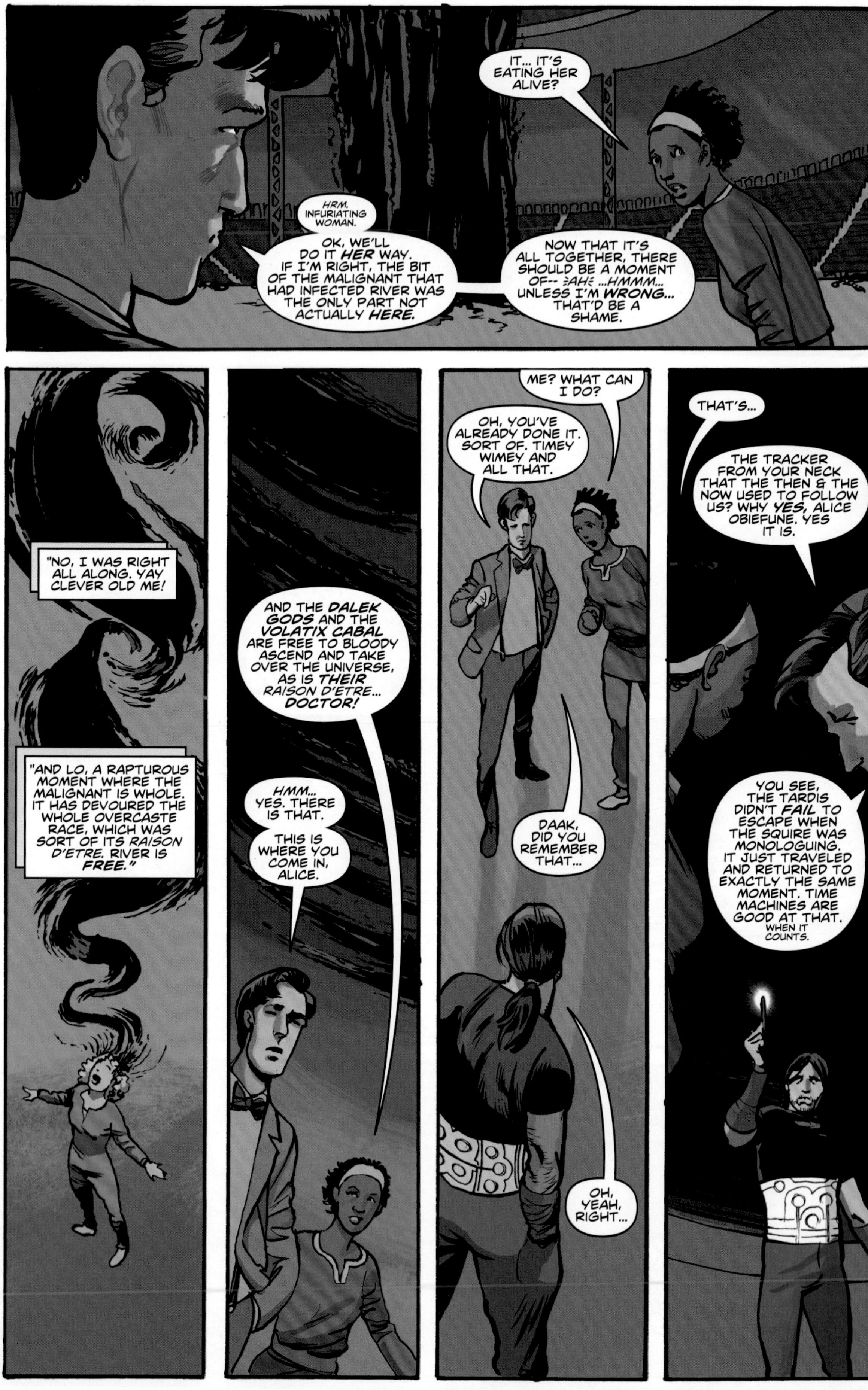
IT... IT'S EATING HER ALIVE?
HRM. INFURIATING WOMAN.
OK, WE'LL DO IT *HER* WAY. IF I'M RIGHT, THE BIT OF THE MALIGNANT THAT HAD INFECTED RIVER WAS THE ONLY PART NOT ACTUALLY *HERE.*
NOW THAT IT'S ALL TOGETHER, THERE SHOULD BE A MOMENT OF-- AH ...HMMM... UNLESS I'M *WRONG...* THAT'D BE A SHAME.
"NO, I WAS RIGHT ALL ALONG. YAY CLEVER OLD ME!
"AND LO, A RAPTUROUS MOMENT WHERE THE MALIGNANT IS WHOLE. IT HAS DEVOURED THE WHOLE OVERCASTE RACE, WHICH WAS SORT OF ITS *RAISON D'ETRE.* RIVER IS *FREE.*"
AND THE *DALEK GODS* AND THE *VOLATIX CABAL* ARE FREE TO BLOODY ASCEND AND TAKE OVER THE UNIVERSE, AS IS *THEIR RAISON D'ETRE... DOCTOR!*
HMM... YES. THERE IS THAT.
THIS IS WHERE YOU COME IN, ALICE.
ME? WHAT CAN I DO?
OH, YOU'VE ALREADY DONE IT. SORT OF. TIMEY WIMEY AND ALL THAT.
DAAK, DID YOU REMEMBER THAT...
OH, YEAH, RIGHT...
THAT'S...
THE TRACKER FROM YOUR NECK THAT THE THEN & THE NOW USED TO FOLLOW US? WHY *YES,* ALICE OBIEFUNE. YES IT IS.
YOU SEE, THE TARDIS DIDN'T *FAIL* TO ESCAPE WHEN THE SQUIRE WAS MONOLOGUING. IT JUST TRAVELED AND RETURNED TO EXACTLY THE SAME MOMENT. TIME MACHINES ARE GOOD AT THAT. WHEN IT COUNTS.

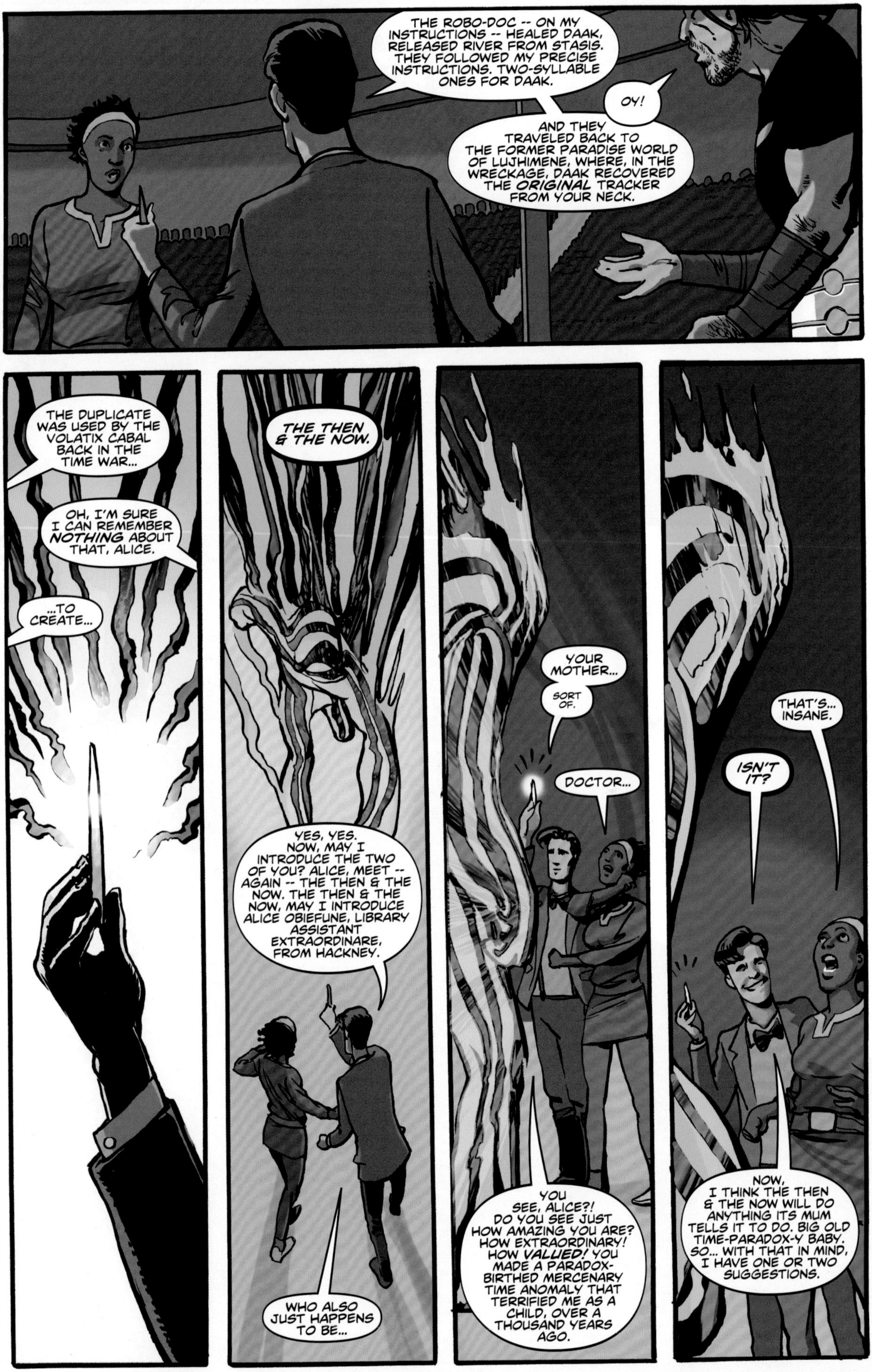
THE ROBO-DOC -- ON MY INSTRUCTIONS -- HEALED DAAK, RELEASED RIVER FROM STASIS. THEY FOLLOWED MY PRECISE INSTRUCTIONS. TWO-SYLLABLE ONES FOR DAAK.
OY!
AND THEY TRAVELED BACK TO THE FORMER PARADISE WORLD OF LUJHIMENE, WHERE, IN THE WRECKAGE, DAAK RECOVERED THE ORIGINAL TRACKER FROM YOUR NECK.
THE DUPLICATE WAS USED BY THE VOLATIX CABAL BACK IN THE TIME WAR...
OH, I'M SURE I CAN REMEMBER NOTHING ABOUT THAT, ALICE.
...TO CREATE...
THE THEN & THE NOW.
YES, YES. NOW, MAY I INTRODUCE THE TWO OF YOU? ALICE, MEET -- AGAIN -- THE THEN & THE NOW. THE THEN & THE NOW, MAY I INTRODUCE ALICE OBIEFUNE, LIBRARY ASSISTANT EXTRAORDINARE, FROM HACKNEY.
WHO ALSO JUST HAPPENS TO BE...
YOUR MOTHER...
SORT OF.
DOCTOR...
YOU SEE, ALICE?! DO YOU SEE JUST HOW AMAZING YOU ARE? HOW EXTRAORDINARY! HOW VALUED! YOU MADE A PARADOX-BIRTHED MERCENARY TIME ANOMALY THAT TERRIFIED ME AS A CHILD, OVER A THOUSAND YEARS AGO.
THAT'S... INSANE.
ISN'T IT?
NOW, I THINK THE THEN & THE NOW WILL DO ANYTHING ITS MUM TELLS IT TO DO. BIG OLD TIME-PARADOX-Y BABY. SO... WITH THAT IN MIND, I HAVE ONE OR TWO SUGGESTIONS.

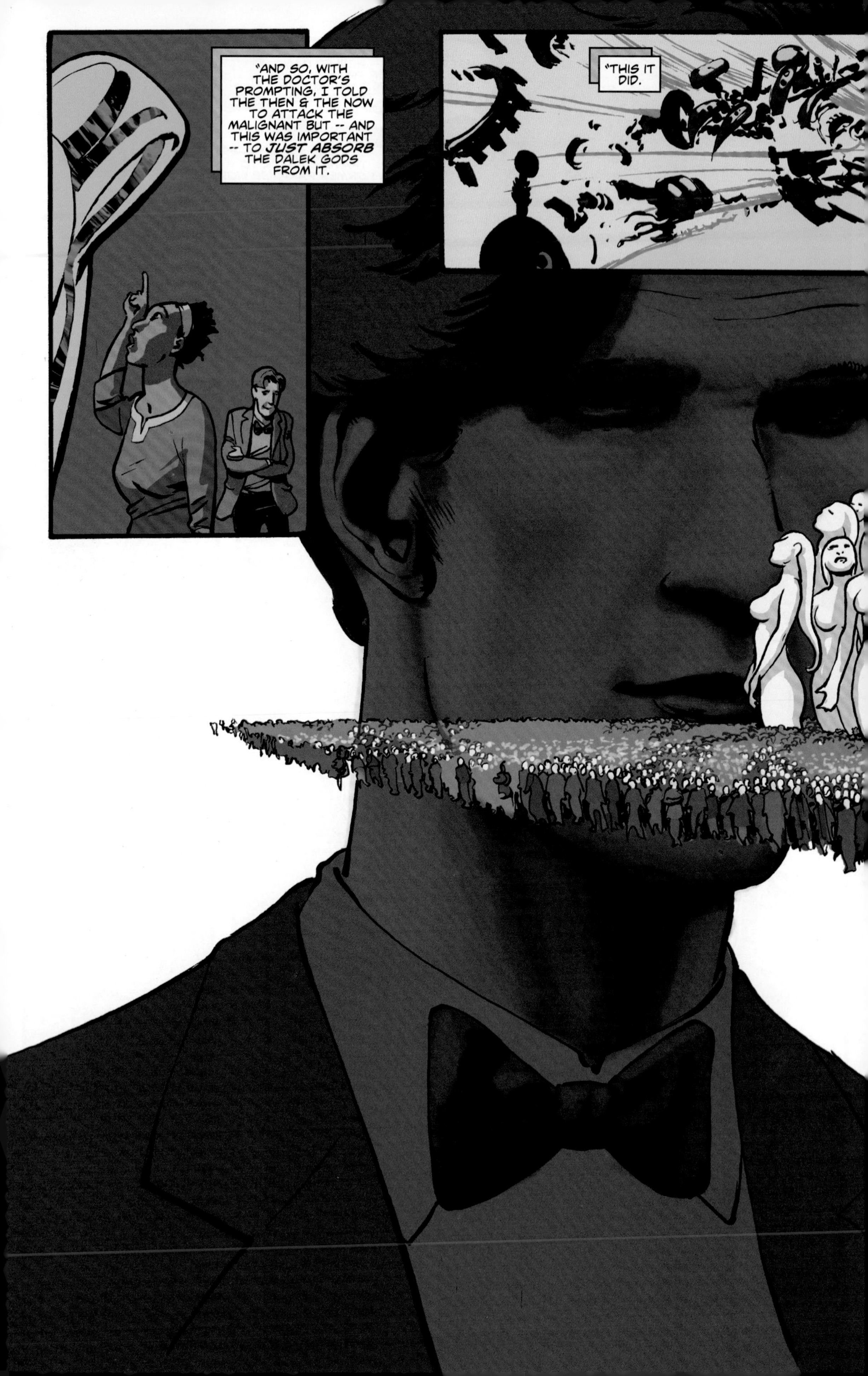
"AND SO, WITH THE DOCTOR'S PROMPTING, I TOLD THE THEN & THE NOW TO ATTACK THE MALIGNANT BUT -- AND THIS WAS IMPORTANT -- TO JUST ABSORB THE DALEK GODS FROM IT.
"THIS IT DID.

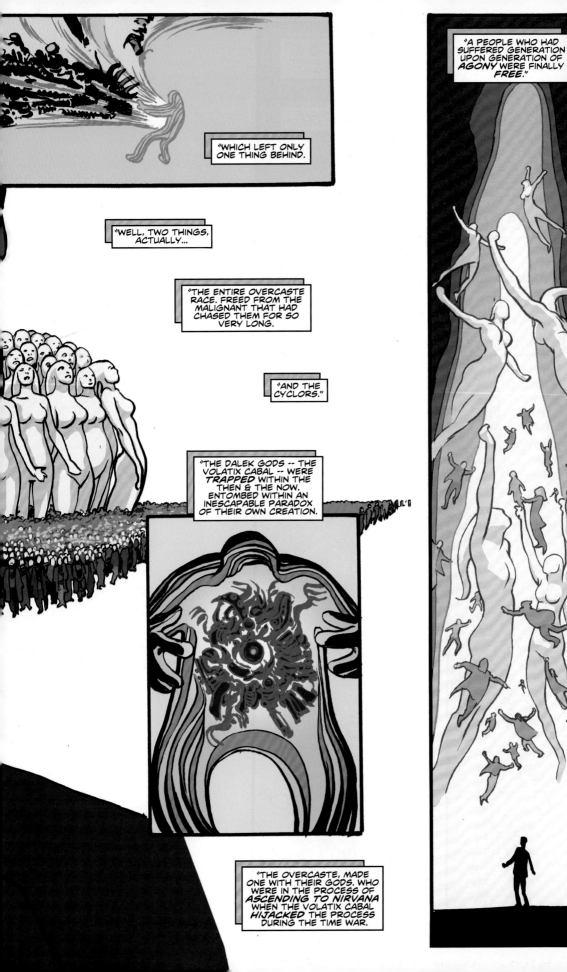

"A PEOPLE WHO HAD SUFFERED GENERATION UPON GENERATION OF *AGONY* WERE FINALLY *FREE*."

"WHICH LEFT ONLY ONE THING BEHIND.

"WELL, TWO THINGS, ACTUALLY...

"THE ENTIRE OVERCASTE RACE. FREED FROM THE MALIGNANT THAT HAD CHASED THEM FOR SO VERY LONG.

"AND THE CYCLORS."

"THE DALEK GODS -- THE *VOLATIX CABAL* -- WERE *TRAPPED* WITHIN THE THEN & THE NOW. ENTOMBED WITHIN AN INESCAPABLE PARADOX OF THEIR OWN CREATION.

"THE OVERCASTE, MADE ONE WITH THEIR GODS. WHO WERE IN THE PROCESS OF *ASCENDING TO NIRVANA* WHEN THE VOLATIX CABAL *HIJACKED* THE PROCESS DURING THE TIME WAR.

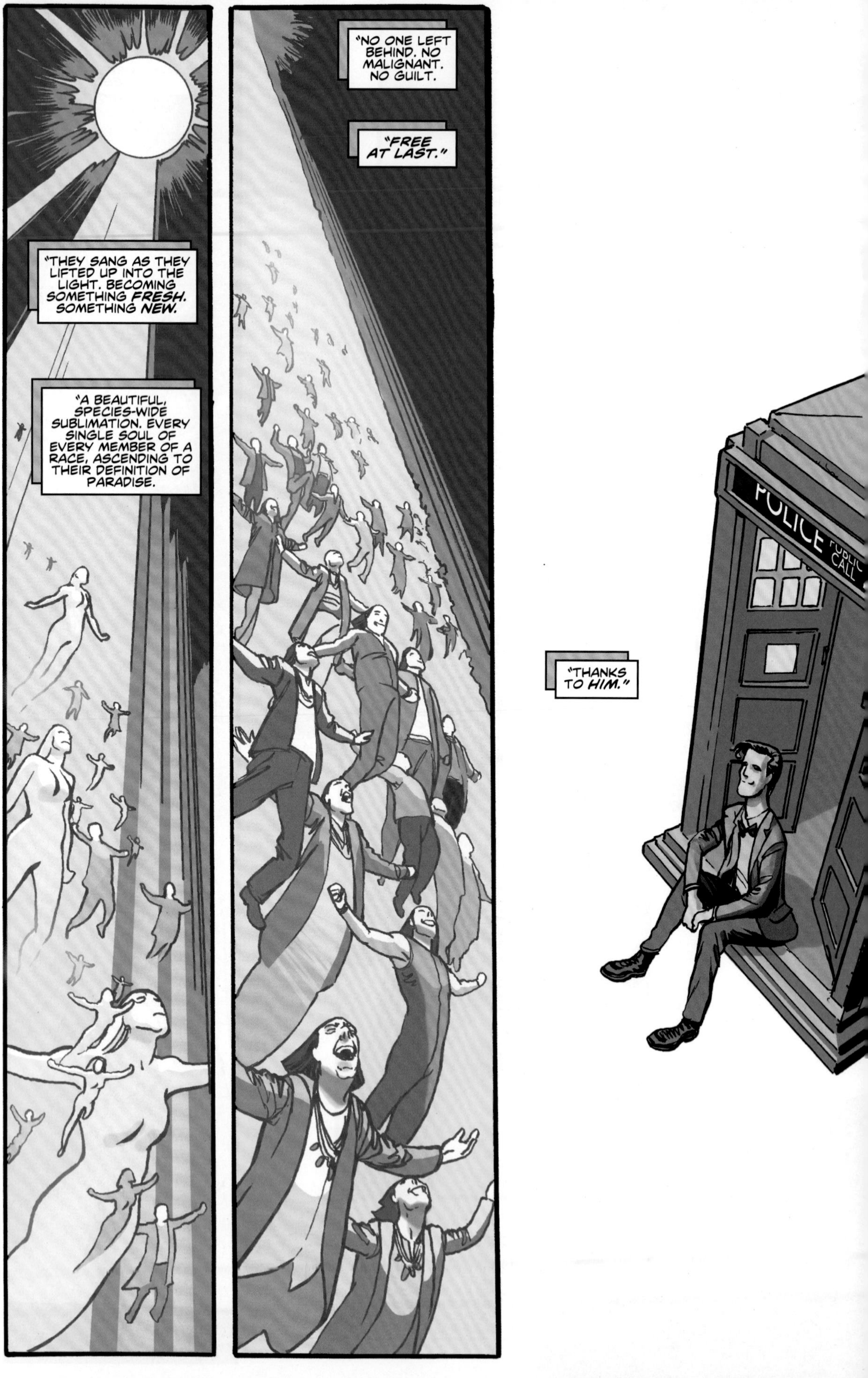
"THEY SANG AS THEY LIFTED UP INTO THE LIGHT. BECOMING SOMETHING *FRESH*. SOMETHING *NEW*.
"A BEAUTIFUL, SPECIES-WIDE SUBLIMATION. EVERY SINGLE SOUL OF EVERY MEMBER OF A RACE, ASCENDING TO THEIR DEFINITION OF PARADISE.
"NO ONE LEFT BEHIND. NO MALIGNANT. NO GUILT.
"FREE AT LAST."
"THANKS TO *HIM*."
POLICE

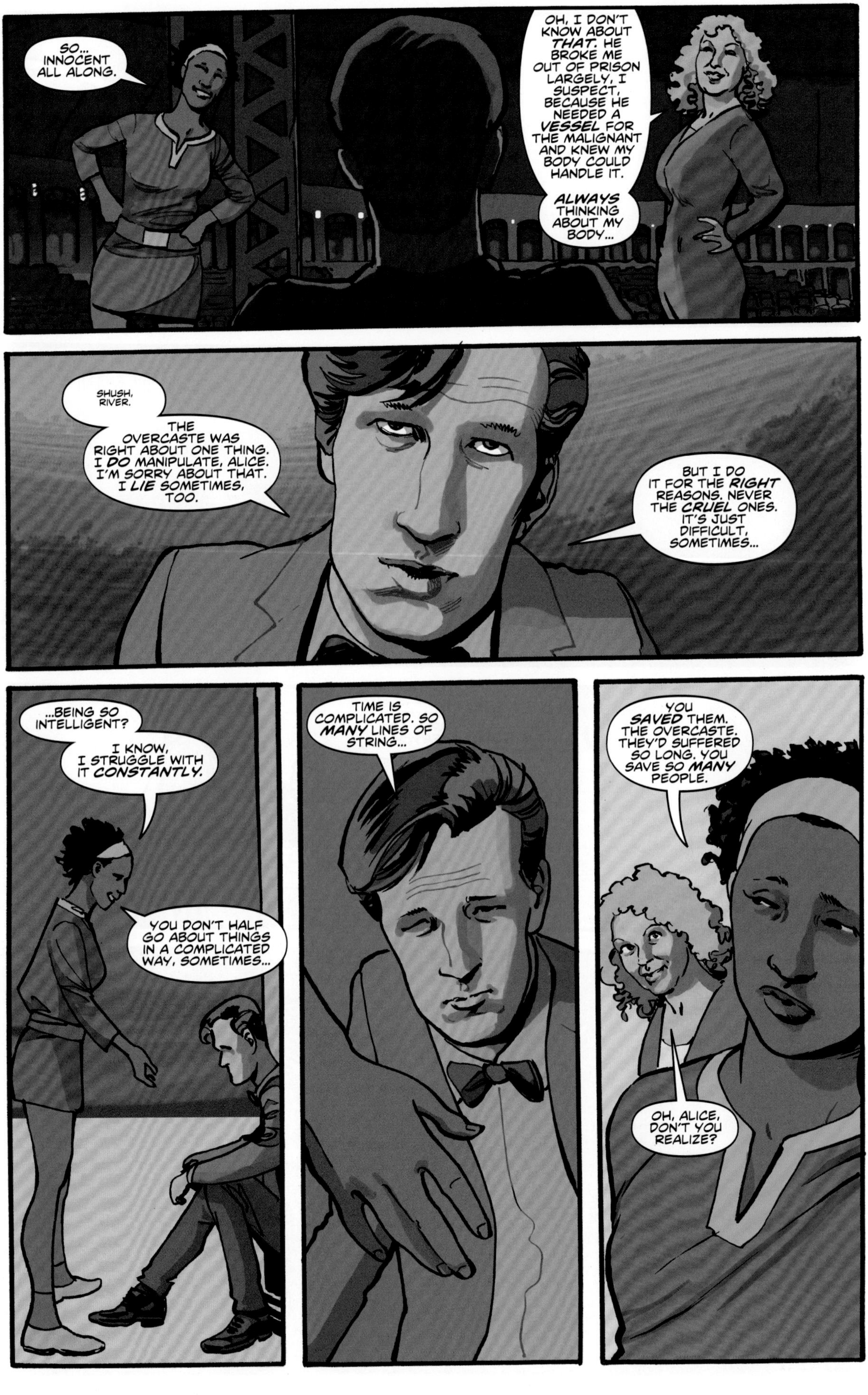
SO... INNOCENT ALL ALONG.
OH, I DON'T KNOW ABOUT THAT. HE BROKE ME OUT OF PRISON LARGELY, I SUSPECT, BECAUSE HE NEEDED A VESSEL FOR THE MALIGNANT AND KNEW MY BODY COULD HANDLE IT.
ALWAYS THINKING ABOUT MY BODY...
SHUSH, RIVER.
THE OVERCASTE WAS RIGHT ABOUT ONE THING. I DO MANIPULATE, ALICE. I'M SORRY ABOUT THAT. I LIE SOMETIMES, TOO.
BUT I DO IT FOR THE RIGHT REASONS. NEVER THE CRUEL ONES. IT'S JUST DIFFICULT, SOMETIMES...
...BEING SO INTELLIGENT?
I KNOW, I STRUGGLE WITH IT CONSTANTLY.
YOU DON'T HALF GO ABOUT THINGS IN A COMPLICATED WAY, SOMETIMES...
TIME IS COMPLICATED. SO MANY LINES OF STRING...
YOU SAVED THEM. THE OVERCASTE. THEY'D SUFFERED SO LONG. YOU SAVE SO MANY PEOPLE.
OH, ALICE, DON'T YOU REALIZE?

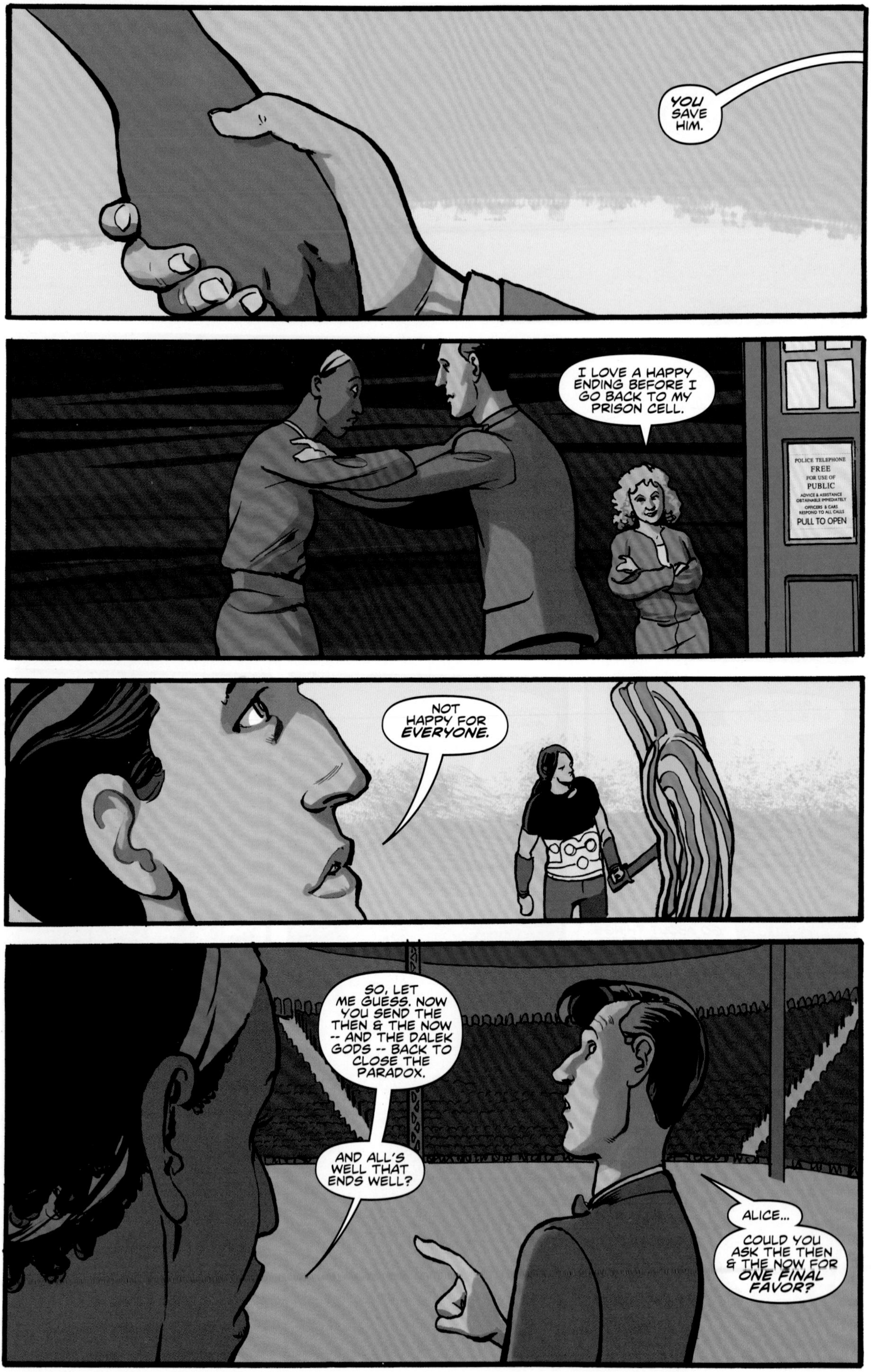
YOU SAVE HIM.
I LOVE A HAPPY ENDING BEFORE I GO BACK TO MY PRISON CELL.
POLICE TELEPHONE
FREE
FOR USE OF
PUBLIC
ADVICE & ASSISTANCE OBTAINABLE IMMEDIATELY
OFFICERS & CARS RESPOND TO ALL CALLS
PULL TO OPEN
NOT HAPPY FOR *EVERYONE.*
SO, LET ME GUESS. NOW YOU SEND THE THEN & THE NOW -- AND THE DALEK GODS -- BACK TO CLOSE THE PARADOX.
AND ALL'S WELL THAT ENDS WELL?
ALICE...
COULD YOU ASK THE THEN & THE NOW FOR *ONE FINAL FAVOR?*

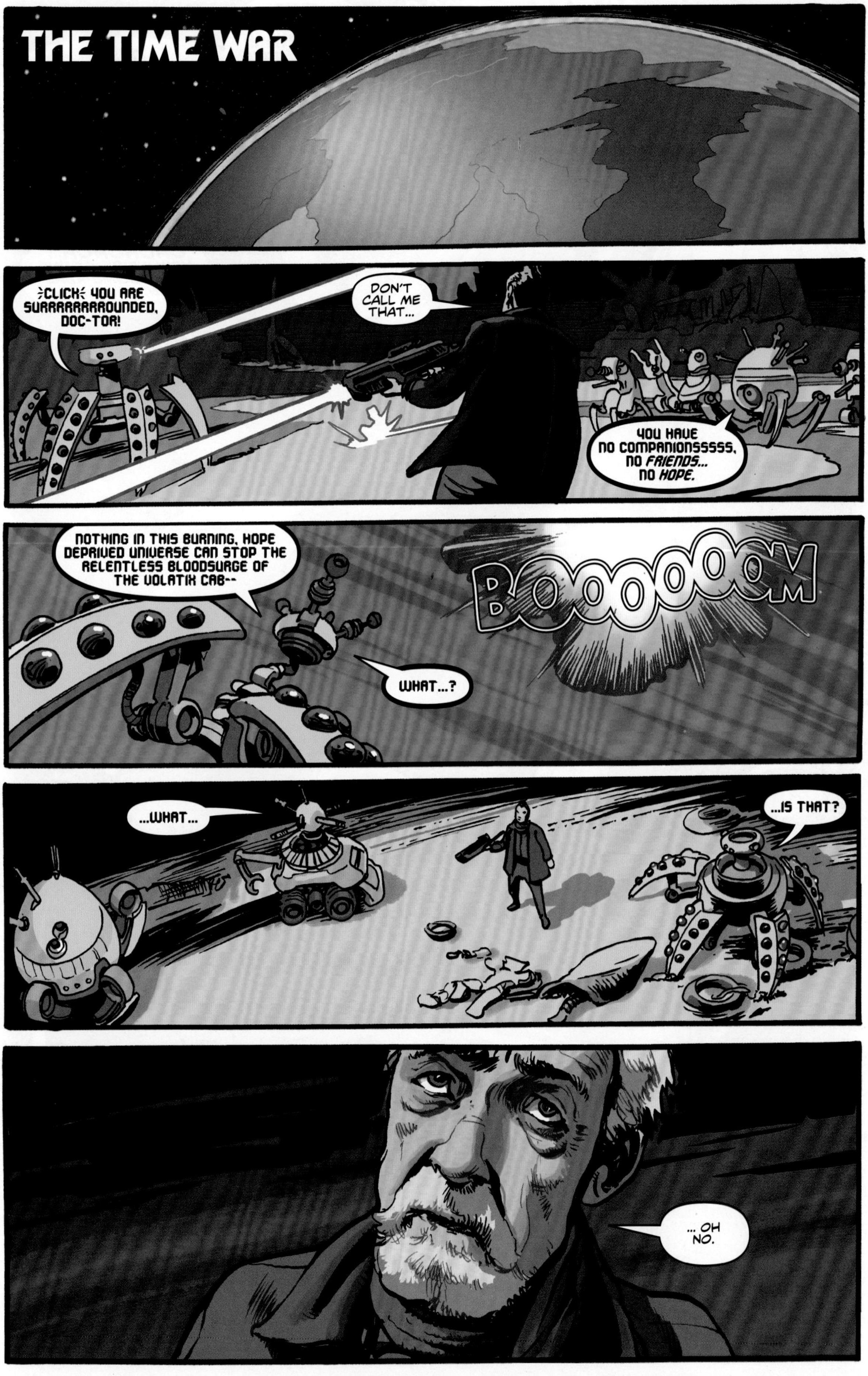
THE TIME WAR
>CLICK< YOU ARE SURRRRRRRROUNDED, DOC-TOR!
DON'T CALL ME THAT...
YOU HAVE NO COMPANIONSSSSS, NO FRIENDS... NO HOPE.
NOTHING IN THIS BURNING, HOPE DEPRIVED UNIVERSE CAN STOP THE RELENTLESS BLOODSURGE OF THE VOLATIX CAB--
BOOOOOOOM
WHAT...?
...WHAT...
...IS THAT?
... OH NO.

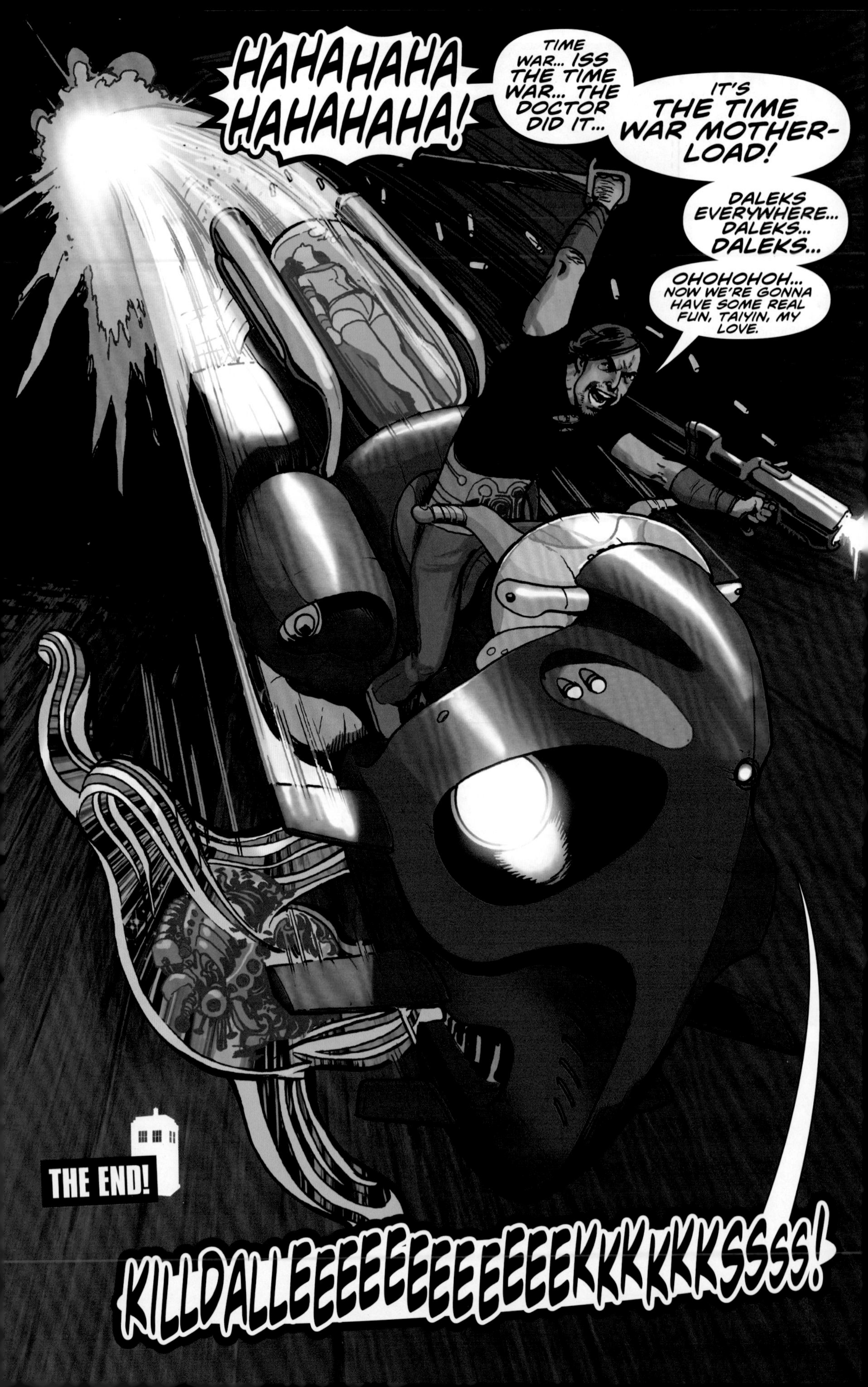
HAHAHAHA HAHAHAHA!
TIME WAR... ISS THE TIME WAR... THE DOCTOR DID IT...
IT'S THE TIME WAR MOTHER-LOAD!
DALEKS EVERYWHERE... DALEKS... DALEKS...
OHOHOHOH... NOW WE'RE GONNA HAVE SOME REAL FUN, TAIYIN, MY LOVE.
THE END!
KILLDALLEEEEEEEEEEEEEEKKKKKKSSSS!

BBC DOCTOR WHO THE ELEVENTH DOCTOR

COVER GALLERY

ISSUE #2.11

BBC THE ELEVENTH DOCTOR ADVENTURES YEAR TWO
DOCTOR WHO
DOCTOR WHO
SI SPURRIER
I.N.J. CULBARD
MARCIO MENYS
POLICE PUBLIC CALL
11 AUG '16 $3.99
COVER B WILL BROOKS
TITAN COMICS

BBC THE ELEVENTH DOCTOR ADVENTURES YEAR TWO
DOCTOR WHO
DOCTOR WHO
SI SPURRIER
I.N.J. CULBARD
MARCIO MENYS
11 AUG '16 $3.99
COVER C STEVE DILLON
TITAN COMICS

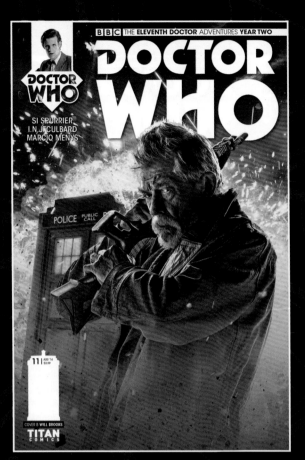

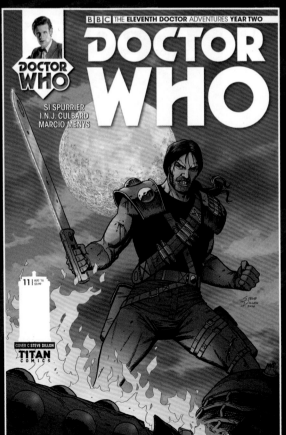

Cover B
Will Brooks

Cover C
Steve Dillon

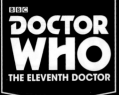

DOCTOR WHO
THE ELEVENTH DOCTOR

COVER GALLERY

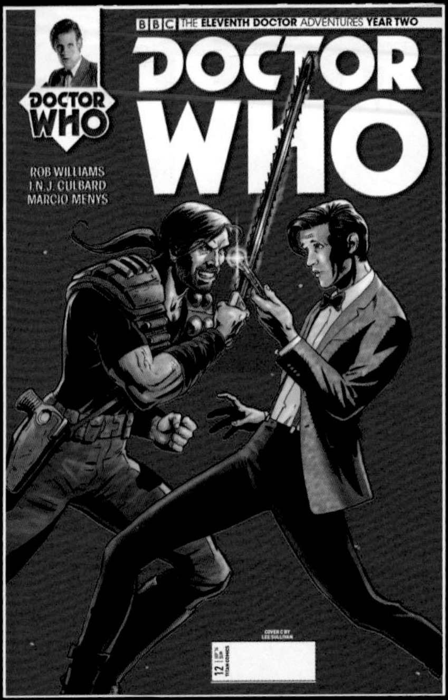
BBC THE ELEVENTH DOCTOR ADVENTURES YEAR TWO
DOCTOR WHO
DOCTOR WHO
ROB WILLIAMS
I.N.J. CULBARD
MARCIO MENYS

ISSUE #2.12

Cover C
Lee Sullivan

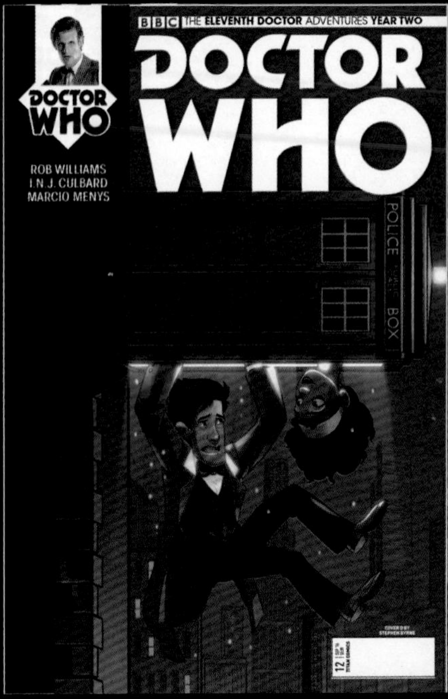
BBC THE ELEVENTH DOCTOR ADVENTURES YEAR TWO
DOCTOR WHO
DOCTOR WHO
ROB WILLIAMS
I.N.J. CULBARD
MARCIO MENYS
POLICE
BOX

Cover C
Stephen Byrne

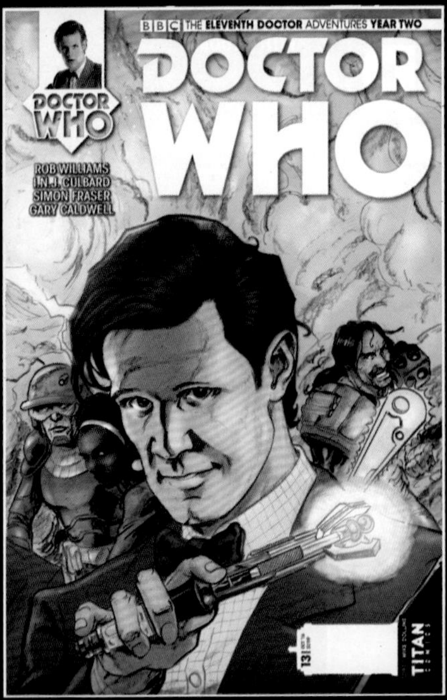
BBC THE ELEVENTH DOCTOR ADVENTURES YEAR TWO
DOCTOR WHO
DOCTOR WHO
ROB WILLIAMS
I.N.J. CULBARD
SIMON FRASER
GARY CALDWELL
TITAN

ISSUE #2.13

Cover C
Mike Collins

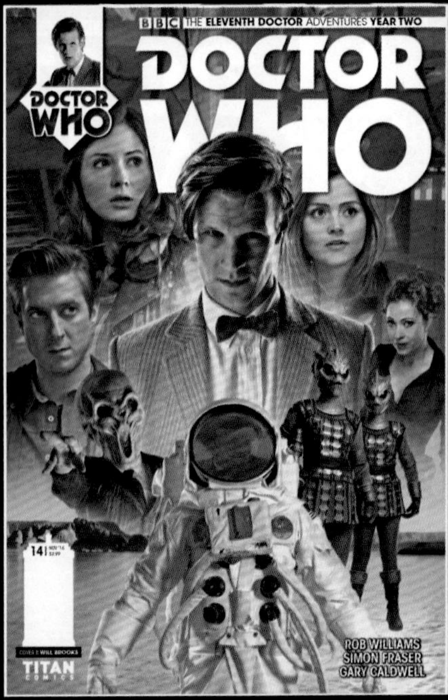
BBC THE ELEVENTH DOCTOR ADVENTURES YEAR TWO
DOCTOR WHO
DOCTOR WHO
ROB WILLIAMS
SIMON FRASER
GARY CALDWELL
TITAN COMICS

ISSUE #2.14

Cover B
Will Brooks

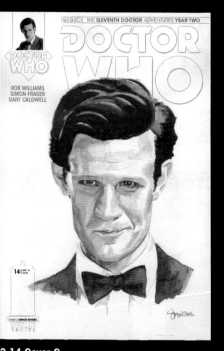

2.14 Cover C
Simon Myers

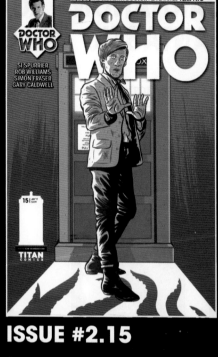

ISSUE #2.15

Cover A
Tom Humberstone

2.15 Cover B
Will Brooks

2.15 Cover C
JAKe

COVER GALLERY

FOLLOW YOUR FAVORITE INCARNATIONS ACROSS THESE FANTASTIC COLLECTIONS!

DOCTOR WHO: THE TWELFTH DOCTOR VOL. 1: TERRORFORMER

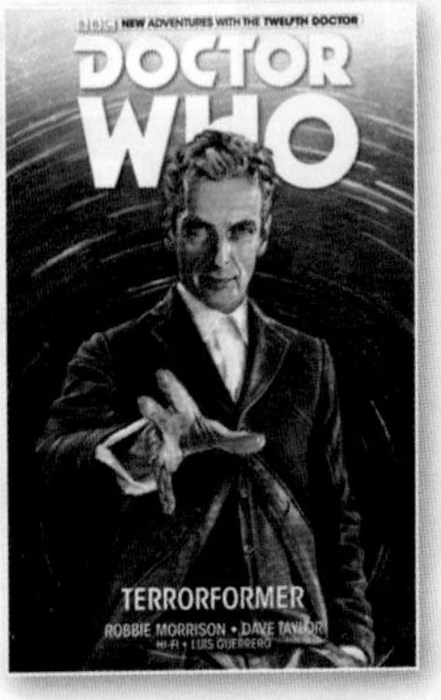
DOCTOR WHO
TERRORFORMER
ROBBIE MORRISON • DAVE TAYLOR

ISBN: 9781782761778
ON SALE NOW - $19.99 / $22.95 CAN / £10.99
(UK EDITION ISBN: 9781782763864)

DOCTOR WHO: THE TWELFTH DOCTOR VOL. 2: FRACTURES

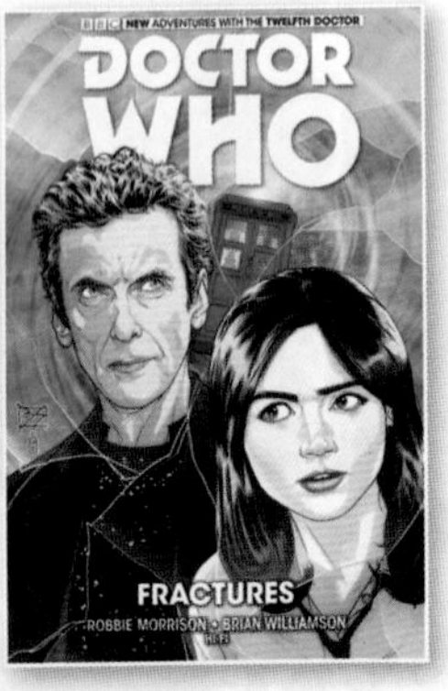
DOCTOR WHO
FRACTURES
ROBBIE MORRISON • BRIAN WILLIAMSON

ISBN: 9781782763017
ON SALE NOW - $19.99 / $25.99 CAN / £10.99
(UK EDITION ISBN: 9781782766599)

DOCTOR WHO: THE TWELFTH DOCTOR VOL. 3: HYPERION

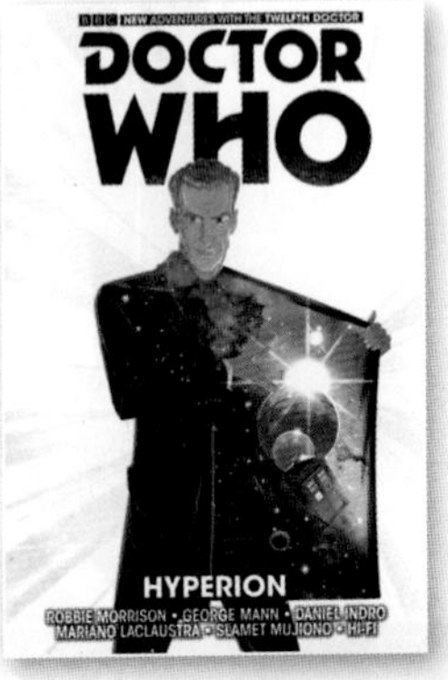
DOCTOR WHO
HYPERION
ROBBIE MORRISON • GEORGE MANN • DANIEL INDRO
MARIANO LACLAUSTRA • SLAMET MUJIONO • HI-FI

ISBN: 9781782767473
ON SALE NOW- $19.99 / $25.99 CAN / £10.99
(UK EDITION ISBN: 97817827674442)

DOCTOR WHO: THE TWELFTH DOCTOR VOL. 4: THE SCHOOL OF DEATH

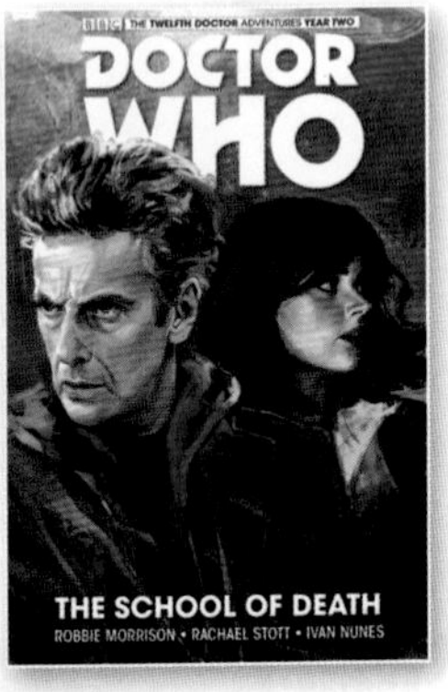
DOCTOR WHO
THE SCHOOL OF DEATH
ROBBIE MORRISON • RACHAEL STOTT • IVAN NUNES

ISBN: 9781785851087
COMING SOON - $19.99 / $25.99 CAN / £10.99
(UK EDITION ISBN: 9781785851070)

DOCTOR WHO: THE ELEVENTH DOCTOR VOL. 1: AFTER LIFE

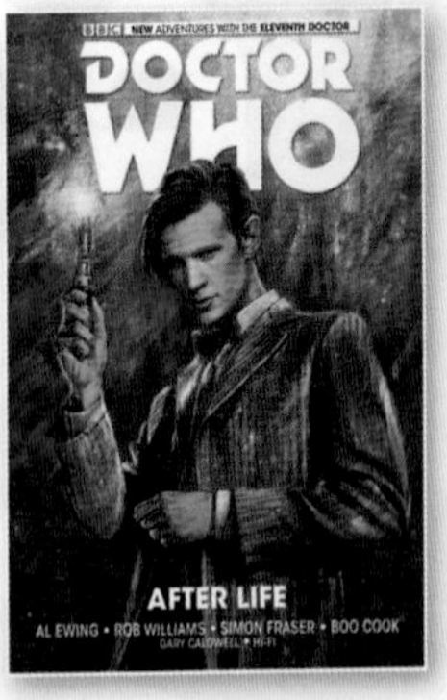
DOCTOR WHO
AFTER LIFE
AL EWING • ROB WILLIAMS • SIMON FRASER • BOO COOK

ISBN: 9781782761747
ON SALE NOW - $19.99 / $22.95 CAN / £10.99
(UK EDITION ISBN: 9781782763857)

DOCTOR WHO: THE ELEVENTH DOCTOR VOL. 2: SERVE YOU

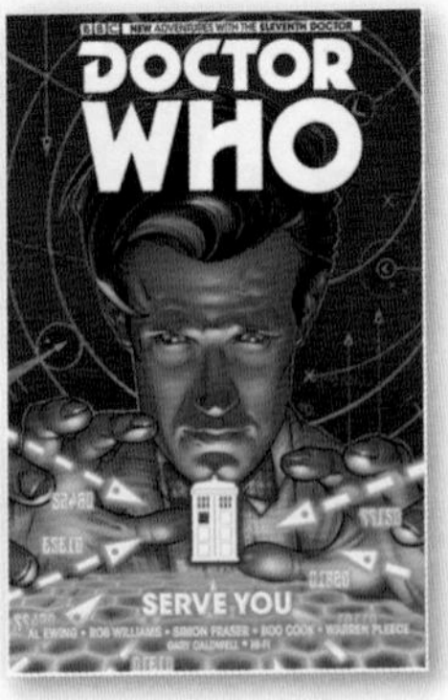
DOCTOR WHO
SERVE YOU

ISBN: 9781782761754
ON SALE NOW - $19.99 / $25.99 CAN / £10.99
(UK EDITION ISBN: 9781782766582)

DOCTOR WHO: THE ELEVENTH DOCTOR VOL. 3: CONVERSION

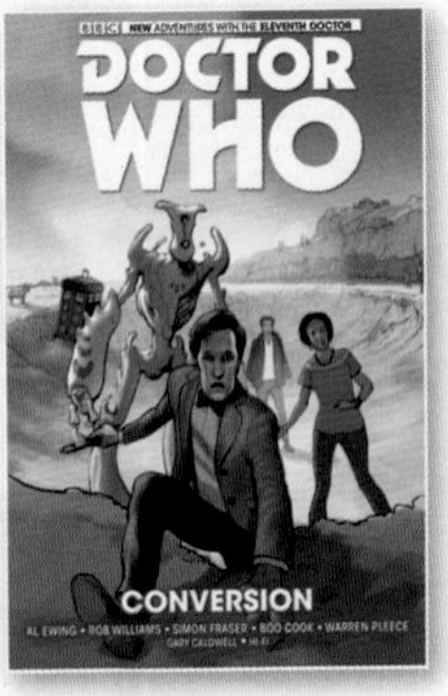
DOCTOR WHO
CONVERSION
AL EWING • ROB WILLIAMS • SIMON FRASER • BOO COOK • WARREN PLEECE

ISBN: 9781782763024
ON SALE NOW - $19.99 / $25.99 CAN / £10.99
(UK EDITION ISBN: 9781782767435)

DOCTOR WHO: THE ELEVENTH DOCTOR VOL. 4: THE THEN AND THE NOW

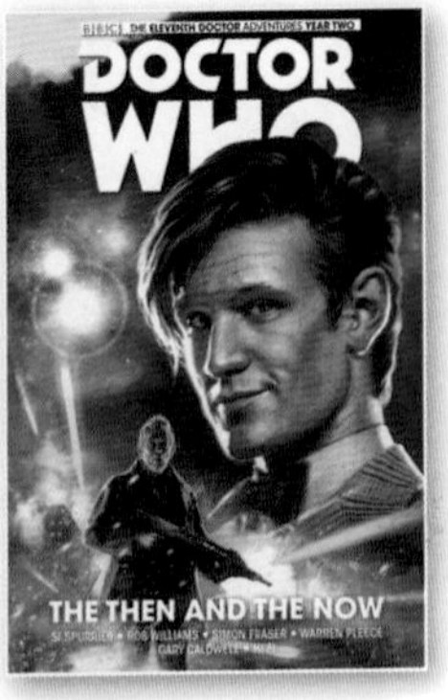
DOCTOR WHO
THE THEN AND THE NOW

ISBN: 9781782767466
ON SALE NOW - $19.99 / $25.99 CAN / £10.99
(UK EDITION ISBN: 9781722767428)

For information on how to subscribe to our great Doctor Who titles, or to purchase them digitally for your favorite device, visit:

WWW.TITAN-COMICS.COM

TITAN COMICS